HUNTING
IN
COUNTY KILKENNY

LE VIEUX SERVITEUR
This small pencil sketch, by the visiting French artist, Monsieur E. Verpilleux, of a kennel-man at Mount Juliet, was one of Victor McCalmont's favourite pictures. Drawn in the 1920s, it stood proudly on his dressing table throughout his life. Although the man's identity is unknown, his image forms the frontispiece of this book as a tribute to all those who worked in hunt kennels both at Mount Juliet and elsewhere.

(Courtesy of Mr. & Mrs. Harry McCalmont)

HUNTING
IN
COUNTY KILKENNY

Caroline Corballis

Foreword by
Robin de Vere Hunt

Published by:
Castlefield Publications,
Gowran, Co. Kilkenny, Ireland.
1999

e-mail: hunting@fresco.ie
http://www.fresco.ie/hunting.htm

ISBN 0 9535750 0 4

Printed and bound by:
Colour Books Ltd.
Dublin 13.

In memory of
Major Victor McCalmont MFH
and
Peter Thomas MFH

CONTENTS

LIST OF ABBREVIATIONS

FLJ	Finn's Leinster Journal
KJ	Kilkenny Journal
KK Mod.	Kilkenny Moderator
LJ	Leinster Journal
NLI	National Library of Ireland
UNC	Unidentified newspaper cutting

LIST OF ILLUSTRATIONS

Colour Plates

ACKNOWLEDGEMENTS

To write a comprehensive history of foxhunting, based on public archives would be virtually impossible. Without the tremendous help of numerous private individuals and without access to their libraries, this book could not have been written. A number of rare and locally printed pamphlets, letters, sets of accounts and other relevant material were kindly lent to me. Also, many precious photographs were entrusted into my care, for the production of this volume. Most of all, I am indebted to those who shared their memories and personal experiences.

Amongst the books consulted, Major James Connellan's *Memoir of the Kilkenny Hunt* published in 1897, to celebrate the hunt's centenary, was the most comprehensive on the subject. It is of particular interest, as he had access to material that is now apparently lost. My investigation will endeavour to avoid covering the same ground and will attempt to bring the history up to 1993, when Major Victor McCalmont (Master of the Kilkenny Hunt) died, symbolising the end of an era. It will also include some details of other packs, who have hunted in the county, over the past two hundred years.

Within the general literature on hunting there are useful works on Kilkenny, such as the Irish section of *British Hunts and Huntsmen* (1911) and Muriel Bowen's *Irish Hunting* (1953). Both depend heavily on Fitzpatrick's *Irish Sports and Sportsmen* (1878), as did Connellan before them. Baily's Hunting Directories, published annually since 1896, are an invaluable source of information for the well-established and registered packs.

The most prolific sources of primary material are the newspaper files, in the Kilkenny County Library. They provide an endless stream of reports of hunt meets, dinners, club meetings, hunting appointments, hunt balls and other associated activities. It is solely thanks to them that we know about the eighteenth century Merry Harriers and other contemporary hunt clubs. Until the 1830s the notices are sparse, but by the mid-nineteenth century every committee meeting is fully reported. Readers are, from then on, supplied with regular "Sporting Intelligence" on each meet, up to the end of the century.

The twentieth century chapters are based chiefly on a series of interviews, conducted over a period of years, originally with the view to writing a short local history. For the chapters on the North Kilkenny Hunt, the Mullinavat Harriers and the Nore Vale Harriers I am indebted to Des McCheane, Owen Conway and Martin Kavanagh respectively. Due to pressures of time and space, the research was confined solely to the mounted packs of foxhounds.

The following have been remarkably generous with both their time and advice: Mr. John Alexander, Mrs. Patricia Bayliss, The Hon. Bryan Bellew, Mr. & Mrs. Charles Blacque, Mrs. Mary Breen, Mr. Tommy Brennan, Mr. George Briscoe, Mrs. Juliet Brown, Mr. & the late Mrs. Gilbert Butler, Mrs. Gillian Butler, Mrs. Mary Cassin, Mr. Owen Conway, Mr. Seamus Corballis, the late Mrs. Isabella Cronyn, Lady Couchman, Mr. & Mrs. Harry de Bromhead, Mr. & Mrs. Rory Dicker, Mr. Jack Dwan, Mr. & Mrs. Paddy Fennelly, Mr. & Mrs. Jim Finnegan, Prof. Flanagan, the late Col. & Mrs. Gabbett, Mr. Michael Gabbett, Mr. Christopher Gaisford St. Lawrence, Mrs. Phyllis Glenn, Mr. Walter Halley, Mrs. Olivia Hamilton, Mr. David Herring, the late Mrs. Marie Heskin, Mr. John Hickey, Mr. John Joyce, Mr. Martin Kavanagh, Ms. Grace Kearney, Mr. John Kirwan, Mrs. Desmond Lambert, Mr. Nicholas Lambert, the late Sir Hercules Langrishe Bt., Mr. Eamonn Lannon, Mr. Edward Law, Miss Melosina Lenox-Conyngham, Mr. Nicholas Marshall, Mr. & Mrs. Harry McCalmont, Miss Yvonne McClintock, Mr. Paddy Macdonald, Mr. & Mrs. Andrew McMorrough Kavanagh, Mrs. Mary Moran, Capt. & Mrs. Tom Morgan, Mr. & Mrs. Michael Morris, the late Mrs. Moylan, Mrs. Maureen Mullins, Mr. William Murphy, the late Col. Newell, Mr. Hugh Newell, Mr. Peter Newell, Mr. Evan Newell, Dr. O'Brien, Mr. Jim O'Connell, Mr. & Mrs. Kevin O'Donnell (Senior), Mr. Michael O'Hanrahan, Mr. Larry O'Reilly, Mr. Noel Phelan, Mr. Tony Power, Mrs. Elaine Reilly, the late Miss Jean Seale, Mr. Felix Sheridan, Judge Peter Smithwick, Mr. Mikey Thomas, Mrs. Peter Thomas, Miss Maura Toler-Aylward, Miss Nicky Toler-Aylward, Mr. Walter Walsh, the Marquess & Marchioness of Waterford, the late Mr. Nicky White, Mrs. Jane de Montmorency Wright, Kilkenny County Library and the Kilkenny Archaeological Society.

It is impossible to include a comprehensive list of members and followers of all the hunts detailed herein and there will be, no doubt, many unworthy omissions and inaccuracies. Apologies to all concerned, though it is doubtful if anyone contributed to foxhunting in County Kilkenny, just to be included in this history.

In particular, I would like to thank Mr. Desmond McCheane for all his encouragement, help and invaluable advice, without which this book would never have been written or published. Also to my long suffering family, my gratitude.

FOREWORD

What an appropriate time Caroline Corballis has chosen to write this history of the Kilkenny hunts, after those golden years when so many famous masters were at the head of affairs.

Great dedication and research have been necessary to write such interesting accounts of the masters and their style of hunting during this long period of time.

For many of us, this book will bring back many happy memories of the McCalmont era; the superb turnout of staff, horses and hounds, the excitement and thrill of riding across this wild and rugged country behind a flying pack of hounds. Also the limitless hospitality for the many visitors who stayed the night at Mount Juliet; waking in the morning to see hounds walking out by the river accompanied by three white coated hunt staff. At the same time on the other side of the house could be seen perhaps twenty-four hunt horses out at exercise, twelve ridden and twelve led by liveried grooms (all male!).

These old masters of bygone days would be horrified if they could return to see all the problems of the present day, modern farming methods, electric wires, motorways etc. All the more credit to masters of the present day who still provide such fine sport in spite of these many difficulties.

Robin de Vere Hunt

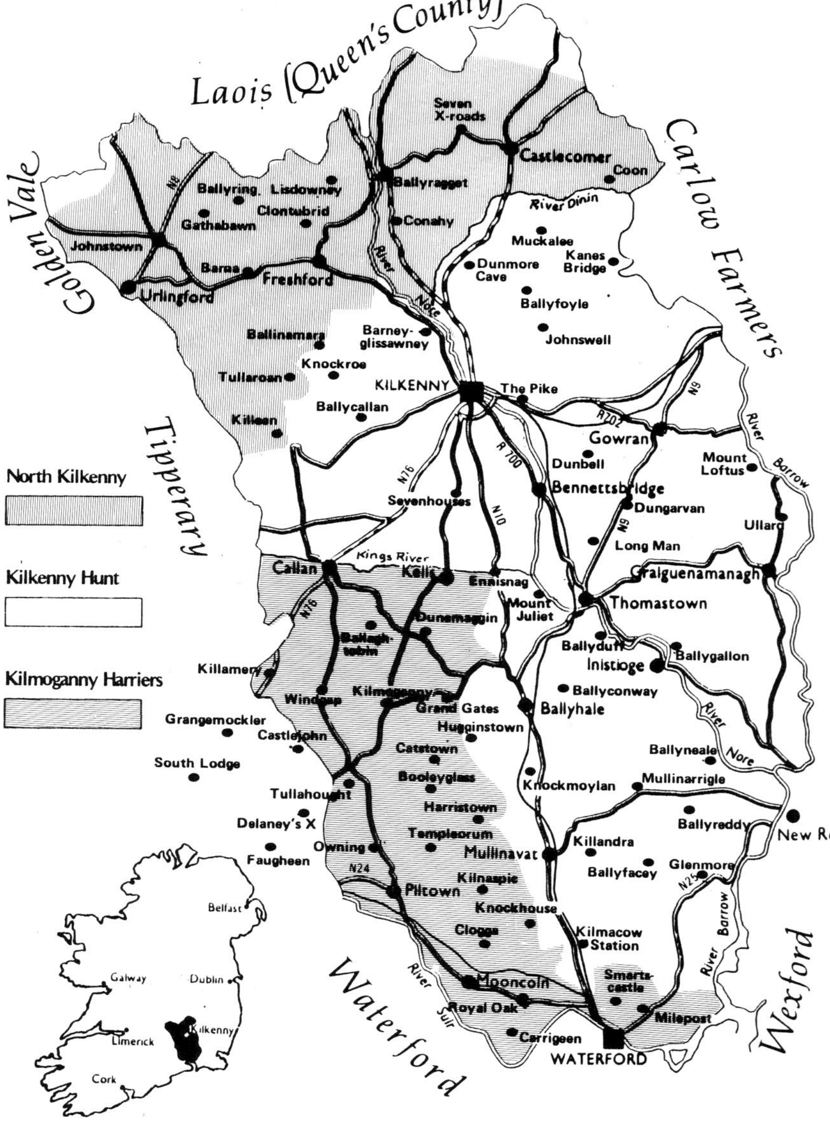

The Hunt Countries of the registered Hunts in County Kilkenny

(Drawn by Des McCheane, outline courtesy of Kilkenny Chamber of Commerce, Ordnance Survey permit no. 6742, 1998)

Chapter 1

Introduction – Origins of foxhunting

Hunting is the most honest, innocent, healthful, noble and pleasant diversion that the earth can afford. (Arthur Stringer, 1714)

Hounds played a prominent role in Celtic mythology. They were probably introduced to Ireland by the Celts between the fifth and third centuries BC, as valuable hunting dogs. They were status symbols for their owners and in all likelihood hunted a variety of game and vermin *(Osborn, 1994).* The Celts are recorded as having hunted foxes on horseback *(Lewis, 1995)* though we know little of their techniques. The legend "Táin Bó Fraích", describes how King Ailill and Queen Medb organised a great hunt in County Roscommon for deer, wild boar, hare and fox *(Kelly, 1998).*

The growth and development of foxhunting evolved gradually. It depended initially on the nature of the countryside, and on agricultural practices, which in turn were dependent on trade and the economy.

During early medieval times the forests were still virtually intact throughout the British Isles and wild red deer were plentiful. In England, they were considered the most noble of the beasts of the chase, and were preserved by the Crown for the King and his favourites to hunt. Nevertheless, poaching was endemic, due to the popularity of venison at a time when fresh meat was not always readily available.

From the late Elizabethan period, hunting was considered a suitable pastime for young gentlemen who had the necessary time, literacy and money. It was admired for its test of courage, strength and agility. Many books were published on the required accomplishments and etiquette.

Some authors advised on the maintenance of hunters, while others cautioned against the popularity of such sports. The Bishop of Gloucester published a sermon in 1616 on "The Fall of Man..." warning against the speed at which followers of the hunt galloped:

> such violent labour, such dangerous riding; the highways cannot always contain them, but over the hedges and ditches... then immediately follows the renting of garment, the tearing of

> flesh, the breaking of legs, the cracking of bones, through stormes and tempests *(Vale, 1977, 147).*

It sounds remarkably like a modern foxhunt and not like the slow and tedious seventeenth century hunting about which one usually reads.

Not all followers of the early packs of hounds were mounted, this depended on their role within the hunt, their social status and the locality in which they were hunting. Hounds were bred for their noses and music, not for speed *(Scarth Dixon, 1912).* The followers' primary interest was the manner in which the hounds worked, pursuing their quarry. Although judging by the above sermon, there were always some individuals who hunted for the thrill of the ride.

The clearing of the forests caused the deer to move to higher ground in more remote areas and they became scarce. Foxhunting thus gradually became popular, eventually replacing stag hunting. As the landscape changed so too did the art of foxhunting. While the forests remained, foxes did not travel any great distance. But as the felling of trees opened up the country they had to break from their cover in the hope of reaching safety elsewhere, giving the followers a run across open country. The new enclosures, both in England and Ireland, created formidable fences which, when met, were jumped from a "flying leap", adding a fresh element of excitement for the mounted followers, and giving the sport a new dimension.

The hare was another traditional and popular quarry. It took a skilled pack of hounds to hunt one and the danger element was reduced to a minimum. Packs of harriers continue to survive, although in the early nineteenth century, a number were pressurised by the dictates of fashion into becoming foxhounds. Others carried on hunting whatever game came their way.

During the eighteenth century foxhunting became regularised and hunt clubs were formed by groups of sporting gentlemen, enabling them to hunt larger tracts of land, beyond their immediate localities. They also acted as focal points for rural society in the gloomy winter months, the gentlemen dining regularly together in their appointed clubhouses. Some clubs occasionally established themselves away from home and provided temporary kennels, lodging and stabling for their members for the duration of their stay.

As the countryside changed and hound breeding evolved to meet the changing conditions, packs became more uniform and faster. It was the

(Photo: Des McChecne)

A wild Irish fox

influence of Hugo Meynell, master of the Quorn (1753-1800), the father of modern foxhunting, that first raised hunting to the level of a highly fashionable sport. He bred a faster type of hound, which in turn put the fox under greater pressure. It was no longer necessary to meet at the crack of dawn to find a fox with a full belly. Meynell's chief interest remained in his hounds and in the manner they worked while hunting. However, the increased pace attracted a new type of individual to the hunting field, one whose satisfaction was in his own personal horsemanship, and the excitement of the ride.

At the turn of the eighteenth century, the shires consisted of great plains of grass. It was cattle rearing country with substantial fences. The thrill of the hard riding and sometimes dangerous jumping, drew some of the wealthiest and most fashionable young men of the day, including the Marquess of Waterford and others with Irish connections. During the winter months, they congregated mainly in the village of Melton

Mowbray from where they hunted with a variety of packs. They became known for their lavish expenditure, reckless riding and outrageous behaviour. By the 1830s, with the advent of ladies wintering in the shires, their behaviour was somewhat modified and "Meltonian" became synonymous with the epitome of excellence in hunting.

It was this new form of foxhunting so successfully introduced to County Kilkenny, that soon set the standard for other Irish packs.

Chapter 2

Foxhunting emerges in Kilkenny

Certainly it is only in Ireland that one sees all that horses are capable of. (Prince Puckler-Muskau, 1828)

References to medieval hunting in Ireland are not easily found, but there are sufficient to show that it was a popular pastime for those gentlemen who wished to partake in such activities.

"Our gentry both native and Anglo-Irish were ardently attached to the chase" wrote Prendergast in his account of accusations made by the Earl of Kildare against Piers, the 8th Earl of Ormonde and Ossory in 1525:

> for taking coigne and livery of all the king's subjects in the counties of Kilkenny and Tipperary, not only for his horsemen, kerne... but also for his sundry hunts... twenty-four persons and sixty greyhounds for deer hunting, another number of men and dogs to hunt the martin, all at the charges of the King's subjects – meat, drink and money *(Prendergast, 1852, 148)*

The Earl of Ormonde expected his hounds to receive from his subjects the same ration as a man, as they were such high status animals. Revered by their owner, they were kept supplied with regular quantities of bread, milk or butter. His three packs hunted deer, hare and the pinemarten implying that each pack was specially bred and trained, with varying attributes, according to their intended quarry. The deer hounds hunted more by sight and the harriers by scent.

It is apparent that the Earl was also fond of his food, because he had a pack of beagles trained to turn for home when they heard the sound of the castle dinner bell. The Earl loved his hunting and is reported to have gone foxhunting *(Somerville-Large, 1995)*. His effigy, in St. Canice's Cathedral, carved during his lifetime, has his favourite hound depicted resting at his feet.

While in Kilkenny during the winter of 1648-49, Lord Castlemaine claimed to have amused himself by regularly foxhunting in the early mornings *(Anon. 1911)*. In 1652, a Kilkenny declaration prevented the

(Photo: Bord Failte)

The Tomb of the 8th Earl and Countess of Ormonde, in St. Canice's Cathedral, Kilkenny. The Earl's favourite hound is at his feet.

transportation of valuable wolf dogs out of the kingdom. They were becoming rare, wolves were being hunted to extinction and the hounds' raison d'être was disappearing. Possibly, explaining the increased interest in foxhunting.

A manuscript, written in Irish, dating from 1679 mentions foxhunting in a poem. It describes "the red fox rockward speeding and horsemen all hallooing" *(MacLysaght, 1979, 135).* Dineley noted that a hunted fox, at this period, seldom ran as far as two miles.

The evidence shows that foxhunting existed in seventeenth century County Kilkenny, although not in a form that we would necessarily recognise today.

The nature of the Irish seventeenth century countryside was essentially a new open landscape with scattered remnants of forest. For example, this would have been the case along the Nore and Barrow river valleys and in the wild areas of the Welsh Mountains, Brandon Hill and the Castlecomer plateau. The countryside was thinly populated and as John Dunne, c.1690, noted in his "ramble to Kilkenny, that enclosures are very rare amongst them; much of their land is reserved for grazing and pasturage" *(Harrington ed., 1991, 63).* Large tracts of the country remained in that state until the enclosure acts were introduced during the reign of George III, who, ironically, is quoted as saying: "I love hunting but I fear leaping. A king and a father... should not ride bold" *(Buxton, 1987, 34).* Although comparatively few enclosure acts were passed in Ireland, there were two which had considerable impact in County Kilkenny, they related to the parishes of Gowran and Callan.

The land was largely undrained and the "going", especially in a wet winter, was extremely heavy and slow, due to the water-logged nature of the soil. When these factors were all taken into account, together with the slow breed of hounds and horses, they dictated a ponderous chase after a fox who was often walked to death. That is, when there was one to be found, as the lack of cover meant that they were becoming increasingly rare.

The clearing of the Irish forests had endangered wildlife to such an extent that a game law had to be passed in 1697, to protect what remained from soldiers and their passion for shooting and coursing. The fox was not included, as it was not thought necessary to protect "vermin" *(MacLysaght, 1979).*

The fox (Vulpes vulpes) was purportedly hunted as a pest, likewise the wolf. Although the latter became exceedingly rare, they survived in Ireland until the eighteenth century. There is reference to Lord Clifden of Gowran, asking for hounds to be sent from Castletown, Celbridge to the Slieve Bloom Mountains to hunt wolves. The infamous last Irish

(Photo: author)

The Kilkenny countryside, near Ballyhale, looking east towards Brandon Hill.

wolf was killed in 1786, by Mr. Watson of Ballydarton, County Carlow, a master of foxhounds *(Fairley, 1984)*. Foxes were classified as vermin because of their unpopular behaviour in killing game fowl, domestic poultry and rabbits, all important items in the countryman's diet.

Eighteenth Century Hunting

Arthur Stringer, an exceptionally observant and accurate naturalist for his day, was born in c.1664. He became huntsman to Viscount Conway on the estate at Portmore, County Antrim and is of particular note as the first to write about hunting (including foxhunting) in an Irish context. His notes published in 1714, devote a chapter to a treatise on foxhunting. It is apparent that he considered foxhunting a well established activity with an open season from Michaelmas to the end of March. He recommended it as "a brave noble chase for such who keep good horses and hounds" and considered it "to be a general advantage to the inhabitants of that part of the country where it is used" *(Stringer, 1977,83)*.

It was his belief that a pack of hounds should be specifically trained to hunt foxes and to avoid other game, something many commentators claim to be a later innovation. On the other hand, his method of drawing a covert was an archaic one. Instead of drawing with the entire pack, he used his "staunchest" hounds and the remainder were kept coupled until the "finders" were in full cry. Only then did the he sanction the gradual uncoupling of the remainder of the pack. His logic being that the less experienced hounds may be tempted by other game in the covert.

Stringer was probably ahead of his time, but by the end of the eighteenth century his methods had become unfashionable. Requirements had altered as hound breeding became more scientific

Evidence for packs of foxhounds in County Kilkenny is scant for the first half of the century. Despite this, there is little doubt that several private packs did exist within the county. The hunting horn of Harvey Morres is dated 1732. The suggestion is that he had a pack of hounds at

(Photo: author)

Jane de Montmorency Wright, a descendant of Harvey Morres, with his hunting horn.

Castle Morres at that time. Lord Carrick and his brother, Mr. Butler Cooper, each kept a pack at Ballylinch and Ballyduff respectively. (The Ballylinch connection is of interest, as the property is adjacent to and part of the Mount Juliet estate, where the Kilkenny Hunt is now based).

(Private Collection)

Harvey Morres

The countryside through which they hunted was virtually denuded of trees and bushes, with the exception of a few newly planted gentlemen's estates. These were generally walled in and self-contained. The rising population resulted in people becoming more and more desperate for fuel and having to gather whatever timber they could find. Arthur

Young travelling, in 1776, from Leighlinbridge, County Carlow to Kilfane, County Kilkenny, saw some "very good crops of wheat, but the country is bleak and wants wood much" *(Young 1780, 20)*. Large stretches remained open, farmers made temporary divisions, during the summer months, with bushes. These factors contributed to the lack of game and created the need to bag foxes and enlarge deer. If Arthur Young were to travel the same route today, he would be astonished at the multitude of hedgerows and the sparsity of people in the countryside.

> Last Saturday a fox was unbag'd at Bennet's-bridge, and hunted by Mr. Agar's hounds of Gowran. He first ran from Bennet's-bridge to Kilfera, from thence to Danesfort, Birchfield, and the Suburbs of this City, from whence he struck off to Castle-Blunden, Sheerman's Wood, Desart, Ballycallen, Pottlerath, Cappagh, Farrenrory, Ballengarry, and Sleaveneman, in the County of Tipperary, where Reynard being hard run and closely pursued, after a chace of about 37 miles, and shewing great sport, he was at length obliged to submit to the superiority of a well scented pack, and was killed. This chace is universally allowed to be the greatest ever run in the County *(FLJ. 9:3:1768).*

Such a hunt was only possible under the slow conditions of the time. On that particular day the meet at Bennettsbridge would have been early in the morning, the horses were unclipped and not very fit by our standards.

A second fascinating account reveals that the same Mr. Agar's hounds had another marathon hunt in January 1774 and this time it was not a bagged fox.

> We hear from Thomastown, in this county, that on Saturday last Mr. G. Agar's fox hounds had the most remarkable long chace… they found a fox in Grennan wood, run him thro' Ballyduffe to Coolnehaw rock, where he attempted to get in, but was prevented by some boys; then across the mountain towards Ross to Listerling; from thence he run within a mile of Mullinavat, and crossing the Waterford road, run by Luke's Well, through Knockmoylan, and just to Newmarket, where he

> gave them a full enterprise; he then run for Clonassy, and gave another enterprise there, and run for Tory Hill, but finding himself too pressed he would not venture up, but ran into Bishop's Hall wood, dodged a little about there, gave the hounds another enterprise coming out of the wood; then run up the hill and got into a rock, the hounds within twenty yards of him. They were running him from half an hour after nine in the morning, until past three in the afternoon. There was not a check of five minutes during the chace. It is computed that he ran upwards of thirty miles. Mr. Agar was the only person in when he rocked *(FLJ. 19:1:1774).*

It is unlikely that they ever went out of a trot, hounds and fox included. Few obstacles would have stood in their way, the only exception would have been old medieval boundary fences. The negotiation of such ditches and other similar obstructions was considered foolhardy, but if unavoidable, the "standing leap" was the recommended practice. "Flying leaps" then becoming fashionable in the English shires were considered dangerous and viewed with great suspicion. A run of over thirty miles across heavy undrained land was an endurance test for all concerned and contemporary English accounts suggest that there was often considerable loss of horses and hounds from exhaustion *(Buxton, 1987).*

In 1777 Lord Clifden of Gowran Castle, offered 10 or 12 couple of his "good running hounds" to Mr. Connolly of Castletown as "there is so little game in this country" *(Mayo and Boulton).* It is possible that his hounds were descendants of Mr. Agar's (also of Gowran Castle), and one cannot doubt that they were indeed of the best stock, judging from the above accounts.

Early Hunt Clubs

As in England, hunt clubs gained popularity in Ireland. They were gentlemen's clubs, to which new members were elected. The Slievardagh Hunting Club in Killenaule, County Tipperary was fully operational by 1768. A toast sung by one of its members makes it clear that their drinking capacity was just as significant as their day's hunting *(FLJ. 18:5:1768).*

In Kilkenny in February 1774, the following notice appeared in the Leinster Journal: "To be sold: 30 couple of harriers – for hare or fox, about 24 inches high and remarkably stout. They go too fast for the owner" *(FLJ. Feb. 1774)*. Obviously, they were a fine privately owned sporting pack.

It has been suggested that these may have formed the foundation pack for the Merry Harriers Club who were established later that year *(Law, 1995)*. The Merry Harriers regularly advertised notices of their monthly meets. These took place between 8 and 10 a.m. generally at Grevine and afterwards the followers dined in the Wheat Sheaf, a sizeable Kilkenny inn, which became synonymous with hunt club dinners over the following couple of decades. In October 1778, they advertised for "a huntsman that can be well recommended for knowing his business, honesty and sobriety particularly" *(FLJ. Oct. 1778)*, implying that they probably raised a subscription to pay a huntsman and

(Photo: author)

Typical Kilkenny gorse covert near Ullard.

to meet other expenses. Their membership was made up of at least thirty prominent individuals who took turns to hold the office of President. Members included a High Sheriff, an MP, leading businessmen and large landowners like James Wemys, George Agar and John Butler. The club remained active until it went into apparent decline c.1785. At about the same time the Sportsman's Club emerged and they too dined at the Wheat Sheaf.

While the official records show that the Kilkenny Hunt was founded in 1797, newspapers of the 1770s and 1780s tell of a hunt named the

Kilkenny Hunt some years earlier. John Butler, nicknamed "Jack the Castle" who had come into considerable wealth through his marriage into the Wandesforde family, "chaired the Kilkenny Hunt at its dinner in the King's Arms in 1773" *(Neely, 1989*). The hunt club appears to have met there on the first Thursday of every month. In January 1775, a newspaper notice stated "The Kilkenny Hunt at Garter Inn on 5th being Club day, and a doe will be enlarged at Dunbell".

No more references to the hunt are found until:

> The Kilkenny Hunt dine at the Wheat Sheaf, 11th Inst. The hounds and a sporting bag-fox at Clifden at 10. Any member not attending or sending apology in writing to the President, to be no longer considered as belonging to the Hunt *(LJ. 9:2:1788).*

The picture emerges of a well-organised hunt, with strict rules, providing social occasions as well as hunting, and like the Merry Harriers, they had a system of rotating presidents. Later that year in October, there is notice of a meet: "Kilkenny Hunt, a fox at Grevine, Sam Waring, President" *(LJ. 11:10:1788).*

The Kilkenny Hunt's choice of meet at Grevine and the presence of a member of the Waring family indicate strong links with the Merry Harriers. The issue is further complicated by an isolated notice in Finn's Leinster Journal of April 1796 of a Merry Harriers meet at Kile-Roe, Sir John Blunden, President (FLJ. 2:4:1796). Had the Kilkenny Hunt been disbanded or did they exist along side the Merry Harriers? William Blunden refers to going foxhunting at Kilfane and Ballytobin in his journal of January 1790, unfortunately he omits to mention with which pack. It is dangerous to make too many assumptions from the above advertisements because they throw up more questions than answers. One can only surmise that the original Kilkenny Hunt Club was run on similar lines to those of the Merry Harriers.

Chapter 3

A New Era – John Power

I never saw a man that loved the work and pleasure of hounds and hunting, that had not many good qualities to him.
(Gaston de Foix, 1387)

The new and speedier hunting, fast becoming fashionable in the English shires towards the close of the eighteenth century, provided the vision for the type of hunting which John Power and Sir Wheeler Cuffe wished to emulate and introduce to Kilkenny. John Power (he was later made a Baronet) founded the present Kilkenny Hunt, the first established county pack in Ireland, on his arrival at Derrynahinch, Ballyhale, in 1797.

Soon afterwards he married Harriet Bushe of Kilmurry, near Thomastown and in 1799 he took a perpetual lease on Kilfane House, gardens and demesne, the adjoining property to his wife's home. Lady Power finally bought out the freehold in 1902/1903 and their descendants continued to live there until the 1970s. Contrary to popular belief the Powers were not local landlords.

John Power, a prominent Whig, was a man of independent means, based on his family's commercial interests in Clonmel. This enabled him to devote himself to his passionate love of hounds and hunting. On his arrival at Kilfane he constructed new kennels to the west of the main house at Sunnyvale, and filled them with the best English foxhound blood available.

It may have been Sir Wheeler Cuffe who was instrumental in introducing Power to the shires, where Cuffe was sufficiently well-known to have been included in the following lines:

> ... Sir Wheeler O'Cuffe
> Who neglecting at Tilton to keep a good luff
> *(Records of the Kilkenny Hunt, 1902-1908, 27)*

Occasionally he deputised as master for John Power and was the first man in Kilkenny to ride a clipped horse (which was not common practice until the mid 1880s) and together with Power, aimed to make

Kilkenny, the Leicestershire of Ireland. It is perhaps worth noting that County Kilkenny has recently been officially twinned with Leicestershire.

Power's contribution to Kilkenny hunting was enormous and had lasting effect, coverts he planted are still drawn by the hunt he founded. He supervised their planting and enclosing, while gradually refining his hunting techniques in accordance with the latest English theories of hound management and breeding. He presided over the hunt during its evolution from a small subscription pack into an important county institution. The changes took place gradually, at first he hunted in the old style over a vast area from Coollattin in County Wicklow, to Durrow in County Laois, drawing the last vestiges of forest, housing the hounds in temporary makeshift kennels. He met at daybreak initially, which was usual practice amongst traditionalists: "He frequently used to shelter from the wind under the lee of a house at the place of meeting 'till day dawned, and was enabled to commence operations" *(Anon. 1897, 12)*. The time of his meets gradually became later as he confined himself to hunting within the county.

Folklore in the Kilfane area still recalls stories from this golden era. Most frequently told is that of the devil's visit, which was recorded as follows by a Gowran schoolgirl in 1934:

> Some years ago, there lived a noble gentleman known as Sir John Power, a predecessor of the present Power family.
>
> He was at that time master of the Kilkenny hounds. One lovely morning of a meet during the hunting season Sir John felt so fit that he made the remark that he would ride against the devil that day. When he was out hunting that day a gentleman rode up on a lovely grey horse and Sir John was surprised to see that the man beat him in every way.
>
> He did some very difficult jumps, he even went so far as to jump his horse through the fork of a large tree.
>
> Sir John had so much admiration for this fine sportsman that he invited him to dine with him among his guests. When the dinner was over Sir John introduced card playing. During the game someone let a card fall and the butler who was waiting on them stopped to pick it up, and to his horror he discovered a cloven foot under the table. He then drew Sir John's

(Photo: Michael O'Byrne. Courtesy of Kilkenny Archaeological Society)

Sir John Power (1st Baronet) founder of the Kilkenny Hunt portrait by J.P. Haverty RHA.

> attention to it and soon the whole company became alarmed to find that their new guest was the devil.
>
> Sir John sent for his own clergyman to use his power to drive him away. He could not get rid of him. He was advised to get the Catholic priest which he did.
>
> The method he adopted to get him out was, first to put his hat in the door way, then he put his stick in the chimney and his gloves in the window. Then he prayed and after some time the devil disappeared through the roof. The exit in the roof we are told is still to be seen *(Folklore Commission, 1934).*

The scorch marks left by the devil making his exit through the roof are still visible, and it is reputed that no one has ever been able to fix the leaks that occur there.

A slightly less dramatic encounter occurred when William Wrixon-Becher, a gentleman actor friend of the Powers, had planned to secretly marry the professional actress, Elizabeth O'Neill. He had arranged a quiet wedding to take place at Kilfane. As luck would have it, he was unaware that his choice of date coincided with a meet of the Kilkenny Hounds at the same venue. A more public occasion could not have been foreseen, his secret was short-lived.

John Power and his son (also John) between them held the mastership of the hunt for fifty-three years, imparting to it great stability under their benign leadership. In effect they placed Kilkenny hunting on a modern footing.

Creation of Coverts and the Nineteenth Century Landscape

Prior to the establishment of the Kilkenny Hunt it was not unusual to hunt a bagged fox. Foxes were rare in the wild and there was little natural habitat within the county. John Power began to take steps to preserve them, and build up numbers for hunting.

When he established the hunt he found the country largely unenclosed. He could: ". . . follow hounds over a district called the Welsh Mountains [a region in the south-west of the county] to the bridge of Waterford without jumping a fence" *(Anon, 1897, 11).* Victor McCalmont claimed that when he was a young man he did not require a horse that could jump while hunting the country south of Stonecarthy,

(Photo: Des McCheane)

Knockroe Covert planted by Sir John Power (1st Baronet).

and parallel and east of the main Waterford/Kilkenny road, thus proving that some of the poorer areas of the county remained comparatively unenclosed right into the twentieth century.

It is unclear at what stage Power began his planting and enclosing program. He is credited with having created coverts at Castlewarren, Bishopslough, Cloghala, Dunbell and Knockroe amongst others. Some of these were patches of natural gorse and scrub which he enclosed and planted *(Anon 1897)*. Artificial earths were constructed within them. He leased Grennan Wood as a nursery for foxes, which when reared were strategically distributed around the country. Some coverts were rented from the occupier of the land who was compensated for loss of use and for the inconvenience of having to tolerate increased numbers of foxes.

The Aher and Clements map of County Kilkenny 1812-1824, has seven coverts marked: Ballykeeffe Hill, Baunreagh, Booleyglass, Bregaun, Newlands and Pottlerath *(Andrews, 1979)*. Unfortunately, the section of the map containing the Barony of Gowran is missing, so the list is not complete. All those planted by Power were within that Barony, with the exception of Knockroe. The latter is omitted on the

Aher and Clements map, suggesting that they only noted the older, mature and probably natural ones.

The establishment of strategic coverts around the hunting country created areas like islands of cover, from which the foxes would break giving the field a fast run in between. If it had not been for these artificial habitats and for the lengths to which Power and others went to preserve them, foxes would have possibly gone the way of the wolf, or like the pinemarten (once common in Kilkenny) become extremely rare.

The more important coverts were managed by covert keepers, who maintained them and preserved the foxes. Elsewhere, for example in England, there are reports of foxes being fed horseflesh to keep the numbers up *(Carr, 1986)* and it is likely that a similar system was in operation here. Most of the coverts mentioned still survive, are owned by the Kilkenny Hunt and continue to be drawn. In Bishopslough, the remains of formal box hedging at the entrance of an earth, may still be seen.

The nineteenth century countryside remained very bare, even though it was now well enclosed. Few hedges were planted, the majority of field boundaries took the form of walls and banks. Big granite walls were characteristic around Ullard in the east of the county, with thin high walls around Ballyconway. Further south and east "murder mile", between Ballyhale and Kilcasy, caused grief to many a hunting horse as they banked the wide walls which continue to Hugginstown. Further again to the south near Mullinavat and over on the New Ross side and along the Suir, were the single banks so beloved of the steeplechasers who raced alongside each other over them. In Knockroe and surrounding areas, the heavier land required the digging of deep ditches and the earth was thrown up in banks alongside them, awesome but not as big as those found in the Booleyglass country. Kilkenny became famous among hunting folk for the variety of its fences.

The constant demand for fuel in a county where turf bogs are rare, where dung was dried and thistles were collected for fuel *(O'Sullivan, 1828)* ensured the banks and walls were kept free of scrub wood. Much land still required draining, making the going very heavy in a wet winter. O'Sullivan entered in his diary on St. Stephen's day 1828, it was "difficult to go hunting with a pack of hounds today, for it is extremely hard for the hunters to follow them, the country is so wet" *(O'Sullivan, 1797, 28)*. A strenuous effort was required by those who followed hounds under such conditions.

Wildlife remained under pressure outside the demesne walls, the human population continued to increase rapidly until the Famine in 1845 and by then 50% of Ireland was under cultivation, and that figure was even higher for parts of Kilkenny *(Smith, 1995)*.

In 1884, both Killeen, near Knocktopher, and Carpenter's Glen, a draw close to Dunmore Park, were described as having virtually no cover *(Butson, 1884-86)*. There was barely sufficient to hold a sporting fox, yet these remained important hunt coverts.

Impact of Hunting on Landowners and Tenants

Most landlords readily agreed to the preservation of foxes and even those who did not hunt made their contribution by donating use of their coverts, rent-free, to the hunts. Vulpicide was regarded by hunting people as the most heinous of crimes. Therefore it is not surprising that it was occasionally used by tenant farmers as a method of making a protest. Such protests culminated in the Land League hunts, where all vermin and game were ruthlessly destroyed with the intention of "getting at" the landlords *(Curtis, 1987)*.

By the mid 1800s a list of Kilkenny Hunt coverts and covert keepers indicate a well-managed hunt *(MS 25043, NLI)*. In Lord St. Lawrence's time, there were twenty-six gorse coverts *(KK Mod. 12:1:1870)* and ten years later in 1869 the country was considered overstocked with foxes *(Anon 1870)*. The keepers acted as important liaison men between the hunt and the tenant farmers. They were well rewarded by the hunt when a find resulted in a good run.

The effect of hunting on the small farmer prior to the Famine is unrecorded. Initially, the small field of followers and the slowness of the chase, imply little damage. The problems began when increased numbers began breaking down fences and carelessly riding across corn. However the effect on crops was minimal as the sport was confined to winter.

Once hunt committees became aware that they were answerable to farmers for damage caused by foxes, poultry funds were set up to compensate for loss of fowl. In the Thomastown district, in the season of 1888-89, £9-10-0 was paid out by the fund, slightly more than the £9 rent paid for the use of Kiltorcan covert.

Nineteenth century cattle held little condition during the winter months and did not require the strong fencing of their modern counterparts. The lack of wire made it possible for riders to choose their own line of country with ease. The only place where wire did have a major impact was along the Dublin to Waterford railway line which split the hunting country in two. On the other hand, foxes soon learned that they could benefit from the railway and would run the line.

Pictures from the last two decades of the nineteenth century, show a countryside remarkably bare to modern eyes. It is apparent that the walls and banks only became "hairy" in the twentieth century, when the demand for firewood declined.

Small Private Packs

Wakefield, in 1812 wrote: "Kilkenny, Carlow and the Western side of the Barrow, south of the Queen's County, abound with county squires... distinguished by a taste for foxhunting" *(Lewis, 1975, 81).* Lewis disputes this on the basis that relatively few hunts subsequently developed in these areas, but the local evidence indicates that in the early nineteenth century Wakefield was correct and a large number of small packs did exist in County Kilkenny.

Private packs of hounds co-existed with the Kilkenny Hunt, they were mainly described as harriers, but if their quarry was not readily available they probably hunted whatever came their way: hares, foxes or even the occasional outlying deer. The manner in which they agreed their country is unknown, but it is likely that the smaller packs just hunted in their own immediate vicinities. The Webbsborough Hunt was one such pack, notice of its first meet was placed in the Leinster Journal in 1805.

> The Webbsborough Hunt will meet on the 1st Tuesday in every month and the first meeting to take place on Tuesday 2nd April next, Lewis C. Kinchella, Treasurer *(LJ. 30:3:1805)*

They were based to the north of the city. In the same year another Kilkenny pack disbanded, that of George Pack of High Street who sold his hare hounds *(L.J. 17:8:1805).* Four years later Mr. Hunt of Jerpoint, a prominent member of the Kilkenny Hunt Club sold his pack of twenty couples of harriers *(KK Mod. 2:5:1827).*

During the late 1820s the Elliotts of Clonmore hunted a subscription pack called the Iverk Harriers *(KK Mod. 2:5:1827)* and Edward Cooke of Patrick Street, founded his pack of "Kilkenny Harriers", obviously with John Power's blessing for he gave them a stag to hunt in February

(Photo: author)

Stone wall country near Ullard. Field enclosures in foreground and Borris Demesne walls in background.

1827 *(KK Mod. 21:2:1827),* a practise that was not uncommon for a master of hounds who wished to bestow a favour upon a smaller pack.

Mr. Cooke's Harriers continued to hunt through to 1858 when it was reported that, "the successful hunting of this beautiful pack has been very remarkable during the season" *(KJ. 13:2:1858)* and "the Merry Red Caps still keep up the sport although the foxhunting season has closed locally" *(KK Mod. 10:4:1858).* Incidental references to other small packs occur regularly in the newspapers, and many were probably short-lived.

Some accounts are more confusing than helpful, such as the following:

> A treat for sportsmen, on Friday, at one o'clock, the Ballydine hounds met at Ballynarahagh, shook a bag fox, and, in a few short minutes had Reynard aground after a run of a mile and a half, although the horses were actually knee deep... Capt.

> Power was as usual in a conspicuous place, with Walter Herbert and young Power... we hear the Capt. intends producing the same pack and one of the same foxes, on the same ground Monday next *(KK Mod. 19:1:1833).*

One can only feel sympathy for the unfortunate farmers and wonder why the Powers and Mr. Herbert, a founder member of the Kilkenny Hunt, were hunting regularly with another pack. Had the Tithe War prevented them from hunting their own hounds, or were they merely visiting neighbours?

Mr. Smithwick's Kilcreene Harriers (1860s–1870s) were an extremely popular pack both with the press and local farmers, at a time when the Kilkenny Hunt was having severe difficulties. Regiments, like the 20th stationed in Kilkenny, had their own beagles to provide sport. Some hunts based outside the county hunted within the county boundaries, for example, the Carlow Hunt occasionally held meets in the east of the county. Violet Martin attended one such meet in Gowran *(Martin, 1888).* To the south, the Curraghmore hunted in County Kilkenny, until the hounds were sold as a direct result of the Land War in 1884.

Chapter 4

The Kilkenny Hunt Club

Laugh and be fat, hunt and be happy. (H.W. Briscoe, c.1870)

In 1797 the Kilkenny Hunt Club based itself in Patrick Street. Mr. James Rice became house-steward to the club, and in 1817 he opened Rice's Hotel (later The Club House Hotel) on the premises *(Kilkenny People, 1992)*. To the present day the two hundred year old Kilkenny Hunt continues to hold its meetings in the Club House Hotel.

Emulating the gentlemen's hunting clubs of Leicestershire, the Kilkenny Hunt Club quickly became fashionable and influential. Unfortunately the original rules have been lost. The only rules in existence date from 1904. Membership was a much coveted honour. The club's function, apart from aiding the master in providing good sport, was to enliven the long winter months in an era when communication and travel were difficult for those living in the countryside. Initially members met for two weeks in November and again in February. They stayed at the Club House, each bringing two or three horses and an assortment of servants and grooms. Some, like the Marquess of Waterford, a well-known Meltonian, brought many more. Each day's hunting was followed by a long dinner and on occasion wild and reckless behaviour – this despite John Power's relative sobriety.

The arrival of the Hunt Club caused much excitement and gaiety. The hounds, the horses and the red coats, all immaculately turned out were quite a sight. In 1819, forty members, all gentlemen, sat down to a dinner chaired by the High Sheriff of Kilkenny, John Flood, at which they presented John Power with a silver candelabra (value 300 gns.) as a token of their gratitude *(KK Mod. 16:2:1819)*. They honoured him as the founder of the club, *(KK Mod. 16:2:1819)*. This would seem to prove that the earlier eighteenth century Kilkenny Hunt Club had previously been disbanded.

As the years passed the club's success attracted gentlemen from further afield to stay in Kilkenny for the hunting season. Hunting provided those who had time and leisure on their hands with an outlet that tested their mettle as well as their purses. In 1816 twenty horsemen out was considered a large field, however, by the mid century after the introduction of the railway to Kilkenny, several hundred were out at some of the more popular meets.

In the nineteenth century, there were only a limited number of ways for a fashionable young man to show off his wealth and it was not long before hunting was considered to be amongst the more agreeable. It encouraged them to live on their estates, to keep active and fit, and attracted others into the county circulating money locally. They competed with each other, testing their prowess in crossing the country, often over-riding the hounds and spoiling the sport for the rest of the field *(Howth, 1894).* It is particularly difficult to establish exactly who was hunting, as the contemporary newspaper reports invariably only mention members of the landed gentry and the aristocracy. Although it is possible to name a large number of the hunt club members throughout the century, this would give a false idea of who actually hunted. Many farmers, merchants and horse dealers regularly hunted, without ever aspiring to being club members, and they remain undocumented and virtually impossible to identify.

Foremost amongst the early club members was Sir Wheeler Cuffe of Lyrath, who remained a staunch supporter for over fifty years *(Anon., 1897).* Others included Sir Nicholas Loftus of Mt. Loftus, Mr. Bayley of Norelands, Sir R. Cox, Bart. and Messrs. Montmorency, Ponsonby and Cooke *(Fitzpatrick, 1878).* The club was supported by a number of non-hunting men who approved of its ideals. They gave the hunt use of their coverts free of charge and donated considerable subscriptions to the hunt.

The extravagant and outrageous behaviour of the hunt club members was typified by the actions of the 3rd Marquess of Waterford. He is said to have ridden his horse upstairs in the Club House Hotel, and jumped the dining room table before returning downstairs. On a separate occasion Captain Machell successfully wagered that he could jump up and stand on the four inch wide mantel shelf above the fireplace. Such high-jinks did not prevent the club members from professing to stand on high moral ground, in the belief that hunting was conducive to the unity and stability of society. The argument was that as hunting was open to all, it promoted good health and a sense of tradition within the community. The club became such a powerful county institution that a grand jury excused Sir John Power (dressed in his hunting coat) from attendance on the grounds that he had "other business" *(British Hunts and Huntsmen, 1911).*

(Private Collection)

The 3rd Marquess of Waterford

The Hunt Club Evolves

Sir John Power died in 1844 and his son, John, succeeded to the baronetcy and to the sole mastership of the Kilkenny Hunt. This he ran with great enthusiasm and skill for five seasons until he found that he was unable to continue and resigned his mastership in 1850. He remained a member of the hunt club and was prominent on the hunting field until close to his death in 1873.

A period of decline set in after the Famine. In February 1855, the hunt committee had to call a meeting in the Club House Hotel to determine that :

> the selection maybe made of some gentlemen willing to undertake the keeping of a pack of foxhounds... in a county where the feelings of the gentry and tenantry has always been in favour of hunting *(KJ. 21:2 1855).*

They failed to find a suitable candidate, and a committee was forced to run the hunt until Lord James Butler took over. The success of the hunt club ultimately depended upon the whims and the fortunes, or the lack thereof, of individual masters. Throughout this period of turmoil club membership continued to be considered highly desirable. It was occasionally conferred upon officers of visiting regiments, Lord St. Lawrence was one such individual. He was from a Catholic family, whose seat was Howth Castle, near Dublin. He was introduced to Kilkenny hunting via his regiment – the 7th Hussars, who were based in Carrick-on-Suir. On becoming master in 1856, he revived the hunt club and bought himself a house in the city, but found it more convenient to live at the "Club".

The excessive behaviour and practical jokes of earlier times were no longer as popular. Nevertheless, for a wager of 100 sovereigns, Sir John Courtney of Ballyedmund, County Cork rode his grey hunter up the stairs and into the club room, jumped a firescreen across the breadth of the room and: "then rode downstairs in the same way, a feat even more perilous and difficult than the ascent, inasmuch as the steps are sheeted with brass" *(KJ. 18:2:1857).* He was much praised for his great horsemanship.

A farewell dinner given in the Club House to honour Lord St. Lawrence was:

> replete with every luxury and delicacy of the season... The wines were abundant and composed of some of the finest and rarest vintages that joyously sparkled. The rich liquid poured out in congenial response to each toast *(KJ. 6:4:1861).*

This dinner was chaired by George Bryan, a fellow Catholic, of Jenkinstown and a former Kilkenny Hunt master. St. Lawrence's departure was apparently accelerated by an unfortunate liaison with a certain Miss Davis *(St. Lawrence notes).*

Henry Briscoe, a first rate master in a similar mould to the two Sir John Powers, had a moderating effect on the club members. An excellent judge of horses and hounds, he encouraged and enjoyed the hunt club dinners but, like his predecessors from Kilfane, he did not over-indulge during the hunting week and retired early to bed.

Practical jokes did not entirely die out. Captain Hartopp in the early 1880s, the first man to introduce polo to Ireland, was remembered for his electrification of the Club House railings. When touched by passersby, the unfortunates received a nasty shock. He also amused himself by feeding cats with fish heads placed on exploding plates *(Bell, 1947).*

Kilkenny Society and Hunting

The conviviality of the hunting field extended to the families of the club members. The influx of visitors added to the sport. In particular hunting officers from various regiments were tapped as a source of eligible gentlemen for daughters of marriageable age, who were encouraged to be seen out hunting. To begin with the ladies travelled to meets in a variety of equipages to view and to be viewed. Some were sufficiently interested in hound work to follow on horseback without actually taking part in the hunt. These fared better, since they travelled the lanes and boreens that the "equipages" found inaccessible. Several cartoons, showing grooms trying, with various degrees of success, to keep their young female charges to the road, appeared in English magazines of the period.

The poor state of the road network was noted too in March 1859, when Lord Waterford was killed in a fall while hunting at Corbally Wood, south of Castlemorres :

> the body having been placed on a bier, was conveyed to the road, as no car could get up the lane, and there it was laid onto a break-carriage belonging to Lord Bessborough *(KK Mod. 2:4:1859).*

This tragic accident caused hunting caps to become unfashionable, both in Great Britain and Ireland. People took to wearing silk hats and towards the end of Queen Victoria's reign the bowler hat became the

(Photo: Des McCheane)

The memorial to the 3rd Marquess of Waterford, marking the site where he was killed out hunting, while jumping a low wall onto a lane.

preferred headwear.

Hunt balls and the hunt steeplechases were the social high points of the year. The hunt balls were attended by the elite, but all were welcome at the hunt races. Racing was an obsession with the sporting public during the nineteenth century. Reports and results of races throughout Ireland and further afield were regularly published in the local press, like hunting they provided a spectacle for all to view.

The Kilkenny Hunt steeplechases generally took place at the end of the hunting season in April and the location varied. They attracted huge crowds of spectators at a time when there was little organised sport.

In 1842 the hunt steeplechase meeting took place at Dunmore, in the north of the county, "the fences were large, but safe and the view from a commanding hill, was uninterrupted and complete". At two o'clock, eight horses lined up competing for a purse of 40 sovereigns, but four refused to jump the first fence. Mr. Hogan's black horse, Jack Hinton, went on to win the race in one heat despite being "well drenched in a drain". The only other race that day was for a purse of ten sovereigns for the beaten horses where Mr. Coghlan's brown mare, Stout, was successful in both heats of this race (KJ. 16:4:1842). The 1845 Hunt Steeplechase race conditions were advertised in the newspapers one month in advance. The stewards were the Earl of Desart, John Power Esq., Horace Rockford Esq. and Theophilis St. George Esq.

Four races were held at the Dunmore meeting in 1864, of which the third was the Kilkenny Hunt Cup. The conditions for the race were as follows:

> Sweepstakes of 3 Sovs. each, with a cup added value £50. For horses, *bona fide* the property of Subscribers, and that have been hunted regularly with the Kilkenny Fox Hounds. Certificates to that effect to be produced, if required, from the Master of the above Hunt. Gentleman riders. Weights, 12st. About 3 miles over the Steeple Chase Course. The winner to pay 3 sov. towards expenses. *(KJ. 9:4:1864).*

Whitefields near Kilfane, Dunningstown and Jenkinstown were all popular venues for hunt races. In 1857 a special train was laid on from Kilkenny at 10.40 a.m. to Thomastown, returning after the Whitefields races at 7 p.m. First class tickets were 2/6d, third class 1/6d. *(KJ.*

2:5:1857). The hounds usually met the day following the races, which in turn coincided with a week of festivities including the hunt ball.

By the end of the nineteenth century the hunt races became known as point-to-point meetings, and they moved to a course near Castlemorres. The hunt was not the only organisation to run point-to-points. The 85th Regiment held one on a course between Adamstown and Brittas in the parish of Tullaroan, and in the early twentieth century the 60th Rifles had another near Uppercourt, Freshford *(Records of the Kilkenny Hunt, 1899-1908).*

Hunt balls were popular social occasions held exclusively for the aristocracy and gentry. The Kilkenny Hunt Ball of February 1845 was held in the Tholsel, in Kilkenny City, the band of the 24th Regiment provided the music. Tickets were 7/6d for gentlemen and 5/- for ladies. "The attendance was numerous and comprised of the 'elites' of our gentry", *(KJ. 12:2:1845).* At least 110 attended.

In 1857 the Monster House advertised the sale of Limerick lace and tartan dresses, head dresses, opera cloaks etc. "for the approaching ball" *(KJ. 18:2:1857).* Henry Clifford also had "ready for inspection, a superb collection of new goods ordered expressly for the approaching ball", confirming that the resident gentry were supporting local businesses. The popular master, Lord St. Lawrence, was credited with "having done much to renovate the hitherto somewhat depressed spirits of our leading aristocracy and making our city a point of attraction with the sporting world" *(KJ. 18:2:1857).* He was also credited with the introduction of "public" hunt balls, meaning that people, other than the friends and relatives of the hunt club members, were welcome to attend.

Over 210 attended the 1857 ball at the Athenaeum, it was decorated with the following mottoes "Prosperity to the Faire City", "Unity and Peace", "Sweet Tallyho" and the more nationalist "Erin go Bragh" and "Cead Mile Failte" *(KJ. 21:2:1857).* The tables were decorated with "rare and beautiful flowering plants from the Marquess of Ormonde's greenhouses". By 1860, the ball had become so popular that a special train was laid on from Waterford "for the conveyance of parties wishing to attend the ball" *(KJ. 4:2:1860).* Tickets for gentlemen had gone up to 12/- but the ladies' tickets were reduced to 3/6d *(KJ. 4:2:1860).* The dancing began at 10 p.m. and continued until 5 a.m.

In 1860 the hounds met the morning after the ball at the Club House Hotel, drawing an enormous crowd. Most of the sporting gentlemen who attended the ball were present the following morning *(KJ.*

8:2:1860), many of whom had come considerable distances from Meath and Kildare, for a week of hunting and associated activities.

During Captain Hartopp's mastership the mounted hunt servants, dressed in livery, distributed the dance programs *(Bell, 1947).* It was as though each ball had to be more splendid than the previous one.

The Hunt Ball accounts survive for 1886. 77 gentlemen's tickets were sold for 15/6d each and 73 ladies' tickets for 12/6d each. The greatest expenses were the supper, drink and band. Lighting cost £12, and ice 10/-. The end result was a deficit of £70-12-0 *(Hunt ball account, 1886)* enough to make any modern hunt treasurer shudder, in an age when the hunt ball is viewed as a fund raising necessity.

While these occasions were of considerable benefit to the local economy, they also encouraged the aristocracy and gentry to be content to remain resident within the county rather than seek their entertainment abroad.

Ladies of the Nineteenth Century Kilkenny Hunting Field

In England a number of women hunted in the eighteenth century, when the pace was slow and the jumping limited. Squires' wives and daughters were not uncommon on the hunting field. As the century drew to a close, galloping over fences became easier for men due to the development of a new flat hunting saddle, but this made life more difficult for the ladies.

The evidence for the Irish situation is difficult to find. The only confirmation found of a woman hunting in County Kilkenny at this early date, is an intriguing newspaper notice from December 1772, it describes the loss of an essential part of a lady's hunting kit:

> ... on Wednesday Dec. the 9th, between the hours of twelve and three, on the road from Maryborough to Kilkenny, a small Pearl Drop was lost from a Lady's Ear, dressed in a light blue habit, much damaged by a late expedition, and mounted on a black horse. Whoever brings the said Drop to I.M. Esq; at his Lodgings in Coal-Market, Kilkenny, shall receive ten Guineas reward, and no questions asked.
>
> As said Drop is a principal part of a Lady's Hunting Equipage, I.M. Esq; requests that it may be delivered with speed *(FLJ. 12:12:1772).*

By 1800 ladies were a rarity on the hunting field. There were a few notable English exceptions such as the Marchioness of Salisbury. She was the first recorded female master of hounds, 1775-1819 *(Buxton, 1987)* and she only retired when in her seventies. It can be assumed that those in upper echelons of Irish society were influenced by the behaviour of their peers in England, where, as the sport developed into its faster format, few women continued to participate. The few who did must have been the most remarkable and exceptional horsewomen. Riding alongside the men, they jumped supporting themselves by grasping the back of their side-saddles with one hand – a feat few men would have been capable of accomplishing.

By 1800 in Kilkenny, women were not encouraged to be forthright in their behaviour and those who were, often suffered severe disapproval from their own kind, as did Lady Loftus of Mount Loftus by Elizabeth Richards in 1807:

> Lady Loftus was another of the company, she is in her climacteric *[menopause]*. She seems to retain all the tastes of youth and to have the silliness of childhood. Her tongue never ceases. She says, she electioneers, is President of the Kilkenny Hunt, takes an interest in county business and is actually carrying a presentment mending a road against her husband, Sir Edward Loftus *(Richards, 1807).*

Whether she actually hunted remains a mystery. The first mention of a woman hunting with the Kilkenny Hunt is in a poem written c.1820:

> For all were most eager to join in the sport,
> Harry Lorrequer's hero we think of with pride,
> And his sister, a Willett, they rode side by side,
> Disdaining restriction and feminine fear,
> She so loved the hunting and always was near
> *(Anon., 115).*

Mrs. Willett was born Rebecca O'Flaherty of Castlefield, daughter of a spendthrift Justice of the Peace and High Sheriff of Kilkenny *(Corballis, 1996).* Obviously an exceptional young lady, for it was not until 1830 that Jules Charles Pellier and Francis Boucher invented the

(Courtesy of Mr. & Mrs. Andrew Kavanagh)

Miss Power dressed in her hunting attire. It is difficult to believe that she actually followed hounds wearing these tight corsets.

third pommel or leaping head that enabled women to jump and ride on a par with men (Buxton).

"The Young Ladies Equestrian Manual" of 1838 recommended:

> no lady of taste ever gallops on the road. Into this pace, the lady's horse is never urged, or permitted to break, except in the field: and not above one among a thousand of our fair readers... is likely to be endowed with sufficient ambition and boldness to attempt 'the following of hounds'.

It instructed ladies on leaping the bar in a riding school and recommended standing leaps to be taught first; they were considered more difficult, but safer than flying ones.

In the 1830s, in the shires, ladies began to spend the hunting season with their menfolk, which had a calming effect on their wild behaviour. Many began to take an interest in attending the meets and watching the hounds work where possible. They are reported as having taken similar interest in Kilkenny and in the latter end of Sir John Power's (1st Baronet) time, he tolerated ladies on the hunting field to a greater extent than many of his contemporary English masters:

> some may have been riding spectators from the road. However, there were two who made themselves conspicuous by their good riding viz. Lady Desart... a most finished horsewoman over a country; and Miss Fetherstonhaugh, a lady from Westmeath, and had the enviable reputation of being able to keep a foremost place in every good run *(Anon., 1897, 56).*

Amongst those who rode with the field under Sir John Power's (2nd Baronet) mastership were the Misses Langrishe of Knocktopher, Miss Smithwick of Kilcreene and Lady Worcester (afterwards Duchess of Beaufort) *(Bowen, 1953).* Augusta Bryan, sister of George Bryan is portrayed in hunting attire in a c.1853 oil painting by Edmund Fitzpatrick, at the enlargement of the stag, but it is note-worthy that she is not depicted in the second painting where the hounds are running.

Newspaper hunting reports do not mention ladies hunting until the late 1850s. It does not necessarily mean that they were not hunting, as they only reported the names of the aristocracy, gentlemen and officers. It is also conceivable that it was considered indelicate for a lady's name to appear in print in a hunting report. The first newspaper report of ladies hunting in Kilkenny describes them as being "in fashionable equipages and on horseback" *(KJ. 29:11:1856).* The following year "Lady Desart mounted on her spirited steed, also joined the sport" *(KJ. 14:11:1857).*

Others felt safer and more secure in their "splendid equipages and gorgeous scarlet hunting costumes", Miss Smithwick on that day is mentioned as the sole lady amongst the field *(KJ. 27:11:1858).* Gradually, the numbers of women hunting increased and by 1861 the

Kilkenny Journal noted several, Miss Smithwick was the most frequently mentioned, hunting in the company of Mr. J.R. Howlett (of Tullaherin) whom she later married.

The new three-pommelled side saddle and the balance strap were introduced c. 1860 and the safety skirt about 1875, giving women

(Courtesy of Mrs. Peter Thomas)

Drawing by Crawford McFall, from Mrs. Solly Flood's scrapbook.

greater freedom and removing the dangers of riding in long and unsuitable skirts while also saving their hunters from sore backs. During the latter half of the century, thanks to these improvements the numbers of women who hunted increased enormously. It was the Empress of Austria who finally made hunting fashionable and respectable for women. She rented Summerhill House in County Meath for two seasons and was a beautiful and an accomplished horsewoman who drew the admiration of all. She also hunted with the Queen's County Hunt adjacent to County Kilkenny.

In general Kilkenny Hunt masters appear to have been tolerant and even welcoming to lady riders. By 1880, at least twenty ladies were hunting with the Kilkenny Hunt in the Ballyragget country *(Butler, 1880).* Sinclair Butson, master, noted in his 1884 hunting diary that "Alice W. Smith rode beautifully all the way on Rufus", on a run from Dunmore Park to Flagmount, where he stopped the hounds after 1 hour 40 minutes, a "distance about 15 miles, very few finished". He also admired the young Hon. Rose Bingham, who got away with hounds near Coppenagh alone with Mr. Spencer and Mr. Pilsworth on January 2nd 1885. Later the same month, she was one of only seven of a very large field who finished a hunt from Ballyfoyle as darkness fell *(Butson, 1884-86).* The fatal hunting accident to Mrs. Crofton in 1897 came as a shock for many, but it failed to halt the influx of the fair sex. She met her fate jumping downhill over a double bank near Booleyglass, during a fine run of 1¼ hours.

It has been suggested that the roots of the women's movement for liberation may be found on the hunting field *(Carr, 1987),* where able and influential women discovered that they were capable of riding as hard as men across country and some, like the Empress of Austria, outrode them all. Today equestrian sports are virtually alone in that women may partake as equals to men and compete directly with them. Their new found independence gave them the confidence to make greater demands for liberation in other spheres.

Chapter 5

Periods of Crisis

It will be evident... that on more than one occasion the Kilkenny Hunt and with it the old Club, was perilously near extinction, and probably has had more hairbreadth escapes than most packs.
(J. Connellan, 1897)

During its first century the Kilkenny Hunt withstood many problems. External factors, the Tithe War, the Famine and the Land League's anti-hunting campaign which coincided with an agricultural depression, all took their toll. A fierce internal dispute erupted, fuelled by some members' political views on tenant rights and the Protestant status quo's rejection of their aspirations.

The fact that the hunt survived these periods of turmoil proved its resilience and ability to adapt. Lessons were learned and the grievances were addressed.

During the eighteenth century it was generally accepted that, legally, one was at liberty to cross anyone's land while foxhunting. After 1809 the laws of trespass applied and hunts became responsible for any damage caused *(Itzkowitz, 1977)*. In effect the rural community allowed hunting to continue regardless. In Kilkenny leases stipulated that the landlord reserved the rights for himself and his heirs to have "free liberty to hunt, hawk, fish or fowl"*(Tighe, 1802, 421)* on tenanted lands. They also reserved the right to make or erect ditches and fences, another indication of the continuing enclosure of land.

Tithe War

The Tithe War was probably the most difficult period with which Sir John Power (1st Baronet) had to contend, but its effect on hunting is virtually undocumented. The following letter from Lord St. Lawrence hinted that all was not well in the early 1830s:

> When the wrath of the peasantry was warmly kindled against the gentry in Kilkenny, many of the latter had to take to the (hunting) field armed, in order to protect themselves from

assault; but the life of the fox and hounds remained inviolate *(KK Mod., 12:1:1870).*

The Famine

By 1845, the hunt had increased enormously in popularity with over 150 red coats counted at one meet *(Anon., 1897)*. Only two seasons later matters had deteriorated, however the following encouraging comment appeared in a local newspaper:

> We are happy to learn that this famous hunt, which for so many years enjoyed the reputation of being the first in Ireland is to meet as usual this season. It was rumoured some time ago that the club was about to be dissolved; but we are glad to see by an announcement of the day and meeting, for this and the next months, that the gentlemen of the county are determined not to lose the high sporting character which they hitherto have gloried to *(KJ. 23:10:1847).*

This raises the question as to what was the root cause of the problem. Was it the Famine? Presumably it resulted in the sudden downturn, but precisely how it affected hunting has not been researched. In 1847 the opening meet was held at Mount Loftus on October 28th. Reports indicate that they still managed to hunt three days a week. Sir John Power (2nd Baronet) resigned as master in 1850 but remained on the committee and continued to take an active role in the running of the hunt.

Meredyth/Bryan Dispute

In 1869, one of the most bitter disputes ever witnessed in Irish hunting erupted in Kilkenny. The main protagonists were the master, Henry Meredyth, and a previous master, George Bryan MP of Jenkinstown. Meredyth was a grandson of Clayton Bayly of Norelands, who was a founder member of the Kilkenny Hunt Club.

Bryan was descended from one of the most prominent Catholic families within the county. A generous man, he kept open house at Jenkinstown, and was generally resident there. He was a keen supporter of the tenant rights movement. Not only had he been master, but he was also one of the main subscribers to the hunt. He rode hard, had his own pack of harriers and held regular race meetings in the park at

Jenkinstown and generally closed his hunting season with the enlargement of a stag especially kept for the occasion. His generosity extended to giving enormous hunt breakfasts. The lavish feasts were held at Jenkinstown, where he entertained on a vast scale in his "usual princely style of hospitality at a splendid déjeuner" *(KJ. Nov. 1861)*. "At least 400 persons of all classes, from statesman... to the substantial yeoman were present on that occasion and of that number fully two-thirds were equestrians" *(KJ. 22:2:1864)*. On another occasion 140 were invited for breakfast before hunting with the Kilkenny foxhounds.

(Private collection)

George Bryan (centre) from a painting by Edmund Fitzpatrick.

During his first years as master of the Kilkenny Hunt, Meredyth showed good sport. Matters appear to have declined when his huntsman, William Boxall, resigned and Meredyth took up the horn himself. By 1867, there was an element of dissatisfaction with the quality of the sport and the manner in which he ran the hunt. This prompted some members to complain to George Bryan. In February 1869 Bryan's friend and ally, Mulhallen Marum, also a hunt member, wrote a letter to "Bell's Life" suggesting that the mastership of the Kilkenny Hunt would become vacant at the end of the season, thus initiating a lengthy and acrimonious debate, which the local and British press reported fully, *(KK Mod. 21:1:1870)*. Of the local newspapers the Kilkenny Journal sided with Bryan and the Moderator championed Meredyth.

Amongst the minority who initially supported Bryan were Sir John Blunden of Castleblunden, W.H Flood of Farmley, E.L. Warren of Lodge Park, H.M. de Montmorency of Tennypark, W.P. Blunden of Castleblunden, Robert Stanyard of Grange, A.W. Mosse of Ballyconra, Ralph Bunbury and John P. Hyland. These were all hunting men (only 30 members out of 85 hunted regularly). Yet in August 1869 most of them had signed a statement of confidence in Meredyth.

Bryan continued to insist that the hunt members in general were dissatisfied with Meredyth's management of the pack and the decline it had experienced since Lord St. Lawrence had handed it over to Meredyth. St. Lawrence had presided over the hunt when "Kilkenny stood forth as the first hunting county in Ireland" *(Bryan, 1870)*. There was also dissatisfaction with regard to the lack of social functions and "the primary cause of the Kilkenny Hunt difficulty... was the UTTER ABSENCE OF SPORT DURING THE PRESENT MASTERSHIP" *(Bryan, 1870)*.

The dispute grew into an extremely unpleasant and vicious one. The 1868-69 season concluded with the poisoning of several hounds at Knockroe covert to the west of the city. Later that year the Kilkenny Journal began to describe the hunt as "Kilkenny Ascendancy Hunt" implying their lack of respect for the land over which they rode and for the people's Roman Catholic religion *(KJ, 27:10:1869)*.

By the autumn of 1869 all attempts at reconciliation had failed and it was clear that Bryan had enormous popular support in the country to the north and west of Kilkenny city. At the second meet of the season on October 29th 1869 at Foyle Bridge, over fifty people obstructed the hunt and the Journal reported :

> two hundred stalwart farmers assemble at the meet to tell the field they are no longer welcome – that the farmers of the Freshford district will not tolerate "Ascendancy" in the hunting field. The neighbouring hills at each covert are lined with brawny men *(KJ, 3:11:1869)*.

It went on to state that over 200 men guarded other coverts in the district. Bryan's position was further entrenched by his founding of the "Kilkenny Tenant League". He took the chair, and Mulhallen Marum was appointed as one of the honorary secretaries. More hounds were maliciously poisoned, and Bryan felt obliged to resign from the hunt club. The fox coverts at Ballyspellan and Knocknamuck were set on fire and some attempts were made to burn those at Punchbowl, Kiltorcan and Clara *(KJ. 22:12:1869)* and a petition was signed warning off Meredyth.

The majority of incidents arose in the neighbourhood of Jenkinstown, so hunting generally took place elsewhere in the county, particularly in the south and east *(KK Mod. 30:3:1870)*. However, a few isolated disturbances are also recorded there. The burning of Sir John's Gorse occurred at Coolmeen, near Ballyhale, where Archdeacon O'Shea was strongly opposed to the hunt.

Hunting ceased in the middle of January 1870 following the poisoning of 19 more hounds. The remainder were threatened with sale. Lord St. Lawrence feared that the 26 gorse coverts would succumb to the plough, if the Kilkenny Hunt ceased to exist *(KK Mod. 12:1:1870)*.

Meredyth was not a man to give up easily, and by the end of the month he hunted again in defiance of Bryan *(KK Mod. 22:1:1870)*, this time however, he stated his intention to resign on May 1st (the traditional date for the termination of a master's contract), *(KK Mod. 22:1:1870)*. In February, Meredyth won a court case over an action taken by Thomas Morrissey after the Foyle Bridge episode *(KK Mod. 9:2:1870)*. Morrissey had been supported in his case by Mr. Maher, Bryan's agent, and a few weeks later the plaintiff was seen out hunting at Kilmanagh on a brown pony *(KK Mod. 2:3:1870)*.

The Solution - a New Master

The internal nature of the Kilkenny Hunt dispute is illustrated by the fact that the Kilcreene Harriers (Mr. Smithwick's pack) and the 20th Regiment's pack of beagles continued to hunt without any obstruction. There was tremendous enthusiasm for Mr. Smithwick's harriers and it is of note that Mr. Smithwick felt secure enough to enlarge a stag at Ballyfoyle, not far from Jenkinstown, on April 18th, 1870. Smithwick fully supported Bryan in his campaign to have Meredyth replaced and their stance was generally recognised as having popular support.

Lord St. Lawrence viewed the issues at stake as being of a religious and political nature and blamed the predominant position of Protestants in the hunting field, where three-quarters of the large estates and probably two-thirds of the Kilkenny Hunt subscriptions were Protestant *(KK Mod. 12:1:1870)*. At the same time he emphasised the amusement afforded to those Catholics who hunted and stressed that their harriers had long enjoyed access to the big Protestant estates. He emphasised that without the goodwill of Catholic farmers there would be no hunting, "so fragile, in reality, is the tenure of fox-hunting" *(KK Mod. 12:1:1870).* If hunting ceased in Kilkenny, it was his belief that most of Meredyth's supporters could afford to hunt in Kildare, Meath or the shires, but apart from Bryan none of the latter's supporters would be in such a position.

It was because of the dominant role of foxhunting within society, that the repercussions of the dispute were so widely felt.

Meredyth's supporters included some Roman Catholic subscribers who effectively closed ranks around their master, prompting Bryan to comment that in "retaining their Master... they have lost their country". Following yet another failed attempt at reconciliation under the arbitration of Lord Cork and Lord Portsmouth, numerous meetings chaired by Sir John Power (2nd Baronet) were held during the summer months in 1870. Little progress was made until a new master, acceptable to all, was found. This was Henry Briscoe who had resigned from the Curraghmore mastership, in favour of the 5th Marquess of Waterford, and was now available. Briscoe was a popular choice, a skilled huntsman with a level head, who was quickly accepted by all.

Although the dispute had split the county in two and caused considerable apprehension in the hunting world and even in the political world, it is remarkable how quickly and conclusively such a bitter row ended. Briscoe was able to hunt through Jenkinstown at the opening meet, in November 1870 without altercation. He was a brilliant sportsman with a keen knowledge of hounds and horses which had been handed down to him by his father who had kept a pack of harriers at Tinvane. (His expertise has remained within the family, as his great grand nephew, George Briscoe has been master of the Tara Harriers for over 50 years).

While agrarian agitation continued within the county, it took one good leader, capable of instilling respect from all sides, to save the Kilkenny Hunt. Briscoe provided the necessary ingredients. He was held in high regard and above all, he provided good sport.

Hunting, although perceived as the sport of the landlords, continued to be tolerated by tenant farmers even in Meath, Westmeath and Tipperary *(KK Mod., 12:1:1870),* where there was widespread unrest. It was not until the Land War that it became a target and even then opposition to the sport was never officially approved by the leaders of the Land League.

Land War

The Land League was founded in 1879. It was founded as a protest movement against landlords and unfair rents. Its birthplace was in Mayo and as it progressed eastwards across the country, it was hijacked by larger farmers and politicians and eventually became less radical.

(The Illustrated London News)

The State of Ireland: Stopping a Hunt, 1881.

Kilkenny was not one of the counties which suffered serious agitation in the early days of the movement. The Thomastown branch was not formed until late in 1880, and that branch was slow to join the renewed demands of the nationalists *(Gulliver & Silverman, 1995).* Agrarian outrages and protests had run at a low level since the Famine and dissension was gradually becoming more political in nature.

The Land League initiated a "campaign to stop landlords and magistrates from hunting across tenanted land" *(Curtis, 1987, 350).* It was not an anti-hunting campaign as such, for the more Catholic based harriers were not disrupted, and the movement even organised its own hunts, which were designed to wipe out all the game in a given area, thereby depriving the landlords from having sport. Thus the target of their objection was not the act of hunting, it was the fact that foxhunting was considered an immensely powerful social institution within certain counties. The Land League provided tenants with a mechanism with which landlords could be opposed through the interruption of an organisation, in which the landlords invested considerable time and money (although the latter was not always readily available).

Parnell and other leaders carefully avoided condemnation or approval of the anti-hunting campaign, which in effect meant such policies were decided upon at league branch level within the individual counties. Parnell was a hunting man who had supported the Wicklow Harriers and ironically hunted in December 1880 with the Curraghmore Hounds while staying with his friend Richard Power MP. Only ten months later while cub-hunting, the Curraghmore Hunt witnessed, the so-called Battle of Newtown Wood in south Kilkenny. Three hundred people were summoned by the bells of Faugheen Church and surrounded the hunt on Thomas Lalor's estate at Cregg. The "battle" only lasted a few minutes, during which a hound was killed and the Marquess was struck on the back by a stone. Meanwhile, four miles away at Tinvane, Henry Briscoe, who had done so much for foxhunting, was buried on the same day.

The unrest caused Lord Waterford to resign as master of the Curraghmore. He closed down his magnificent hunting establishment on which he spent £6,000 per annum *(Curtis, 1987).* Eighty horses were stabled there and his kennels held sixty couples of hounds. It had not been a subscription pack, apart from collecting cap at each meet, he financed the entire hunt himself, however he was not prepared to hunt without the full support of his tenants. This support had been withdrawn

(Courtesy of Kilkenny Archaeology Society)

The first known photograph of the Kilkenny Hounds: Captain Hartopp on left, Dan Carroll (first whip), Jack Tydd (huntsman) and Ben Capell (second whip), 1880-1881.

after he proceeded, on his agent's advice, against some half dozen tenants for non-payment of rent. It coincided with the imprisonment of several of the leaders of the Land League. By November 1881, Lord Waterford had sold his dog pack and moved with his best hunters to the shires where he hunted with his father-in-law, the Duke of Beaufort *(Curtis, 1987)*. Some of the Curraghmore hounds and horses were moved to Tinvane, from where Briscoe had hunted them in the time of the 4th Marquess. The bitch pack was lent to Lord Lonsdale for the remainder of the season and was subsequently lent to Thomas Springfield. He became master of a much dwindled subscription pack, based at Tinvane, which carried on against the odds until March 1884. Hounds were poisoned and protests continued. The entire pack was finally sold in England for £2,000 *(Curtis, 1987)*.

Lord Waterford's reaction to the anti-hunting agitation was precisely that which the majority of contemporary economists and local traders feared most, i.e. those who could afford to hunt elsewhere would do so, and become absentee landlords. Employment would suffer and money in circulation would be in short supply. Following their success at Curraghmore, league branches elsewhere planned to disrupt other hunts.

The Kilkenny Hunt - targeted by the Land League

The Kilkenny Hunt ran into trouble when Sir John Blunden sold the interest in the holdings of some tenants. The local league branch recommended that farmers in the vicinity should not allow hunting while the hounds remained kennelled at Blunden Villa.

The hunt encountered further trouble on November 2nd 1881 at Sir John's Gorse, Coolmeen, near Ballyhale. The same covert had been burnt twice during the Bryan/Meredyth dispute in March 1869 and 1870. On this occasion, a visitor (a Waterford corn merchant) who had applied for Kilkenny Hunt membership lost his temper with the agitators. This was deplored by those present who wished to remain on the best possible terms with the neighbouring farmers and as a result Thomas F. Spencer was refused membership. He was most aggrieved and accused the Kilkenny hunt members of snobbish behaviour. The hunt committee responded by inviting farmers to a meeting to "persuade them of the benefits of hunting to the community" *(Curtis, 1987, 372)*. The Kilkenny Hunt refrained from hunting for some weeks during

(Courtesy of Mrs. Peter Thomas)

A meet of the Kilkenny Hounds at Kilkenny Castle in 1882.

(Courtesy of Mrs. Peter Thomas)

James Connellan with his five favourite hounds, at Coolmore, Thomastown.

December, as did the Queen's County and the North Tipperary hunts. Other packs were worse off, the Kildare Hunt had to abandon hunting for the rest of the season, and the Curraghmore, Killimer and Wexford hunts all ended up selling their hounds. There was a general fear amongst the hunting community that it might cease entirely. Only four out of approximately twenty fox hunts remained unscathed by the Land League, they were the Meath, South Union, Louth and Scarteen *(Curtis, 1987)*.

The Kilkenny Hunt resumed hunting in January 1882, but the agitators persisted. While hunting near Thomastown on March 9th ten hounds were poisoned. This led to Captain Hartopp's resignation and he left for India *(Bell, 1948)*. He had been offered the mastership of the Kilkenny Hunt, prior to Briscoe, and had refused it. He was a man who liked to enjoy himself and not someone who wished to embroil himself in the fraught politics of hunting. A fine horseman, he probably recognised his limitations as an Englishman hunting an Irish pack of hounds in troubled times.

The pack entered a period of decline following Briscoe's death. The agrarian unrest had aggravated the hunt's already perilous state and the effects of the Land War took a long time to heal. This made the position of master an unenviable one. It was difficult to attract a suitable candidate, who possessed the necessary knowledge as well as money.

The hunt continued to struggle on, initially under the guidance of a committee. Financial and other problems plagued a succession of masters throughout the 1880s. Sinclair Butson encountered opposition between Killeen and Kiltorcan in November 1884:

> On our return there were about 20 boys (school boys) shouted and threw stones at the hounds and some women came out shouting and in fact were worse than the men *(Butson, 1884-86)*.

Lord Desart became master from 1882-84 "showing good sport under most trying circumstances" *(Anon., 1897, 88)*. It was a most difficult period, "and it seemed inevitable that the affairs of the hunt must be wound up, and the pack dispersed in order to meet outstanding liabilities" *(Anon.,1897, 90)*.

In 1886 Robert Challoner Knox became master. He was a colourful character, his home at Caherlesk was not far from Callan. In his youth he had been a keen cyclist and had hunted regularly with the Kilkenny Hunt during the mastership of Col. Frank Chaplin *(Challoner Knox, 1876)*. He was Lord Desart's agent, and was granted permission to erect temporary hunt kennels at Desart Court in 1886. The financial accounts survive for the year of his mastership. They include itemised construction costs (£18-13-3) for the erection of the kennels. What is clear from the accounts is that Major James Connellan, in his capacity as honorary secretary, was heavily subsidising Challoner Knox's mastership. He lodged personal cheques to the hunt accounts for a total sum in excess of £400 during the course of one season. Chally Knox, as he was generally known, became a Colonel in the Kilkenny Militia. Subsequently he was the cause of a major county scandal, having been accused of cheating Lord Desart's estate of a substantial sum of money. The Marquess of Ormonde, the Protestant Bishop of Ossory and Sir Hercules Langrishe stood by him and protested his innocence throughout the whole bitter controversy. *(Butler, 1986).* Under these circumstances it is not surprising that Chally Knox remained master for only one season. He was quoted in 1887 as being extremely pessimistic about the future of hunting and he believed that it could easily be

(Courtesy of Mrs. Peter Thomas)

James Connellan and the Kilkenny Hounds.

stopped in Kilkenny, by local farmers *(Curtis 1987).* Connellan took over from him and began what was to prove a crucial mastership for the future of the hunt. He bought the hounds from Edmund Smithwick and paid off the £106 outstanding to the Smithwick family for their keep. Connellan worked hard to prevent the hunt's collapse, running it on a tight budget, and in a diplomatic fashion for three seasons. It is thanks to him, the anonymous author of the *Memoir of the Kilkenny Hunt*, that we have a good record of the first hundred years of the hunt, and in which, apart from including his own picture, he omits any mention of himself. Luckily his daughter, Margarite Solly Flood, enlightens us:

> he really only took over because there had been financial and other difficulties. He hunted a very large area that, in those days, often entailed overnight train journeys for himself, all the hunt horses and temporary housing for hunt servants and hounds. He was a very keen man to hounds and showed very good sport but, characteristically, recorded none of this in his history *(Solly Flood, 1978, 53).*

He finally ensured the hunt's future by handing it over to his cousin, Capt. Hercules (Herky) Langrishe in 1890. On his retirement, Connellan was presented with a silver monteith and two old Irish goblets, by the hunt members as a token of their appreciation. The Smithwick family also received a presentation of silver in recognition of their role in saving the hunt for future generations.

Chapter 6

Stability under Hercules Langrishe

Hunting is all that's worth living for—
All time is lost wot is not spent in 'unting. (R.S. Surtees, 1805-64)

The Langrishe family had lived at Knocktopher Abbey since c.1700. They had a long history of activity in county politics and had been instrumental in the repealing of the oppressive penal laws, which had so restricted the activities of Roman Catholics.

When Captain Hercules Langrishe took over the reins of the Kilkenny Hunt, he was to be the first of four remarkably wealthy and talented foxhunting men, who provided long-term stability for the sport. Foxhunting in Kilkenny entered the twentieth century in a strong and secure position.

There was some doubt as to whether Herky was a suitable candidate, however as the Kilkenny Hunt still required substantial funding to keep it viable, and as he had just come into a considerable amount of money through his marriage to Helen, daughter of the Rt. Hon. Fitzwilliam Hume-Dick of Humewood, County Wicklow, it was agreed he should become master.

Herky soon won over those who were not enamoured with the idea of him hunting the hounds. He had previously hunted his own pack of harriers and gained from the experience. T.M. Fergusson described him as "Just a real wild good-looking Irishman" *(The Hexham Courant, Nov. 1932).* He became a good, fun-loving master of hounds, who subsequently turned out to be a fine amateur huntsman. He was witty, good company and determined to give sport at all costs, particularly as the sport had been poor for a number of years. He was a virtuoso on the hunting horn, and was capable of blowing "Gone Away" on his gun barrel. His favourite horse had a stiff off-foreleg, with no movement in the knee. When the horse jumped, it swung the leg over everything. Herky always maintained that it was the best horse he ever had.

His young wife, Helen, was an enthusiastic rider to hounds. Carrying his second horn, she followed Herky over everything. She never took her own line, but still had many crashing falls, breaking a large number of bones. She was remarkable for her stamina, was never known to be

(Courtesy of Kilkenny Archaeological Society)

From left to right: P.F. Dalton, H.R. Langrishe MFH, P. McGrath and W. Stacey, 1892-93.

tired, and seldom missed a day's hunting either with the Kilkenny or with the East Kilkenny hunts. After a long day in the saddle, she would regularly take her dogs for a lengthy walk around Knocktopher. Likewise she was not opposed to hacking long distances on her own. One evening, after a particularly good day with the Kilkenny, she rode into the yard at Shankill Castle, at about 6 o'clock. The hounds had run into County Carlow. Being very light, riding only about eight stone with her side-saddle, she would not get off her horse. She merely requested a chilled drink of water for her horse, which Jimmy Kilcoyne, the groom, provided whereupon she went off singing with a sixteen mile ride ahead of her to Knocktopher. She arrived home at 10 o'clock that night and, as telephones were not in general use, she sent a postcard which arrived the following day at Shankill, to say that she had reached home safely. Helen did not always see eye to eye with her husband, possibly due to the fact that he was partial to spending her money.

Herky believed that hunting should be fun, he was most amusing and thoroughly enjoyed life. He had the reputation of being a "divil" who could cause chaos on purpose and enjoy every moment of it. On one occasion when he had planned to catch the evening train to Dublin after hunting. Unsure as to how he could make a discreet departure from the field; towards the end of the day he dashed around to the back of the covert and blew "Gone Away", as only he could do, and rode flat out with the hounds for home. He was on the train by the time most of the field reached Knocktopher. When one old groom was asked if the story was true the reply was, "Ah sure there is no craic now, you would not mind what Sir Herky would do, he would do anything, he was great gas". Herky believed that it was the duty of the master to provide sport whenever possible.

On another occasion, it was arranged that the Kildare Hunt should be invited down to Kilkenny for a joint meet:

> there was always a certain amount of rivalry between the two packs and so we in Kilkenny, having heard that the Kildare ladies were preparing to show us a thing or two, were warned to keep our best horses for the occasion as each lady rider might have a possible Kildare opponent. As I had only one horse, the choice did not arise but I was quite confident that my 17 hand determined old "Speckles" was more than equal for any Kildare challenge, realised that if it came to a conflict that weight would tell and that all I had to do was to stick in my saddle. Unfortunately it turned out to be a pretty wet day and, as the previous night had been even worse, foxes had been stopped in. Poor Herky frantically drew covert after covert blank and his field was growing fewer and fewer when suddenly from a small gorse covert the pack opened up and screamed away. One of the first fences ahead was a big double bank and my opponent and I "happened" to be riding side by side as we reached it. It was the sort of fence Speckles loved, a big clean jump to the very centre of the bank followed by his usual grunt and having a good look ahead before taking off for about 20 yards across the field. We jumped together, but what would have been the lady's next move, I never knew and I felt very proud of my old man and not a little pleased with myself. We had a very fast run for about 20-30 minutes and then the scent seemed to suddenly fail. As it was pouring by then, the two masters decided that was enough and the sodden members

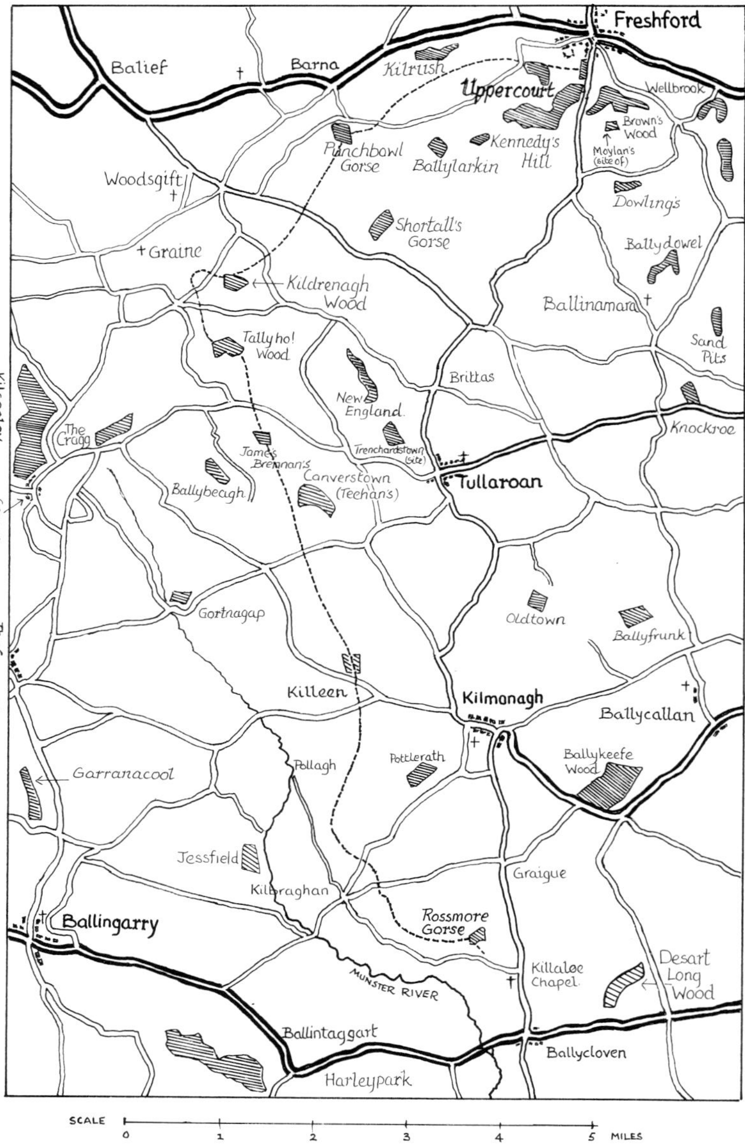

(Map based on Ordnance Survey permit no. 6742)

The line that hounds ran on the last of the famous Rossmore hunts, as drawn by Tommy McCheane.

> of the Kildare hunt repaired to the station, removed as much as possible of their soaking hunting clothes, and departed for home. It was a long time before any of us knew that Herky decided, on account of the previous night's storm and rain, that, at any cost, there must be a run of some sort and so arranged that, if the day was really bad, he would "draw" this certain gorse from which a well laid drag had been laid and so the Kildare could see and hear the Kilkenny hounds at work. There was an old porter in Kilkenny Station for years who was friends with everyone... and a short time after this hunt I was talking to Andy and mentioned to him what bad luck it had turned out so wet, but his view was quite different – 'Bad luck, is it? I never had a grander day watchin' Lady May-O strippin' to the skin in the Lady's room *(Solly Flood, 1978, 55).*

After several seasons hunting hounds, Herky's sporting attitude began to attract significantly larger fields. He was well able to manage them, thanks to his sense of humour and his good nature. His fame as a character was not just limited to hunting, his unprintable after dinner antics in male company were legendary. Foxes were still relatively scarce, blank days were not uncommon, but where a fox was found there was every chance of a long point. The famous Rossmore Hunts from the covert at Rossmore to Tallyho and elsewhere are well described by Muriel Bowen and others. They took place during the seasons of 1894-1896. They were a remarkable series of hunts. The best was the sixth and last which, unfortunately, the master missed due to illness while in London. The run is described by Commander Forbes, "Maintop":

> It took place on January 3rd, 1896. J. Dalton, first whip, carried the horn, and Col. Challoner Knox acted as Master on this memorable occasion, for the run is considered by many who saw it to be the finest foxhunt in their recollection. The old fox was now well known by appearance to many of the field and spectators, and may be described as a rough, shaggy-looking dog fox of medium size. He was not found in Rossmore, having left on hearing the foot people near the gorse; but hounds got strong touch of him in covert, and put him on his legs in a small patch of gorse bushes about three

> hundred yards south-east of the covert through which he passed when found. The pace was very fast from the first, and, after crossing over the west shoulder of Pottlerath, hounds ran by the very border line of Tipperary for some distance before bearing away to Killeen, through which covert he passed this time; sportsman had to gallop up alongside the covert, for a hat in the air told the fox was away; the time to this point was thirty minutes. In another half hour exactly, hounds dashed into Tallyho Wood, and the horsemen dismounted as they arrived – all except a small body who followed into the wood, to find that the earths had been dug up to rid them of badgers, and the fox was away at the top end, bound for Woodsgift. Before reaching this he turned back, and, passing down to Tallyho, permitted the large field, now assembled, to nick in. The chase then led through the hollow Kildrina Wood to the Punchbowl, where the covert keeper, hearing hounds, had stopped the earths. On then, past Kilrush, to Uppercourt Wood, out behind the house, at least 1½ brace of fresh foxes divided the hounds, and they were stopped, after 2 hours and 5 minutes. The distance was accurately measured by a walking party two days later, and proved to be 18½ miles, while the point is 11¼ miles *(British Hunts & Huntsman, 1911, 484).*

Local Politics and Attitudes to Farmers

Matters had greatly improved since the days when Challoner Knox believed that hunting had no future. The "short-lived opposition to hunting has died out" announced the sporting press. The hunts continued to preserve foxes from being poisoned, shot or snared, and, in return, they were prepared to compensate farmers for any poultry lost. George Butler, honorary secretary of the hunt in Herky's time, considered that the hunt's relationship with farmers was not bad and, as he managed the poultry fund amongst other duties, he would have had a good insight. The country was divided up into nine districts and the district managers all ran accounts dealing with covert rents, earth stopping expenses etc. which were then submitted to George Butler who made payment by cheque.

Lord Desart, in his autobiography, refers to those who might be found out cub hunting at the turn of the century, "farmers on home-bred hunters, boys on foot or on donkey back, a few gentlefolk, a priest or

Lady Helen Langrishe. (British Hunts and Huntsmen)

Sir Hercules Langrishe. (British Hunts and Huntsmen)

two – naturally on their way to some parish call" *(Desart & Lubbock, 1936, 208)*. A number of farmers hunted, not just to bring on young horses, but for sport they would join in on their cart horses if the hunt was in their vicinity. In 1898 at a meet in the Ballyfacey/Glenmore locality, a farmer unhitched his horse and rode him to hounds bareback, finished the hunt and was given the brush *(Poe album)*. It does not sound like the all exclusive field that might have been found in contemporary England.

Transport and Country

Herky had a great love of cars, he owned the second motor-car imported into Ireland. Cars were already making their appearances at hunt meets in Kilkenny by 1903, when a hunting correspondent expressed delight on being given a lift to a meet at the high speed of 17 mph. However, the same correspondent's luck ran out the following year when he had to hack home 14 long miles, even though there had been a "brace of motors" at the meet *(Records of the Kilkenny Hunt, 1902-08)*.

Mrs. Solly Flood (then Margarite Connellan) recalled her hunting days with Herky. He "was the first Master that I remember when I started to hunt in the Christmas holidays and, on leaving school, I hunted regularly each season". She lived at Coolmore, near Thomastown, from where the horses were hacked to meets between Mullinavat and Kilkenny with their rugs rolled up and fastened to the front of the saddle. Sometimes they were hacked by grooms, otherwise by members of the family and on the occasions when the horses went ahead with the grooms, she travelled with her father in a fast American trap. Hounds moved off sharp at 11 a.m. but it was always important to try to find out in advance from Herky where he might end up at the end of a day's hunting:

> so as to make arrangements with the groom where to drive to stable our horses and traps, so as to be near enough not to have too long to ride back on tired horses. I remember long exhausting hacks between coverts as well as arriving home with rather sore "behinds" on very tired and often stumbling horses and often going in that horrible trot known as "hound jog". I have done more than 15 miles of that misery more than

> once ... We had marvellous fun, not only the hunting, but, at the end of a long day, we often had a huge tea of poached eggs and bacon, cold ham and every conceivable variety of buns, cakes and huge cups of tea in the nearest house available while our grooms rode our tired horses home and we followed in our various vehicles. These "teas" were not confined to Knocktopher. Kilfane, Ballylinch, Kilmurry, Coolmore, Mt. Juliet etc. all took their turns *(Solly Flood, 1978, 53).*

At the turn of the century the country around Foyle Bridge was described in a newspaper article as: "Magnificent country, grand, undulating Freshford hills with ne're a bush or tree to intercept the view, fine big grassy fields divided formidable looking walls, and hardly a house or cabin in sight. What a country to hunt a fox in!" The only covert in the locality was six acres of gorse at Ballyspellan, "40 minutes of the very best that man or woman could wish to ride over fine country from Ballyring...and on through Seskin where wire caused a good deal of obstruction..." *(McMorrough Kavanagh album)*. Further south was:

> glorious hunting country... with sound, and fairly narrow, stone-faced banks, big double banks often with narrow ditches on both sides, huge stone walls (in the Knockmoylan country) like a double bank, lots of high and mostly uncut, thin hedges through which there seemed no way over and so, sometimes, one had to try and crash through with a prayer that one's hat would not be torn off or that one's face would not be a mass of scratches if, and when, one emerged on the far side still in one's saddle! If there was any wire it was certainly not the horror of the barbed variety. I feel, from a hunting point of view, the greatest asset of all were the very wide, often twelve foot, grass verges which made it so easy for the hunt to follow hounds *(Solly Flood, 1978, 54).*

Hunt Finances

Herky spent the bulk of his money on hunting and on sailing, to the detriment of his family. He was an accomplished yachtsman and, influenced by observations made sailing, he cast his hounds according to the wind. At the time he died there were seven mortgages taken out on Knocktopher Abbey and he had squandered most of his wife's fortune. The last mortgage he arranged was to fund a new yacht. His lack of concern over such matters permitted him to lead a charmed life, while having wonderful fun at the same time. Despite his personal financial instability, he succeeded in placing the hunt on a sound footing. He was a popular master and his determination to show sport attracted almost 100 subscribers, greater than any number achieved during the remainder of the twentieth century. What is almost more remarkable, is that the subscription rate he struck stayed virtually constant for half a century. The balance sheet for 1896 gives an income of £1275-2-10 and that of 1952 shows receipts of £1363-12-8; reflecting two things, firstly that Herky was attracting considerable income for the hunt and secondly it indicates the extent to which the McCalmonts were subsidising the Kilkenny Hunt at the later date.

The hunt club once again became active, the number of members increased and they were now expected to pay a surcharge for the privilege. A small rule booklet was printed for their use, outlining the nine hunt club rules. Fund raising was successful through a variety of schemes. Apart from the hunt ball, there was a Ladies' Fund run by Mrs. Crofton. Miss H. Poe realised £5-7-0 through the sale of hunting maps and a novel idea in 1897 was the introduction of a Carriage Fund collected by Mrs. L.J. Watters, from those who regularly drove to see the hunting. She raised over £7 from about 20 subscribers, mainly ladies.

Puppy Walking

Puppy walking has always played an important part in the rearing of the Kilkenny Hunt hounds. Mrs. Solly Flood gives an amusing insight into puppy walking as she knew it in Herky's time:

> I think one can say that a great many followers were involved with the hunt during a good part of the year. Hound bitches whelped any time from April to July and six puppies was quite a common litter. During those months, it was the kennel huntsman and his underlings who had all the worry and work but, as soon as the puppies were weaned and doing well, no time was lost in placing them out to walk, or in ordinary language finding a home for two puppies with a follower of the hunt or a good natured farmer who would feed them well, give them as much freedom as possible and have enough affection

(Courtesy of Mr. & Mrs. Harry McCalmont)
Captain Hercules Langrishe and the Kilkenny Hounds, c.1906.

to give them confidence and would themselves, have enough tolerance to put up with the exuberant spirits and mischief they would often do. I remember one couple that we had who had a glorious day when they found the dairy door slightly open and demolished 18lbs. of lovely fresh butter which the dairy maid had just made and left to harden on the stone cold shelves of the dairy. Of course, if they could find a newly dug and planted flower bed on our ornamental terrace, it was just asking to be rooted up and used for the burial of any newly discovered treasure. In spite of their naughtiness, they really were great fun and as a child I never remember Coolmore without its Dainty, Dauntless, Consul, Rossie etc. How long the puppies remained in their foster homes depended on when they were born, how well they were being done by their walker and, I am afraid, in some cases on the patience of the said walker. At a time the Master and Kennel Huntsman thought suitable, there was the Hound Puppy Show when neighbouring

> Masters or Kennel Huntsman judged the new entry. Everyone had a wonderful meal and speeches were made before the presentation of prizes and ending perhaps with a few walkers suggesting their own particular puppies had done so well, it might be best for them to learn more discipline in the kennels! However the young entry remained in their temporary homes until as late as January and February or even much of the following spring and the packs throughout the country owe much to the owners of the happy homes so many of their "babies" had" *(Solly Flood, 1978, 55).*

Cub Hunting

Cub hunting in Herky's time was not for morning slouches, a 5 a.m. start to the day was virtually mandatory. There were several reasons for this, the scent was supposed to be better and would enable the young entry to follow the example of their peers more successfully. The flies would become a nuisance once the dew had evaporated and the sun would not be too hot for the young hounds when it came to hacking home, tired and thirsty. Herky expected each hound in the pack to be capable of travelling over 100 miles a day, so it was essential to harden their pads gradually. Hounds, horses and people all travelled long distances to and from meets, they were much fitter than their late twentieth century counterparts. The hounds were big-boned and quite different from what was soon to appear in Kilkenny under a new mastership. Once again, let us return to Mrs. Solly Flood, as she remembered those early mornings when Patrick Darcy, the butler at Coolmore, would wake her and her brother at 5 a.m.

> It was poor Darcy who had the thankless task of getting us out of our beds. The routine was Darcy banging on our bedroom doors announcing it was 5 a.m. or what ever hour my father thought necessary. After the knock "Are ye getting up?", "Yes, Darcy, I am awake" and then turn over to sleep in two minutes, a slight pause and Darcy again "Ye are not getting up, jump so that I will hear ye". To my shame, I remember once, in desperation, leaning out of bed, picking up my bedroom slippers and flinging them as hard as I could with the lie "Can't you hear me jumping?". To Darcy's everlasting credit, I think he always did manage to produce a couple of heavy-eyed,

rather sulky, 'keen hunting children' in time to scramble on to their ponies following their father *(Solly Flood, 1978, 56).*

Opening Meet in Patrick Street, Kilkenny.

The opening meet continued to take place at the Club House Hotel, Kilkenny, in early November. Moving off at 11 a.m. it suited those who travelled with their horses by train. Outside cars would meet the hunting trains and the grooms would bring the horses through the town to the meet. "The opening meet meant much rivalry between grooms about the perfection of the horses in their charge and the owner's 'turning out' as well as they could possibly afford – shining top boots and tall hats, snowy white stocks, yellow waistcoats and the lady riders in the best cut and smartest riding habit they had" *(Solly Flood, 1978, 56).* Patrick Darcy took special pride in turning out the Connellan family well for hunting. A large number of onlookers would gather for the occasion and follow the hunt as far as they were able.

Point-to-Points and Hunt Balls

In much the same way as the opening meet signalled the start of the season the point-to-point races heralded its close. In Herky's time the location of the course varied according to the wishes of the hunt committee and the farmers over whose land it was to be held:

> The course was marked by white flags on the left and red on the right of the riders, hung from tall poles...and the judges were mounted on a farm cart exactly opposite the winning post. The races always included a Hunt Heavyweight, a Hunt Lightweight, in which only horses certified by the Master as having hunted regularly were allowed to enter, an open race in which horses and riders of any description, (other than jennets and mules) could compete and finally a Farmers' Race during which there was the most betting and yelling. As all the woman rode side-saddle until after the 1914 War, there was no special ladies race, but anyone who had hunted during the previous season and could cajole their best young man to act as jockey could enter *(Solly Flood, 1978, 57).*

Tents were erected for the use of the jockeys and for the officials. The point-to-point was a popular country event which attracted large crowds including "fiddlers and peddlers with their baskets of oranges, buns, apples and a very bright pink sweet known as 'Peggy's Leg'." *(Solly Flood, 1978, 57).*

The annual hunt ball remained one of the high-lights of the Kilkenny social calendar. In the 1890s the ball had become grander than ever. Sir Hercules and Lady Langrishe presided over the evening with the Marquess and Marchioness of Ormonde, who were treated like royalty. Mrs. Solly Flood recalled a wonderful picture of the hunt ball, then a young girl accompanied by her chaperone:

> As far as the young members of the hunt were concerned, the great event of the year was the Hunt Ball. When I was first old enough to attend, it was held in the Court House in Kilkenny. There was a wonderful floor which was somehow hung on chains and almost completely covered the whole of the big central entrance hall, except for a small raised platform at each end which was carpeted, had comfortable sofas and chairs for the chaperones and room for the musicians. The rest of the floor space was perfect for all the different and gay dances – Polkas, Waltzes, Barn Dances, Lancers, Fox-trots etc., followed in very quick succession accompanied by the most fashionable band in Ireland. This band was conducted and led by the owner himself, a beautiful violinist called Clarke Barry whose headquarters were in Dublin and who played for every big ball in the country. It would be useless to try and describe the various rooms and curious cubby holes which were used on Ball nights for purposes for which the Law Courts never designed them! Sufficient to say that we danced in the big entrance hall, supped in the spacious Council Chamber and sat out in any and every possible spot including the Court Room. I have no recollection as to how, or if, it was heated and how the dozens of sofas and chairs etc. were produced but anyway everyone enjoyed themselves far too much to be critical. At every dance, no matter how small, there was always trays of dance Programs placed as near to the entrance as possible and one picked one on the way to the cloakroom. The programs were very small and each had a tiny pencil attached and, on the inside of the doubled card, were on the left Nos. 1-20 with

(Courtesy of Miss Maura Toler-Aylward)

From left to right: Sir Hercules Langrishe, Mrs. Terence Langrishe, Lady Langrishe and Mr. Terence Langrishe, post 1926.

small lines beside each number and on the opposite side, the type of dance and tune to be played was printed. Thus armed, and accompanied by your chaperone, you emerged into the ballroom and hoped to be immediately surrounded by young men clamouring for a dance and, if possible, your special young man of the moment begging to be allowed to take you into supper. I was quite a tolerable dancer and therefore did not have the misery of sometimes having no partner and propping up the ballroom wall, but Caroline Marsh, my childhood friend, was such a beautiful dancer that, if there had been twice as many numbers on the Program, they would have all been claimed before she had got as far as the ballroom.

Officially the hunt balls started at 9 p.m. but the dancing did not begin until Mr. Clarke Barry decided that there were enough couples. Herky and Helen Langrishe arrived any time between 9 p.m. and 10 p.m. and greeted their friends while awaiting the arrival of Lord and Lady Ormonde and their party at about 10 p.m. They were escorted by the Master and his wife to the raised platform at one end of the hall. Lady

Ormonde and Lady Langrishe wore their tiaras, all the girls were in their very best and at least three-quarters of the men were in their attractive hunt evening uniforms, scarlet tail coat with pale blue facings (the special Kilkenny Hunt colour), brass Hunt Club buttons, black trousers, white waistcoats, stiff white shirts and collars and ties and both sexes wore kid gloves when dancing. To open the ball, Herky led out Lady Ormonde and Lord Ormonde led out Helen in a sort of quadrille or lancers in which four couples faced each other and danced a square dance, which included the 'grand chain' by which partners were swapped. It was the most suitable dance for the elderly and the hall looked really lovely with as many lancers as it would hold all obviously enjoying themselves. As soon as the opening quadrille was over, the waltzes, fox-trots etc. were soon in full swing and it was really exciting and huge fun. Waltzes were the most enjoyable and popular and with Mr. Clarke Barry's gorgeous band playing lovely Strauss music, one could not ask for anything better.

I don't remember by whom or how the suppers were run but, at midnight, Herky led by Lady Ormonde and Helen was led in by Lord Ormonde and, with a selected party, sat down at the table at the far end of the Council Chamber. As many people as could be seated at the same time took their places down the long tables the whole length of the room, champagne corks 'popped', supper was served and the champagne was supplemented by white and red wine and minerals etc. There was no such thing as 'a bar' but I expect the men fortified themselves with an odd whiskey and soda as the night wore on sometimes until 5am. When finally Mr. Clarke Barry firmly played 'John Peel' with the master blowing 'Out of covert' on his hunting horn and then, automatically, it all ended with the national Anthem. We all then staggered to the cloakroom, retrieved our warm coats and, jostled by the crowd outside the Court House, looked for the vehicle that was to drive us, either to our homes or, if possible, a bed as near Kilkenny as we could find. In later years (when I think the old dancing floor had collapsed) we had two hunt balls in the long Room at Knocktopher Abbey, twice at Kilcreene and twice in the Picture Gallery at the Castle *(Solly Flood, 1978, 57-58).*

(Courtesy of Mrs. Phyllis Glenn)

The Castlecomer and Queen's County Hunt on April 5th 1902. From left to right included in the photograph are: Mr. Mowbray Brown (huntsman), Mr. Dobbs, Mr. W. Edge, Capt. R.H. Wandesforde MFH, Mr. Raskell, Miss Maude Campbell, Miss Eva White, Miss Draper, Mr. McCreery, Mr. W. Dobbs, Dr. O'Hanlon, Miss McCheane, Master Christopher Prior-Wandesforde (on donkey), Mr. Tommy McCheane, Mrs. Prior Wandesforde with Miss Vera Prior-Wandesforde (child) and Master Ferd Prior-Wandesforde.

The Castlecomer and Queen's County Hunt

Herky did not hunt the whole county. The Kilkenny Hunt boundaries were constantly being redrawn, depending on the resources of its masters and the location of the kennels. The Knocktopher kennels were too far south to hunt the north of the county regularly. This made way for Richard Prior-Wandesforde of Castlecomer, who obtained a loan of certain coverts in the north-east of the county in 1898.

His family estates stretched for miles around the town, and included several coal mines. The permanent grassland country was well stocked with foxes mainly because of the woodlands at Castlecomer, Jenkinstown and Uskerty, as well as a certain amount of wild covert.

(British Hunts and Huntsmen)

Richard Prior-Wandesforde of Castlecomer.

This had not always been the case, as when the Queen's County pack had folded in 1877, it had been feared that the fox would become extinct in the area without the management of an active hunt.

Richard Prior-Wandesforde acquired an unhunted portion of Queen's County (County Laois), in 1899. He had for some years hunted a scratch pack of harriers made up of various kinds and breeds of dogs, with which he hunted hares. Sealy Dobbs, was first whip and one of the grooms acted as second whip. They turned themselves out well, wearing a grey frieze frock coat and a scarlet waistcoat with brass buttons. From this scratch pack the Castlecomer and Queen's County Hounds emerged. He hunted them himself, crossing the country at speed, and by carefully avoiding interfering with his hounds, he produced some good sport. Mowbray Brown, "a silvery voiced white haired, red faced professional... a lovely figure of a man with a glorious voice for hounds" *(Dobbs)* was engaged as the kennel huntsman. When Prior-Wandesforde retired in 1902 he lent his hounds to the new masters, Hervey Knox Browne and Henry Childers (a relative of Erskine Childers). The latter acted as second whip for two seasons. They were both renowned for their bravery in crossing the country. It was a small hunt, consisting of about 20 couples of hounds, mostly drafts.

> Walking puppies in that part of Ireland was not a success. The small farmers had enough to do to feed themselves and children, but the MFH got a few out, the bag at the end of the season was never a big one as there were so many stone drains and other places unstoppped, also the peasants were not keen on digging or even putting a terrier in *(The Hexham Courant, Nov.1932).*

Hounds were kennelled at the coal mining centre of Massford, near Castlecomer, and so they remained until 1909 when Isaac Bell reclaimed the country on behalf of the Kilkenny Hunt. Richard Prior-Wandesforde remained the owner of the pack, and renamed the Queen's County pack, they continued to hunt. Mr. Knox Browne was a clear headed huntsman, who was always with his hounds. One of his best runs was a seven mile point from Swiftsheath.

(Courtesy of Mr. Nicholas Lambert)

Nicholas Lambert with his hounds and kennel huntsman at Dysertmore.

Mr. Lambert's Hounds

The southern portion of the county had been originally leased to Lord Waterford in 1843, by Sir Charles Nugent Humble. The country had officially become vacant in 1884 following the dissolution of the Curraghmore Hunt, due to the actions of the Land League, which it is estimated, resulted in a loss to the local economy of £30,000 per annum. Small packs such as Nugent Humble's (1891-1893) and Lord Duncannon's Harriers (1898-1906) hunted parts of the country and some of it was also hunted by the newly formed Waterford Hunt, which replaced the disbanded Curraghmore Hunt.

By 1894 Herky realised he was over-stretching himself by hunting so much of the county, so he gave up the "Ross country", making way for the New Ross Harriers. The 5th Marquess of Waterford, prior to the Land League days, had managed this country extremely efficiently with the aid of Ambrose Lambert of Dysertmore. They had planted the three coverts of Mullinahone, Weatherstown and Ormonde's Gorse, and replanted Brownstown Wood and Knockbrack, all at the expense of the Marquess. The master of the New Ross Hounds was Nicholas (Nick) Lambert, son of Ambrose. Tempted by the plentiful supply of foxes, the result of the work put in by the previous generation, he soon abandoned hare hunting. In 1904 they became known as Mr. Lambert's Hounds and, with the agreement of his great friend Herky, they continued to draw the coverts of south-east County Kilkenny.

The hounds were an uneven pack with drafts from the Kilkenny Hunt and from Robert Watson in Carlow, but they were a good working pack. Nick, riding at over 14 stone, was always found following quietly just behind them. He ran his hunt from home on a very tight budget, which necessitated much improvisation. With the help of E. Brian (kennel huntsman) and Mr. Brian (whip), he hunted his twenty-five couple of hounds twice a week. Nick and his light-weight first whip had a good understanding of each other and of hunting the fox. Once, when his first whip met with an accident, Nick who found him lying on the ground, asked if he was hurt, to which came the reply "Yes, Sir, I am unconscious" *(Worcester Smith, 1925, 159)*. Lambert lived for his hounds and hunting, remaining a bachelor until the age of 53. As a result of overspending on the hounds Lambert, short of fuel to heat the house, is reputed to have burnt the stairs in Dysertmore. "And didn't I spend it well?" he is supposed to have said.

Margarite Solly Flood recalled, "Nick was the finest huntsman I have ever known, his hounds loved him and both his own and his

(Courtesy of Mr. Nicholas Lambert)

Nick Lambert with four of his best hounds.

(Courtesy of Mr. & Mrs. Harry McCalmont)

A meet of Mr. Lambert's Hounds at Tullogher. From left to right: Mrs. Newport, Mr. Lambert MFH, Mr. Orr, Mr.Cormac (whip) and Mr. Tighe.

hounds' voices had to be heard to be really appreciated". *(Solly Flood 1978, 59).* He treated the people of the countryside with the utmost respect, showed some excellent sport and was well-liked.

In 1905 Major-General Sir Hugh and the Hon. Lady Rose McCalmont, a family new to County Kilkenny, rented Mount Juliet from the Earl of Carrick. Lady Rose was a great hunting enthusiast, she had hunted in Kilkenny prior to her marriage, and her determination to return to Kilkenny was soon rewarded with a run of one hour and twelve minutes with Mr. Lambert's hounds. "They found in Garrandarragh by Pipemore Rocks, ran through Ballykenna, through Ballyconnaught to Brabstown over the Arrigle river to Smithstown

Gorse and on by Three Friars Cross to Glenpipe through Mullinakill and killed in the open in Ballykenna" *(inscribed on seal)* on December 15th. Having been presented with one of the fox's pads Lady Rose had it mounted on a silver seal.

During the season of 1907-08 Herky was ill and spent most of the winter in England. Not for the first time, this forced him to look for a deputy to hunt the hounds. Previously Major Connellan and Col. Challoner Knox had stood in for him, during his absence. This time he looked to his good friend and neighbouring huntsman Nick Lambert, who resigned as master of his own pack in favour of Lord Southampton. By deed, Herky made over the ownership of the hounds to his wife, Helen. This turned out to be a rather unfortunate move as she and Herky tended to disagree on many matters, particularly when it came to her husband's deputy.

(Courtesy of Mr. & Mrs. Harry McCalmont)

Nicholas Lambert, huntsman of the Kilkenny Hounds, 1907-1908.

Langrishe / Lambert dispute

Towards the end of the 1907-08 season, Helen Langrishe wrote to Nick Lambert and accused him of putting down hounds without her prior permission or that of her agent Capt. Lindsay, of Ballylinch. She also alleged that he refused to have any dealings with her. She was particularly aggrieved at the lack of consultation, as not only did she own the hounds outright, but at that stage she was entirely responsible for the financing of the hunt in her husband's absence. Unfortunately for her, Herky, as master, had written to Nick the previous November, from the Marlborough Club, in London and had given him full permission to treat the pack as though it were his own, acknowledging Nick's expertise and experience, granting him "absolute control in kennel and field". He sadly wrote at the end of the same letter "I don't suppose that any human being can realise how much I miss my hounds", *(Legal correspondence, 1907)*. Mrs. Langrishe chose to ignore her husband's wishes and the dispute continued for some weeks, until the following proposal made by her was accepted by Mr. Lambert:

> I offer that the hounds and horses and servants continue to have their head quarters here. That Mr. N.J. Lambert hunt the hounds and have absolute authority in the field and in the kennels, except having the power to dismiss any of my servants without my sanction.
>
> The stable department and horses to remain under my control and management and in my absence in that of any gentleman I may select.
>
> I will purchase another horse for Mr. Lambert to ride, and will stable, feed, groom, and bring to and from meets three of his own horses.
>
> That as Mr. Lambert stated he would have to reside in apartments in Thomastown he be paid £2 per week. That the hunting appointments be settled by him in conjunction with the Hon. Sec. of the Kilkenny Hunt *(Legal correspondence, 1908)*.

It was an unnecessary row, the hunting season was about to end and Herky was about to retire. Would Nick Lambert have continued hunting the Kilkenny Hounds if this disagreeable episode had not taken place? On his retirement Herky was presented with a two and a half foot silver gilt fox, that took pride of place on the side-board at Knocktopher. Herky and Helen continued to hunt both with the Kilkenny and the East Kilkenny Hunts and their son, Terence, later became a member of the Kilkenny Hunt Club, although he never crossed the country in the same style as his parents had done in their hey-day.

The hunt required a new master, they looked to a young man who was then hunting the Galway Blazers with considerable success. His name was Isaac Bell.

Chapter 7

Focus on Hounds with Isaac Bell

It arn't that I love the fox less, but that I love the 'ound more.
(R.S. Surtees, 1805-64)

The new master, Isaac Bell, was a nephew of the New York newspaper magnate, James Gordon Bennett. He lived in Paris with his mother before being sent to school at Harrow, where he was in the same house as Peter Solly Flood, Margarite's brother. While he was there, his mother indulged his love of hunting and hounds. As it had become clear from early on that it was his ambition to hunt hounds, she ensured that he had access to the best packs available, namely the Warwickshire and the North Warwickshire.

Later, at Cambridge, his mother made it possible for him to keep half a dozen hunters for his own use, allowing him to hunt with the College Drag hounds. There he whipped-in to James de Rothschild. In addition, he managed some days with the Cambridgeshire, Oakley and the Fitzwilliam hounds. While at Cambridge, Bell and some of his fellow students bought twenty race-horses, solely to run in flapping races, organised by themselves. A successful point-to-point rider, he won the Cottenham Cup. Also a fine, athletic polo player, he had his own polo team, the Old Cantabs. The team was made up of some of the best 10 goal players of the time. He did not play for England, because of his American citizenship. Having reached the top, he stopped playing because his polo team were winning everything and it seemed to be both sporting and sensible to retire.

He completed his education in Melton, from where he hunted virtually every day of the week with the Quorn, the Belvoir and the Cottesmore. He became a first class rider across country. He visited the best kennels, observing everything, taking into account the characteristics he would demand from his hounds, when his turn came.

In 1903 he accepted the mastership of the Galway Blazers and the opportunity to hunt his first pack of hounds. The idea of being able to make all his mistakes as far away from the shires as possible, particularly appealed to him. Galway, before the days of modern transport, must have appeared to be very far away. By 1905 his natural

(Courtesy of Kilkenny Archaeological Society)

Isaac Bell on Alligator.

talent was evident. Hunting fashionably bred hounds out of Tynedale bitches, he provided them with a twelve mile point from Caheroyan to Dartfield.

Ikey's arrival in Kilkenny in 1908 as the new master and huntsman following the retirement of Herky Langrishe was viewed by most members of the hunt with scepticism. Here was just another keen, wealthy, young American who, like Butson, the master twenty years earlier, had hunted hounds in Galway. Little did they realise that this glamorous and charming young man with a zest for life, though initially to be reviled for his unorthodox approach to hound breeding, was destined to become one of the most revered and admired huntsmen and a foremost breeder of foxhounds, in the twentieth century. The Kilkenny hunting field was about to experience a revolution in fox-hound breeding and they were to be the first to benefit from Ikey's experiments.

On October 26th 1908, the hounds met as usual for the opening meet at the Club House Hotel and the new master attracted a large field. They found immediately in Knockroe, from where they ran to

(Courtesy of the Newell family)

The opening meet, November 1909, at the Club House Hotel, Kilkenny photographed from an upstairs window in the Hotel.

Ballydaniel and back across the Tullaroan road before running out of scent. The young Dermot McCalmont observed that it was "a very fine piece of hound work" as there was virtually no scent.

A month later at Kilkieran Cross Roads, they found in Carpenter's Glen, went away quickly through Ballyfoyle Glen and on over Brown Mountain and reached Revanagh in 50 minutes. There followed another 17 minutes of a twisty hunt. Afterwards, Major Arthur McMorrough Kavanagh (a future chairman of the Kilkenny Hunt), heard that the fox had been killed by a sheepdog and hidden by some men. On December 4th in the same year, Ikey had a five mile point from Woodsgift, a 50 minute run took them from Ballyring to Attanagh Station. The new master had every reason to be pleased with his debut. The following season the good sport continued with a ten mile point from Castlewarren, just north-west of the Kilkenny/Dublin main road, to Rossmore near Carlow *(McMorrough Kavanagh, 1904-1940)*. This hunt may be the legendary Kilkenny hunt that took place in three counties, as they found in County Kilkenny, ran through a section of County Carlow and finished in County Laois.

Bell had a different style to that of his predecessor, but the initial concern of the subscribers was short-lived. When the fit and wiry young man arrived at a meet, he would speak to everyone, and particularly to the farmers who were present. Slapping his pockets he would enquire "any cigs?" and having established the whereabouts of the local foxes, he would continue chatting to one and all, until it was time to move off.

(Courtesy of the Newell family)

Looking down upon the hounds at the opening meet 1909. Photographed from an upstairs window in the Club House Hotel.

Like Herky, he too used a system of area managers to mind the country. He expected them to work hard, on behalf of the hunt, particularly in the summer. He was good to those who supported him and on one occasion rewarded three keen hunting farmers, John Kirwan, P.M. O'Keeffe of Castlefield and a member of the O'Donnell family, with a hunting holiday in England. John Kirwan, became a successful racehorse trainer, and when he died in 1950, a wreath was laid "to a great sportsman from Ikey Bell".

When buying horses, and Ikey bought large numbers, he made a point of purchasing them locally, thereby enabling farmers to reap some benefit from the sport. Those horses that turned out to be unsuitable for his requirements were sold at the local fairs, these were often colourful events. He recollected that at the Mullinavat fair, stallion owners would tie their charges to the stone cross and let the horses fight it out, which ever one was the most successful would then be in the greatest demand *(Bell, 1947).*

Point-to point races always included a farmers' race, which attracted great interest. For many it was a show-case for the horses they had bred and the rivalry, as to who would have the best horse on the day, was intense. Bell's first point-to-point races were held at Lacken, near Bonnetstown, on April 1st 1909. Five years later, at the point-to-point, the Hon. Lady Rose McCalmont won one of the first ladies' steeplechase races riding her own horse *(Worcester Smith, 1925).* The venue moved around the hunting country each year and was dependent on the goodwill of farmers owning land in an adjacent block. In the year that the races were held at Bishopslough the course ran over parts of land owned by no less than ten farmers, who were listed as follows: Miss Mary Walsh, Messrs. Pierce O'Keeffe, James Downey, Andrew Dullard, James Lalor, J. Blackmore, Andrew Murphy, William Costello, T. Hanrahan, John Dowling and James Murphy *(UNC).*

Isaac Bell found that Kilkenny was superb scenting country. The south of the county was lightly stocked and generally the banks were inviting. Most had little or no growth on top, the exception was on the Tipperary border, where they had been planted with thick blackthorn towards the end of the nineteenth century. Naturally this acted as a hindrance to hounds. The Kilkenny countryside remained very bare outside the surviving demesnes. South Kilkenny had clean single banks with no sceachs (hawthorn) or gorse growing on them, and most fences were kept neatly trimmed. In a county with few turf bogs there was

(Courtesy of the Newell family)

Ikey Bell's sister jumping a Kilkenny ditch in style.

constant demand for the trimmings which were used as fuel. The furze (gorse) was regularly cut and bruised as fodder for horses. Ikey recalled Rossmore covert as very thick, "cut and laid" *(Bell, notes).*

The permanent grassland was divided into small enclosures, the boundaries of which could be jumped anywhere. This facilitated fast riding over fly fences and on a good day the south Kilkenny country rode like a point-to-point race, attracting riders from New Ross and Wexford where the banks were much larger. Wire was not unknown, Worcester Smith recalled being wired in when hunting with the East Kilkenny Hunt and, on another occasion, he lost hounds for a brief period when he stopped to cut wire, but generally there was not sufficient to hinder hunting.

Controversial Hound Breeding

Ikey Bell was always ready to make changes if he thought that the quality of the hunting would be improved. From his earliest days, he had been considering the type of hounds he would like to breed. The first change he made in Kilkenny was to move the kennels further north. He built new kennels and stables at Birchfield, on the outskirts of Kilkenny City. He then initiated hunting four days a week, as opposed

(Courtesy of Mr. & Mrs. Harry McCalmont)

W. Kimble (second whip) with the Kilkenny Hounds.

to the three that Herky had hunted. He lived at Birchfield until after his marriage in 1909 to Evadne (Dolly) Cane of St. Wolstan's, County Kildare, an All Ireland Croquet Champion. They moved to the nearby Kilcreene House, once the property of another Kilkenny Hunt master, Henry Meredyth. The kennels were retained at Birchfield, where stabling for fifty horses was provided.

Foxes were still not particularly plentiful, blank days were not uncommon and it was felt that there was still a need for the hunt to actively preserve foxes. In County Cork there was such a dearth of foxes, in the early 1900s, they had to be imported from Wales *(Viney, 1997)*. So Ikey continued Sir John Power's policy of planting coverts and installed some artificial earths in strategic coverts, like the Greenwood at Shankill.

Cub hunting was carried out from the end of August through to the opening meet around November 1st. The hour at which they met varied during these months. Ikey's earliest recorded cub hunting meet was on September 4th 1913 at 4.30 a.m. at Mount Juliet *(McCalmont, 1913-1920)*.

Rather than always having a groom following the hunt with his second horse, the master would ensure that, at a certain covert, the earth stopper had a fresh horse waiting for him. Twelve mile hacks between draws were not unknown and fit horses were required. The Rock, always a sure find, on the Laois/Kilkenny border near Gathabawn was one of Bell's favourite coverts. He liked to leave it to the last draw of the day, to the chagrin of those with only one tired horse, after hacking perhaps from Castlecomer, and in no condition for the helter skelter across the country on a four o'clock fox.

Ikey's respect for his hounds was immense. He considered that on a long hack between coverts, the pace should be varied. "A continual jog at exactly the same pace is boring to hounds – and like one's guests one must try never to bore them" *(Bell, notes).* Being tone deaf, he knew his hounds' voices only with difficulty, but he believed their hearing to be extremely acute and was convinced that hounds disliked being shouted at, so he refrained from ever doing so. A genuinely compassionate man, he would often dismount after a day's hunting and walk home with them for a mile or two.

(Courtesy of the Newell family)

The 1909 Kilkenny Hunt Puppy Show.

As he gained experience Ikey realised that he only wanted to hunt the best hounds. He appreciated that most foxhound strains in the best kennels were over 100 years old and he felt it timely to introduce a new strain. In 1911 Ikey had 50 couples, of which 12 couples were dog hounds, mainly of Southwold blood. He embarked on a hound breeding program, developing a smaller type of hound suitable for the hills found in the county. He believed that a leaner, more active hound with greater pace was required. A white hound, Belvoir, which was hunting superbly with the neighbouring East Kilkenny pack, confirmed his belief that it was necessary to return to a type of foxhound that had been bred in the previous century. Belvoir had been sent to Nick Lambert by Sir Edward Curre *(Bell, 1947).* Ikey made investigations, liked what he saw and arranged to visit Curre, and was deeply impressed by his pack of pure Welsh Hounds. On his return to Kilkenny he began to introduce the Welsh cross, as a way to regain those attributes lost through the dictates of fashion:

> to get back some of the very first English working strains... which had remained unpolluted by a craze for show which became menacing after 1900 *(Bell, notes).*

The puppy walkers immediately preferred the Welsh cross hounds, believing them to have better temperaments, to be more intelligent, good companions and more affectionate.

It is difficult now to appreciate what a radical move this was and to understand the deep hostility felt towards him by the establishment. His detractors, led by Lord Bathurst, were certain that the Welsh hounds were prone to riot and would hunt anything from rabbits to cats. He was described as a menace to foxhound breeding, but Ikey preferred to think of himself as a menace to foxes. During the summer months, the showing of hounds at Peterborough was the high-light of most masters' lives, but to Bell it meant little. He had regularly attended Peterborough from the age of seventeen, but his sole interest was in breeding the best performing hounds for the hunting field. He was now demanding concentration, speed and endurance. He disliked the massive, straight, big-boned foxhound that was so popular at the turn of the century, but to consider otherwise was regarded heretical by the establishment. Despite his disinterest in showing, hounds, influenced by Ikey's new ideas, were winning at Peterborough by the 1930s. Sir Peter Farquhar

(Courtesy of the Newell family)

Isaac Bell MFH.

(Courtesy of Miss Maura Toler-Aylward)

Mrs. Isaac Bell and General Godley.

was one of his earliest and most ardent disciples, the new Welsh bloodlines were spread through the Portman and Badminton kennels.

The Kilkenny Hunt was the first hunt to experience hunting with the fore-runners of the modern foxhound. Hunt members appreciated the good sport provided by the new fast, active hounds with their good cry. "The only test of hounds... is to breed the ones who do it best in the field, and not to the show bench" *(Bell, notes)*. Many newspaper reports describe what seemed endless red letter days.

For the privileged, motor transport was coming into common usage and Bell made the most of it, even the hunt terriers travelled by motor-car. Some hunters were still transported by train. The railway line had split the hunting country in two since the 1850s, and it was still used by the wealthier members of society to transport their horses to meets at some distance from their homes. The railway also enabled visitors from Kildare, Carlow and Waterford to hunt their own horses in Kilkenny with ease. Nonetheless most hunters were still hacked to meets.

Distemper was a hound disease for which there was no cure prior to the First World War. Ikey described the heart break it could cause:

> after the young hounds came in, in February and early March distemper would be rife, perhaps 30 couple bleeding at the nose, passing blood, fever raging. The staff hunting 4 days a week would be up nursing 7 nights a week and in the morning probably wheeling out... 4 or 5 couples each morning to be burnt in the destructor and by [the] end of April, having bred a lovely entry of some 40 couples, it was a case of having to go to Rugby Hound Sales and putting down £600 to £700 to put your entry back to 20 couples.
>
> Many a treasured strain was lost thus, and after three bad distemper years a great kennel of hounds would become a third class one.
>
> Looking back, I do not know how the hunt servants pre First World War stuck it out! There were some 'Giants' those days *(Bell, notes).*

Hunting and the First World War

Bell, an American citizen, served with the Royal Naval Reserve during the First World War. Dolly, his wife, took charge and acted as master in his absence. She was a remarkably capable lady, and although she did not hunt the hounds, she was an efficient organiser and succeeded in keeping the hunt going, thus enabling Ikey to provide sport when home on leave. The hounds were hunted by Mr. J. Higman during his long absences. The pack was reduced to 26 couples and a minimum subscription of £5 was expected from those who wished to hunt. In an effort to economise on petrol, a scarce commodity during wartime, Bell bought an old hearse, and placed the whip's horse between the shafts to draw the hounds to the meets. He was never afraid of innovation. The whip, who had to drive them, suffered silently in his embarrassment. On days when there was no hunting, the hunt horses were put to work either ploughing or pulling carts.

The following letter of appreciation was written to Ikey on July 13th 1916, sent from John's Bridge, Kilkenny:

> Dear Mr. Bell,
> Some short time ago the sporting farmers and other well-wishers of the Hunt in the county decided to make you a little presentation in recognition of your courage in keeping the Hunt going under trying conditions as prevailed since the beginning of the War. Knowing as they do the enormously increased cost of keeping up the Pack and the depressing effect which sadly depleted 'Fields' must have upon you they deem it right to offer you this small token of their appreciation of your self sacrifice, and of the high regard in which you are personally held by them. The general feeling is that since you came to the county you have worthily upheld the great traditions of the Kilkenny Hunt, and shown sport that in its best days has never been excelled; and it is hoped that when the War is ended you will be in a position to carry on with even greater success than you have already attained.
>
> We have been directed by the committee to send you the amount subscribed viz., £131.18.1, and have great pleasure in enclosing you a cheque for the amount.

The letter was signed by John Barry, E. Drennan, Jas. Dillon, T. Hogan and Thomas Brennan. Dolly Bell carefully pasted it into her scrap album and was obviously grateful.

Among the many interesting people who were hunting in Kilkenny early this century was Col. Sir Hutchinson Poe, of Heywood, who had no right leg from the hip down, he had lost it in the Sudan. His specially made saddle had two pommels. He was "over banks... all right, but at stone walls found it awkward" *(The Hexham Courant, Nov. 1932).* When he fell off, his leg had a habit of continuing on with his horse. Another, Denys Corbett Wilson of Darver House, was remarkable for having been the first man to fly from England to Ireland across the St. George's Channel. He caused consternation in 1912 when he landed his plane on Lowhill, to visit the Hon. Eda Bellew at Firoda, a remote shooting lodge. No one in the area had ever seen a flying machine before. He was equally reckless in the hunting field, "flying" across the country on his well-bred hunters. The present day Kilkenny Airport is named after him.

Prior to the war, most women rode side-saddle, although a few

(Courtesy of the Hon. Bru Bellew)

Denys Corbett Wilson (mounted), the first man to fly the St. George's Channel, talking to Mr. McMorrough Kavanagh of Borris .

chose not to do so. Dolly Bell always rode side-saddle, and Ikey, concerned that ill fitting saddles would irritate the horses' backs, had a new one made to fit each of her hunters. Doctors had warned that riding astride would have dire effects on women's health, but when these warnings were discovered to be ill-founded, increasing numbers preferred to ride astride. Betty Purdon, born in 1902, never learnt to ride side-saddle, she and Joan Butler were probably amongst the first ladies to hunt astride in Kilkenny.

It is always difficult to establish how many members of the farming community were hunting or supported a particular hunt. Their names are not recorded in newspaper reports and their personal records generally have not survived. Nonetheless, an unusual record exists in the form of an address from the "Farmers and Sportsmen of the Ballysallagh district", which reads as follows:

Dear Sir,
We the Farmers and Sportsmen of the Ballysallagh district,

(Courtesy of the Newell family)

Meet of the Kilkenny Hounds at Freshford.

> Co. Kilkenny hail with pleasure your reappearance amongst us after a most dangerous illness. Signed on behalf of the district:
> Patrick Heffernan (Chairman), John Barrett (Secretary), James Byrne, Thomas Brennan, Martin Brennan, Patrick Brennan, Michael McDermot, William Manning, James Manning, William Meany, Thomas Hogan, Michael Hogan, James Ronan, Patrick Brennan JP, Pierce Comerford, Gerald Doyle, John W. Buggy, Francis Byrne, Peter Byrne, James Hoban, John Hoban, Jeremiah Hoban, Nicholas Rice, James Murphy, Thomas Ronan, Thomas Comerford, Edward Hogan, Thomas Kavanagh.

They presented him with a large silver tray with a perimeter of miniature silver posts and rails. History does not relate details of the "dangerous illness" from which he recovered. Some of the above signatories went on to form the Johnswell Harriers.

The hunt suffered some harassment from Sinn Fein activists during 1919 and on January 16th 1919, Ikey did not draw Sir John's Gorse to avoid giving them the opportunity of saying that they had stopped the hunt. Later in the month the meet was changed from Mullinavat to Ballykeeffe Cross due to further Sinn Fein threats *(McCalmont, 1913-*

1920). The threats did not amount to much, and the hunt avoided the altercations that affected contemporary packs elsewhere in Ireland, possibly aided by the fact that the American master tended to turn a blind eye to the insurgents, who made use of Kilcreene House from time to time.

Sir Alfred Munnings in Kilkenny

By 1920 Bell had become somewhat of a personality in the hunting world, albeit an infamous one in certain circles. The former war artist, Sir Alfred Munnings, was commissioned by Bell to paint his portrait in Kilkenny. Munnings had been living at Lord de Rothschild's house, where he had carte blanche to paint any horse or person he wanted.

The timing of his visit to Ireland was unfortunate. The Bell family were in the midst of a domestic crisis, following the death of their youngest daughter. The tragedy put an enormous strain on the marriage. Furthermore Ireland was in the middle of the War of Independence, from which Kilkenny was not immune and to cap it all the weather was atrocious.

Munnings rose to the challenge. His preference was for painting out of doors whatever the conditions, but not even he could proceed with this commission without retreating indoors. He painted the hounds' portraits by placing them individually on top of the piano in the dining room. However, the master of the Kilkenny Hunt was less co-operative, possibly because he was asked to pose for the artist, on a wooden

(Courtesy of the Newell family)

Drawing the Kilkenny Hunt country towards Ballyragget.

(Courtesy of Mr. & Mrs. Andrew Kavanagh)

Miss Maisie Power.

rocking horse. During his stay at Kilcreene, Munnings completed the commission, painted many sketches and started work on one of his best known pictures, the Kilkenny Fair. The latter was the result of a visit to the fair with Ikey on a truly foul day. Naturally Ikey was in search of good horses, but the artist was so enchanted by the atmosphere of the event that, what started off as a fun sketch became his diploma work and was exhibited at the Royal Academy in 1923. The painting was presented to the Academy by the artist in 1925 and it was exhibited again the following year. The grey horse, depicted in the Fair painting, was bought by Bell and Munnings. Ikey later shipped him to the artist, in England, complete with a new set of clothing. Lady Munnings and the same grey horse appear in many of her husband's later paintings. He always remained most grateful to the Bells for their generous hospitality. Some time later Ikey unwittingly caused consternation in Kilkenny. "No sign of master, believed drowned" was the local evening paper's headline which so amused Bell following his "disappearance". Hounds that day, had found in a bog near Swiftsheath. They had crossed the flooded river Dinan into Lower Dunmore and run through the dairy farm, before heading for the larger river Nore,

(Courtesy of the Newell family)

Meet of the Kilkenny Hounds, during Ikey Bell's mastership, at Thomastown.

also in flood. They crossed the Nore into Thornback, near Three Castles. Already wet, Ikey entered the water in the hounds' wake, his mare however lost her footing and was turned over in the fast water. The master being a strong swimmer reached the river bank and was helped up to safety, sadly losing his good presentation hunting horn in the process *(UNC)*. His horse was carried half a mile downstream and brought ashore at a weir. She was recognised as Ikey's, thus giving rise to the above newspaper headline. Three years later his hunting horn was returned. Some boys swimming in the river had discovered it at the bottom, and although somewhat worn, it went straight back into active service.

Ikey Bell's Legacy to the Sport of Foxhunting

For personal reasons Bell and his family decided to leave Kilkenny. He cub hunted until 31st October 1921, resigned on November 2nd and handed over 35 couples of hounds to Major Dermot McCalmont. The Bells settled in Wiltshire, where he hunted the South and West Wilts, one of the oldest packs of foxhounds in England. They retained their lease on Kilcreene House and made frequent visits back to Kilkenny.

Naturally he continued with his hound breeding program using the Welsh Cross blood. He found it resulted in hounds that required less casting than the pure bred English. His principle reason for favouring the cross was that when hounds were having a bad day, he believed them to have the ability to allow the huntsman to alter their mood, to get their concentration back in order to pick up the scent again:

> Somehow I found whenever difficulties occurred, that difficulties and disappointments which would 'get heads up' in a pure English pack... hounds with a tint of Welsh in them, would not 'get heads up'. For the latter sort, when any such mishap occurred, would not forget they had been hunting, and keep on trying *(Bell, notes)*.

After a crashing fall in 1932, he retired from the South and West Wilts. He tried hunting side-saddle for a short period, but finally suffering from severe arthritis he accepted defeat. He blamed it on an after dinner fall, received from leaping a piece of furniture many years earlier.

Like Herky, for whom he had great respect, he was a good yachtsman

(Photo: T.J. Moran. Courtesy of Mr. John Kirwan)

From Left to right: T. Brennan, Isaac Bell, John Kirwan, Mrs. Bell and J. J. O'Donnell at a point-to-point.

and Ikey owned two yachts named Foxhound and Bloodhound He remained an American citizen all his life, and was the first American to become a member of the Royal Yacht Squadron. After giving up hunting hounds, he found more time to enjoy his sailing. Using the finest English hull, made by Camper and Nicholsons and the best American sails available, he won the Fastnet race with Bloodhcund. The innovative yacht design was so successful that he was accused of having an engine secreted away on board. He subsequently sold Bloodhound to the Duke of Edinburgh in the early 1960s.

Latterly, he went to live near Lismore in County Waterford. Shortly after the Second World War, a Mercedes was an uncommon sight on Irish roads, but Ikey had one of these splendid motors and regularly drove up to Kilkenny to follow Dermot McCalmont's hounds. He worked closely with Capt. Evan Williams on the breeding of the Tipperary pack, with success both on the hunting field and at Peterborough. He also took particular interest in the West Waterford hounds, taken over by Tom and Elsie Morgan in 1954. Ikey recognised Elsie's natural rapport with hounds and together they bred a unique

(Photo: A. Alexander)

Ikey Bell with the Kilkenny Hounds, Castlecomer, May 1st 1917.

(Photo: A. Alexander)

Meet of the Kilkenny Hounds, Castlecomer, May 1st 1917.

pack using Fell blood as an out-cross, instead of the Welsh blood he had previously used. No stud book sires were used for the pack. The Morgans gave up the West Waterford foxhounds in 1988 and the outstanding pale hounds went to America to Ben Hardaway's Midland Hunt. Hardaway had been an admirer of the West Waterford hounds, ever since Bell introduced him to Tom and Elsie in 1962. The hounds are considered to be deer proof and are highly thought of in the USA *(Hardaway, 1997).*

Ikey Bell's influence is evident to this day in that only 5 or 6 Irish packs still hunt Old English Hounds. The Welsh blood which he pioneered, received official respectability when the Foxhound Kennel stud book was opened up to the modern foxhound. His receipt for the ideal hound recommended:

> perfect wearing nails and toes, springy pasterns, perfect shoulders, and lithesomeness, wiry bone (not excessive nor overweight) and courage *(Bell, notes).*

In addition to hound breeding Ikey had an indirect influence on the breeding of the Irish Draught horse. Bred in County Tipperary, Bell's well-known hunter, Lawton's Last, was a foundation sire of the Irish Draught Horse. An amusing anecdote recounts how, while at full gallop hunting on Lawton's Last, Ikey was momentarily distracted surveying the field behind him when the horse took off and cleared a substantial iron gate. The field was most impressed and congratulated Ikey on his courage. In fact, the horse was so impulsive, it had been too late to stop him.

Tom Hutchinson had a similar problem in the Knockdrinia point-to-point, as the horse was regularly exercised there and knew every inch of the country. In the middle of the race he went for home.

Ikey hunted hounds on Lawton's Last for several seasons, and the combination succeeded in winning at least one point-to-point. The horse remained on loan to Ikey and he took him to England and hunted hounds on him with the South and West Wilts. He then returned him to his Kilkenny home and Tom Hodgins stood him for several seasons. Lawton's Last left a good line of jumping horses behind him including Young Lawton. The Bells were long remembered with affection by the members of the Kilkenny Hunt. Their daughter Diana, a winner of more than 48 point-to-points, married Col. Willie Newell in 1945. Although

(Courtesy of Mr. & Mrs. Harry McCalmont)

Charles Morris in 1921, first whip and kennel huntsman to Ikey Bell and Dermot McCalmont.

it was more than 20 years after Ikey's resignation, 56 hunt supporters made a presentation to them on the occasion of their marriage.

Ikey maintained that Kilkenny was the best scenting country he ever hunted. He was master in Kilkenny longer than anywhere else. He and Dolly Bell are buried in the graveyard at St. Canice's Catherdral, in Kilkenny City, not far from his old home.

The city had been a most suitable central location from which to hunt the county. Bell, more so than most masters, had hunted almost the entire county, the exception being the coverts in the east, which were lent to the East Kilkenny Hunt.

The East Kilkenny Hunt

Herky's health had been causing concern, it became necessary for him to go a London hospital and it was apparent that it would be some time before he hunted hounds again. Nick Lambert gave up hunting his own pack, to hunt the Kilkenny Hounds on Herky's behalf, for the duration of the 1907-1908 season. The consequent availability of Mr. Lambert's Hounds presented an opportunity to Lord Southampton who had been looking for a small and comparatively unknown pack to hunt.

Southampton is understood to have fled to Ireland under an unidentified black cloud. Hence the Spy cartoon in which he is depicted as "the Sinner". He rented Kilfane House (the former home of Sir John Power). A keen hound man, he had been master of the Grafton and the Woodland Pytchley 1895-1907 and a Captain in the 10th Hussars (as was a former Kilkenny Hunt master, Capt. Hartopp). He was tall, thin and athletic, and like Hartopp and Bell, a keen polo player. He purchased some of Nick's hounds and bought more from Lady Craven and kennelled the 45 couples at Kilfane.

Ikey Bell gave Lord Southampton permission to draw the coverts on the east side of the county. In 1910 the Carlow Hunt still claimed part of the east of Kilkenny country, around Gowran and Shankill. Gowran had been one of their regular meets for many years. At a later date a small section of this country was still in dispute between Mrs. Hall, master of the Carlow Hunt and the Kilkenny based Mount Loftus Harriers. Southampton carried on leasing Kilfane and spent every winter there with his wife and two small daughters until the outbreak of the First World War. Margarite Solly Flood remembered him for his athletic qualities:

> One day when hounds had found, the far side of Kilfane and were running fast through boggy ground being cheered on by the Master who was riding a big long-tailed chestnut. Suddenly I saw Lord Southampton's tall figure disappear and the hindquarters and long swishing tail of his horse only showed on the far side of the fence. I was certain that he had a bad fall and then, to my amazement, I saw his horse up again cantering across the field with his rider running beside him and, before they reached the next fence, he had vaulted back onto the saddle without a pause and still so interested in his hounds' work that I do not think that he even knew what had happened *(Solly Flood, 1978).*

Foot followers, while enjoying the hunt, often had a certain compassion for the fox, as instanced by the following encounter between Barney Kennedy of Gowran and Lord Southampton. The latter had been invited to cub hunt in the demesne:

> The hounds were giving tongue when his lordship thought he heard the 'gone away'. He galloped out and got onto the road somewhere, when he met a local celebrity called Barney Kennedy. Lord Southampton raced up to him and said: 'Have you seen the fox?' 'The fox,' said Barney, 'a little red fellow, low down on the ground, with a long nose, standing-up ears, and a long bushy tail.' 'Yes, Yes!' said Lord Southampton. 'No, sir,' said Barney, 'I didn't see him'. *(UNC).*

Nick Lambert was not without his hounds for long, as by 1912 he was hunting them again and in March that year they had one of their best days, they met at:

> Cat's rock and found in the covert of that name. The fox led by Rahillakeen over Tory Hill, nearly to the railway at Rahard, and to the right by Ballyhomuck, back to Cat's Rock, where Mr. Lambert discovered that it was a vixen, so hounds were stopped after hunting for twenty-eight minutes. They found another in Ballyquin and ran by Ballintlea with a point for Killandrew Gorse, but the fox bore left by [the] church, then kept on under Tory Hill, continuing by Pollard's Gorse at Ballyfacy. Going to the left by Darbystown and Smithstown, they reached Mullinarrigle, where the hounds pulled their fox down in the open, after a capital hunt of an hour and forty minutes, during which they covered at least fourteen or fifteen miles *(UNC).*

It is unclear what role Nick Lambert played in the East Kilkenny Hunt while Lord Southampton was master, however it is apparent that he was frequently hunting the hounds and probably became joint master at some stage.

The indefatigable Lady Rose McCalmont enjoyed her sport with both the county pack and with the East Kilkenny. In 1913, the hounds found

(Courtesy of Mr. & Mrs. Andrew Kavanagh)

Lord Southampton and the East Kilkenny Hounds.

in Luffany and ran to Prospect, she had the pleasure of taking the fox from the hounds and presenting Mr. Lambert with the brush. The entry in her hunting diary noting the occasion is proudly written in red ink. Her husband, Sir Hugh, only hunted because he considered it his duty, rather than a pleasure. His dislike of hunting is well illustrated in his biography:

> One day Sir Hugh was out with the hounds a farmer accosted him and complained of damage which was alleged to have been done by the hunt. After some altercation – Sir Hugh was wont to be a little quick-tempered under such circumstances – the man threatened that he would have the General prevented from riding across country in future. 'You're the very fellow that I have been looking for for years,' exclaimed Sir Hugh; 'for were it not for my wife and son I would never leave the road' *(McCalmont, 1924, 284).*

(Courtesy of Mr. & Mrs. Andrew Kavanagh)

The Hon. Lady Rose McCalmont and in the background, Mrs. Walter McMorrough Kavanagh.

Lady Rose had been busy grooming their son, Dermot, from "being a small boy with a rather loose seat on either 'The Kaffir' or 'Puffin' to become a very good race rider and man to hounds" *(Solly Flood, 1978, 61).* She ensured that he became master of the East Kilkenny in 1913, joining Nick. Lord Southampton retired just before the First World War. "A farmer said (at a presentation that the farmers and followers gave him before going back to England): 'we are real sorry to lose you, not because you are a Lord, but because ye are a gintleman'." *(The Hexham Courant, Nov.1932).* Nick was in charge once again, only this time he was better funded. The kennels apparently returned to Dysertmore.

In the 1913-1914 season, Dermot and Nick hunted three days a week. Dermot had ten hunters available for his own use and he hunted the bitches, Nick – the dog pack. They leased the Bessborough country in 1913, hunted it one day a week and their original country on the other two days. Dermot had 54 days (including cub hunting) that season with the East Kilkenny and 25 days with the Kilkenny and still had time for 7 days hunting elsewhere *(McCalmont, 1913-1920).* He showed sport early in his career as a huntsman. The following report is of a meet at Mount Neil:

> The first thirty minutes was practically without a check, and the point 7¼ miles or 12 as the hounds ran. This is Captain McCalmont's first season as a huntsman, and every credit is due to him for the way he stuck to hounds throughout, and handled them on a twisting line at the end. Stephen Donoghue; the Tetrach's jockey, was out, and no one saw the hunt better *(UNC).*

The East Kilkenny Hunt point-to-point was held in Tullogher on April 8th 1914. Lady Rose won the Ladies' Race on her hunter, Monkey Puzzle, over 3½ miles. A large number of spectators attended the meeting, many from New Ross:

> The course presented a gay and brilliant spectacle, and everybody, including the bookmakers, appeared to be in the best of humour. The entries for the different races were fairly large, and there were satisfactory fields *(UNC).*

Hunting activities were soon curtailed as the First World War intervened. Dermot managed only six days hunting in the 1914-1915 season, one of which was blank:

> Owing to the war, it was decided at a meeting of the Irish M.F.Hs. – held in Dublin at the end of August – that hunting should be carried on in order to keep down the foxes. It was in no way to be looked on as a sport but rather as a means of giving employment and as a school for training future cavalry horses. No proper season was to be opened. N. Lambert hunts the hounds and carries on, roughly 2 days a week, during my

> absence. I was from Aug. 1st – Sept. 28th doing adj. of the S.I.H. in Dublin and then left to do A.D.C. to General Sir Horace Smith Dorrien Comd. 2nd Army Corps in France *(McCalmont, 1913-1920).*

Dermot managed no further hunting until after the war. In 1918 he came home from East Africa en route to Mesopotamia and resigned his mastership of the East Kilkenny Hunt that year.

The East Kilkenny Hunt remained a popular pack until it was disbanded in 1921, when Dermot took over the county hounds and Nicholas Lambert gave up hunting to sample married life for the first time at the age of 53. The country reverted to the Kilkenny Hunt. A presentation was made to Nick from the East Kilkenny supporters and the names inscribed on it give an indication of those who followed the hunt: Paul Anderson, T.H. Anderson, Earl of Bessborough, Lord Bellew, T.A. Colfer, Arthur Dobbin V.S., J.E. Deane Drake, Capt. R. Gethin, Daryl Gallwey, Paul Hunt, J.L. Handcock, W. F. Hearn, J.B. Hearne, Miss Howlett, P. Kennedy, Sir Hercules & Lady Langrishe, Terence Langrishe, H.H. Langrishe, G.H. Lambert, Anthony M. McCann, Major Dermot McCalmont, J. McConkey, A.J. Mockler, Frank Marsh, Capt. H.J. Newport, Miss Power, R. H. Pilsworth Jnr., A.D. Place, P.D. Place, P.J. Place, P.J. Roche and Dr. M. Walsh.

Chapter 8

The Splendour of Mount Juliet under Dermot McCalmont

Neither hedges nor ditches will set us our bounds
If our horses are good we'll keep up with the hounds.
(Old Yorkshire song)

In 1905 the McCalmont family from County Antrim, in Northern Ireland, rented Mount Juliet from the Earl of Carrick. The Earl had decided, following the death of his father in 1902, that the prospect of living in the large, uncomfortable and old-fashioned house did not appeal to him. He could not afford to modernise it. His father had lived there as a virtual recluse, tolerating the cold and the damp. The house was so uncomfortable that whenever Herky Langrishe went to stay there, he would bring his own supply of coal for the fire in his bedroom. On one unfortunate occasion, as his suitcase was being carried up the stairs, it split open and the coal fell out.

Sir Hugh and Lady Rose McCalmont immediately rectified the situation by lavishly revamping the entire property and they subsequently purchased it in 1914.

The Kilkenny hunting fraternity have to be grateful to two determined ladies, Mrs. Bell (Ikey's mother) and the Hon. Lady Rose McCalmont (Dermot's mother). Independently, both ladies encouraged their respective sons to become outstanding hunt masters. Lady Rose was a descendant of the Persse family, who had been associated with hunting in County Galway for over two hundred years.

Sir Hugh McCalmont preferred the subtler and more refined pleasures of life. It appears that he gave up hunting in 1910, though this did not in any way diminish his wife's enthusiasm for field sports. It was not unusual to see her marching into the house with a couple of dead rabbits that she had just shot. She had a "passion" for hunting, as she once told Mrs. Toler-Aylward of Shankill Castle. She was never to be out-done, once when asked why her only child, Dermot, was so small, she retorted "How do you expect a horse out of a pony?" A brave rider across country, she sang as she jumped and always rode side-saddle. In 1914 she won one of the first Ladies' Steeplechases to be

(Courtesy of Mr. & Mrs. Harry McCalmont)
Sir Hugh McCalmont looked forward to the day when he was no longer expected to hunt.

held at a Kilkenny point-to-point.

Dermot, born in 1887, is reputed to have become the richest commoner in the British Isles after the death of his uncle, Harry McCalmont of Cheveley Park, who had died without issue. Well known on the English Turf as the owner of the Derby winner, Isinglass, Harry McCalmont's large fortune was left to his widow, Winifred, who in turn left the entire estate to Dermot in 1920. Like his uncle, Dermot took an interest in flat racing, and in 1913 he became the owner of one of the fastest two year olds of all time, the Tetrarch, or as he was more familiarly known, the 'Spotted Wonder' because of his unusual colouring. Throughout his life-time Dermot was to enjoy many racing successes. In the same year as the Tetrarch achieved fame, he became joint master of the East Kilkenny Hunt *(Solly Flood, 1978)* and, at the outbreak of war, he joined his father's regiment, the 7th Hussars. Nicholas Lambert deputised for him while he was away serving in the army.

THE SPLENDOUR OF MOUNT JULIET UNDER DERMOT McCALMONT

Dermot married the beautiful Lady Helen Conyngham in 1918, like her mother-in-law, she also rode side-saddle. A very elegant and generous person, she encouraged Dermot to live and entertain in considerable style at Mount Juliet.

Dermot succeeds Ikey Bell

The future of the Kilkenny Hunt was landed in Dermot's capable hands in 1921 when Ikey Bell left for the South and West Wilts. Dermot McCalmont rose to meet the challenge. Ikey's standards had been high and the sport good, the post demanded total commitment from the new master. Dermot possessed a number of the necessary qualities required to succeed Ikey and ultimately surpassed the subscribers' high expectations. As Nick Lambert disbanded his pack, Dermot took back the East Kilkenny country and set forth to hunt the entire county.

On taking over the Kilkenny Hunt, Dermot continued to employ Ikey's hunt staff, including the kennel huntsman, Charlie Morris. He then set about running the hunt in a style as yet unknown in Ireland.

His opening meet was at the Club House Hotel on November 7th 1921. Hounds found in Sutcliffe's and ran around it all day, not perhaps the most inspiring start. But by the following January, from a meet in Mullinavat, they ran from Clonassy via Clontubrid to Ballinaboola, a three hour hunt *(McMorrough Kavanagh, 1914-1940).*

Advised by Charles Sturman of the Heythrop, Dermot built new kennels at Mount Juliet to the highest standards of the day. On June 5th 1922 the hounds were moved from Brownstown, where they had been kennelled for the last years of Ikey's mastership, to Mount Juliet. *(McCalmont, 1921-1926).* Dermot also consulted Sturman on the breeding of his hounds, using Heythrop and Brocklesby blood.

The resulting hounds were not only successful on the hunting field, but also won numerous prizes at the Clonmel hound shows. Dermot showed hounds for the first time at Clonmel in 1925, and picked up four second prizes. The following year Champion and Chaser won the best couple of unentered dog hounds and Chaser won the best unentered dog hound, the first of many show triumphs. Throughout the 1920s and early 1930s outbreaks of distemper often decimated puppies out at walk and on occasions whole kennels suffered. Kilkenny was no exception, and Dermot first used the distemper vaccine with success in 1933.

At the end of a good run early in his career, Dermot, determined to be seen to do the right thing, asked Herky Langrishe to whom the brush

(Courtesy of Mr. & Mrs. Harry McCalmont)

Dermot and Lady Helen McCalmont with their son, Victor, in 1925.

should be given. Herky, in his light-hearted manner, made the suggestion that he should "give it to the first girl who will give you a kiss!" Of course there were those who were unable to accept the new regime with grace. Lady Langrishe had some difficulty and was prone to making rude comments in a loud voice for all to hear. Despite her reluctance to tolerate change, she continued to hunt long after Herky had retired.

Surprisingly perhaps, in view of the political climate, Dermot was able to note in his hunting diary of the 1922-23 season "no trouble of any kind was met in any part of the country" *(McCalmont, 1921-1926).* Generally the hunt was welcome throughout the county, though sometime later a case involving the erection of a barbed wire fence in

Castlegarden, near Kilfane, ended up in the courts. Some farmers had not realised that the Free State had recognised and retained the old British code of law and mistakenly thought that they could take matters into their own hands. Also it was not always appreciated that, while many landlords had sold out to their tenants, they had retained the sporting rights over the properties. An additional problem for hunting was the large number of small landowners created by the breaking up of the big estates. They all had to be dealt with individually, increasing the work load for the area managers.

Lady Helen's enthusiasm for riding to hounds matched that of her husband. Including cub hunting, she hunted 100 days during the 1924-25 season in Kilkenny. Lady Rose had missed several seasons due to an accident. Having moved to Mooresfield House in Kildare, she hunted with the Kildare Hunt and the Naas Harriers, making occasional forays back to see her son hunt the Kilkenny hounds.

Cub hunting took place virtually privately, with few out apart from those who had been personally invited by the master. Dermot usually met between 7 and 9.30 a.m. depending on the month, he did not feel it necessary to cub hunt as early in the day as Ikey Bell did.

He financed everything to such an extent that in 1925 there was an upheaval. Certain hunt members felt that the pack was about to become a private pack. The decision was taken that the hunt would remain the county pack and cap would continue to be collected. That year, Davy McMinn of the Dumfriesshire Hunt was engaged as the second whip. He proved himself and graduated to first whip and kennel huntsman in the autumn of 1927. Charlie Morris injured his pelvis when hunting the hounds during the Major's absence the previous season and was unable to continue his job. Davy had a good voice, and a wonderful "Holloa". The Major would tell him "Davy, get me those hounds!" Davy would jump a five-barred gate off the road, get the hounds and jump back over the gate without hesitation.

Military Precision

The size of the Mount Juliet operation was enormous, there were few estates in Ireland that could rival it. Over 100 men were employed on the property, the excellent terms of employment ensured their loyalty and respect. Such was the air of permanence about the place that no one foresaw the day when there would not be a McCalmont in Mount Juliet. Dermot ran the stable yards and kennels with military precision, no

(Courtesy of Mr. John Kirwan)

Kilkenny Hunt point-to-point races in the 1920s. From left to right: Baroness Prochazka, Mrs. H. Newport, Lady Helen McCalmont, Mrs. Newport, the Countess Dowager of Desart, Lady Ainsworth, and the Hon. Lady Rose McCalmont.

effort or expense was spared to ensure that the Kilkenny Hunt benefited from the highest possible standards. There were over sixty hunters, showjumpers and racehorses at Mount Juliet and there were two grooms in charge of each stabled horse. The kennels alone accounted for the employment of more than seven men. The stable lads, many of whom were local, had lodgings in the hunters' yard, the latter was superbly laid out with wonderful stables, saddle-rooms and wash boxes. A diary was kept in the yard noting the day when each horse would go hunting and the name of the person due to ride the horse.

Every detail was so well organised that the property worked like clockwork. On Thursday evenings the pay sheets from each section of the estate would be sent to Isabelle Cronyn, Dermot's private secretary. Davy McMinn would have made out all the men's hours for their work

(Courtesy of Miss Maura Toler-Aylward)

Major Dermot McCalmont, Master of the Kilkenny Foxhounds.

in the kennels. Every Friday, the wages were collected from the bank in Thomastown by Isabelle in her pony and trap, she always travelled alone and never once feared for her safety.

Dermot made some adjustments to the manner in which the hunt previously had been run. A hunt meeting was held every November at Ballylinch, to discuss the arrangements for the forthcoming season. The committee was made up of members of the Hunt Club and their role in the administration of the hunt became less important as Dermot assumed responsibility for most of the work. The club dwindled until, prior to the Second World War, there were only five members remaining: Arthur McMorrough Kavanagh (hunt chairman), Gilbert Butler (hon. secretary), Willie Pilsworth (former hon. secretary), Jack McEnery and one other.

(Courtesy of Miss Maura Toler-Aylward)
Victor McCalmont with his parents, Lady Helen and Dermot.

Whenever possible Dermot always hunted the hounds himself, considering it a very serious business. His largesse ensured that everything was done to perfection. With the aid of the resources provided by the McCalmonts, Davy McMinn built up an excellent rapport with farmers, and thereby was able to reduce the workload of the area managers. However, time spent on looking after the country, although essential and extremely beneficial to the hunt, did result in his increasing absence from the kennels.

Dermot could be tough on people if he objected to their actions. He distrusted those who did not hunt and had little in common with them. He could be very dogmatic in his views. It was these very characteristics that enabled him to provide Kilkenny with a hunt that was second to none. On the other hand the generosity of Dermot and Lady Helen knew no bounds to those who served the hunt well. In 1929 Tommy McCheane, an area manager in the northern end of the county for many years, and Betty Purdon received a gift of a Morris 12 motor car on the occasion of their marriage – by no means an isolated incident. Betty, who kept a remarkable hunting diary from 1920-1970, thought little of hacking over twenty miles from Freshford, to meets beyond Kilkenny City.

Hunting in the 1920s

From the early 1920s, foxes, scarce heretofore, were slowly becoming more plentiful *(Fairley, 1984)*. In the 1922-1923 season Dermot reckoned the Uppercourt area to be the only part of his country, still lightly stocked with foxes. The chances of hounds changing foxes or dividing increased.

The roads were rough and full of potholes. During the winter months, many towns within the country, were only accessible by roads that were little more than mud tracks, with deep cart ruts. Major improvements came with the introduction of motor vehicles although it was many years before they were all tarred. Even relatively important roads like that from Callan to Carrick-on-Suir remained un-tarred during the 1930s. Motor traffic was still in its infancy and one would be unlikely to encounter a motor car, even on a long hack between Windgap and Callan. The comparatively small amount of motor traffic was

(Courtesy of Miss Maura Toler-Aylward)

A meet at Farmley, the home of Signor Brunelli and the Countess Brunelli Konigsegg. From left to right: John Alexander, Signor Brunelli, the Countess Brunelli Konigsegg, Lady Helen McCalmont, HSH Prince Leyen of Austria and Count Orssich.

considered a problem as the exhaust fumes from vehicles were said to put off the hounds and destroy their noses.

Although the hounds were walked to many meets, the McCalmonts were amongst the first to make use of motorised horseboxes to transport their hunters. The family always had a couple of motors, usually Rolls Royces, following the hunt. There is an intriguing entry in Major McMorrough Kavanagh's hunting diary for October 23rd 1924: "killed with the help of the Rolls Royce and Brown". Sadly, we are not enlightened as to how this came about!

The few motorised horse-boxes that were in use during the 1930s, were not always reliable. On its way to a meet at Jenkinstown, the McMorrough Kavanaghs' box broke down near Dunmore, it was still not fixed later that day, so their horses had to be sent into Kilkenny for the night. Trains also continued to be used. After a hard hunt in January 1931, from Sir John's Gorse to Knocktopher Bog, across the famous single and double walls, and over the rough heather and rocks so typical of that country, the tired horses travelled home by special train. A pleasant end to the day for them, as it had been a bitterly cold and wet day. On other occasions, hunters were transported from Carlow by train and stabled at McCreerys', (now the Sycamores housing estate) on the outskirts of Kilkenny *(McMorrough Kavanagh, 1926-35)*.

Dermot loved to ride at speed. Davy McMinn responded to this and went like a bullet across country, nothing would stop him bar the loss of his horse, and he had scant regard for the good horses he was mounted on. Joane McMorrough Kavanagh noted on February 3rd 1930 "Davy broke his horse's neck". Another day after a fast run from Dunamaggin to the top of Newtown Hill, a distance of about 7 or 8 miles, Davy got off his horse on the top of the hill and it dropped stone dead. Later that year, on March 18th at Fox and Goose, they hunted for an hour and twenty minutes from Smithstown to Gowran. They then drew:

> Bishopslough where we found and had a brilliant hunt up into the hills through Hughes's Bog, towards Kilfane...and around back to Dungarvan 56 minutes...hounds simply flying without hesitation. The country was quite easy to cross and one could not want a better hunt *(McMorrough Kavanagh, 1926-35)*.

That was one of the best days of the 1929-30 season. The following winter, Betty McCheane recorded " a gruelling run over heavy country"

(Courtesy of Miss Maura Toler-Aylward)

A meet at Flood Hall. From left to right: Sir Hercules Langrishe, Major Horace Colmore (partly hidden), Lady Langrishe, Lady Helen McCalmont, the Hon. Lady McCalmont, Master Victor McCalmont, Miss Greta Cameron, Mr. Terence Langrishe, Mr. C. Cameron, Mrs. Terence Langrishe, Mr. Grigg (junior), Mrs. Grigg, Miss "Tommy" Grigg, and Major Dermot McCalmont.

of 1 hour 40 minutes as one of the best days "for a number of years past", with very little wire. The papers reported the same run from Dunmore as 2 hours long. On January 11th 1932 hounds ran from Sugarstown into Bishopslough so fast that it was described as being more like a point-to-point than a hunt. It had been too fast to see or hear hounds. Later the same day they had another very fast seven mile point from Aylwards. The 1937-38 season, was described as:

> Cub-hunting started on August 31, and the regular season finished on March 22. Hounds were out 116 days. They killed 35 brace of foxes and marked 33½ brace to ground... there

(Courtesy of Mr. Nick Marshall)

Oliver Dixon and Mrs. Binty Marshall, both having won first prize, at a show in 1929.

(Courtesy of Miss Maura Toler-Aylward)

The Kilkenny Hunt Puppy Show. From left to right: Dermot McCalmont, Mr. Bob Pilsworth, Lady Helen McCalmont, Mr. O'Gorman of New Ross, Major J.B. Loftus. In front: Victor McCalmont.

> were no blank days...the best hunt of the season took place on January 12, when, finding in Killeen, hounds ran very fast for seventy minutes over the cream of the country, and were almost in view of their fox when he saved his brush in a drain *(The Hunting Diary & Guide).*

During the 1930s the hounds were very fast – too fast some said, and had become relatively silent. Dermot travelled fast from covert to covert and it was sometimes difficult to be sure if hounds were hunting or not. At that time, Kilkenny hounds were rarely seen to be puzzling out a line, they were quickly picked up and cast elsewhere. As the emphasis was on speed, fun and going like hell, Dermot did not always bother to account for his fox. On good scenting days hounds were at their best; when scent was breast high they flew. The field needed to be quick off the mark.

The annual point-to-point took place on a variety of courses around the hunting country. The 1926 meeting held at Ballyfacey, had only 26 runners in five races. In 1927 Rathielty in the north was the venue, followed by Knockadrina and Dunmore.

Victor's Beagles

Dermot and Lady Helen's only child, Victor, was born in 1919. His early childhood was influenced entirely by hounds and horses, to the degree that his parents' Christmas card of 1927 jointly depicts the prize winning dog hound, Trumpeter, with the eight-year-old Victor.

In 1929-30 Victor hunted 14 days with his father's pack and it was not long before he hunted his own pack of beagles. Always well mounted, he hunted the country within easy reach of Mount Juliet, from Tullaherin to Kells and Knocktopher. When the beagles met in their locality, Bertie and Jim Finnegan from Stonyford acted as whippers-in. They principally hunted hares, but one day when they were hunting well, in the direction of Kells, they realised to their horror that they were hunting a cat. It saved its skin by climbing a tree.

Special meets of the beagles were arranged when visitors like Teddy Lambton (son of the trainer, George Lambton) were visiting Mount Juliet. At the end of the Christmas holidays one such meet was planned, they had received permission to draw one of the Kilkenny Hunt fox coverts. Tom Hutchinson was determined that they would have sport that day, and without Victor's knowledge, arranged a drag. It was laid

(Courtesy of Miss Maura Toler Aylward)

Victor McCalmont with his mother, Lady Helen and Mr. Richard Gore at a Kilkenny point-to-point.

by Pat Hutchinson. While hunting the aniseed line, the hounds gave no tongue, Victor's suspicions were aroused and it looked as though all was lost when he ordered Jim Finnegan to stop them. Jim rode ahead to carry out his instructions when, as luck would have it, he saw a large red fox in the field ahead of the hounds. He gave them a good run to the far side of the Callan road.

On poor scenting days, the beagle followers were not averse to creating their own diversion, such as racing each other to the nearest road, perhaps a couple of miles across country. On one occasion, taking a short cut to Stonyford, they came to the King's River. Victor sent Jim across first followed by Bertie Finnegan. Bertie's black mare tried to jump the river but failed to make it. Hearing the splash, Jim looked around but all he saw was his brother's hat in the water. Horse and rider were submerged, though all eventually reached the other side safely.

Every summer a gymkhana was held on the inch, beside the River Nore, at Mount Juliet, in aid of the Kilkenny Hunt Covert Fund. Music was supplied by the St. Joseph's School band from Clonmel and the Clashganny Pipers' band. A variety of competitions included a bicycle point-to-point race over one mile, a donkey show, mounted obstacle races and open jumping which had a first prize of £30.

The Hunt at its Twentieth Century Zenith

Style was important to Dermot. He would arrive at a meet beautifully turned out, in his snowy white breeches covered with a silk apron depicting a fox's or a hound's mask. This protected his breeches, until

(Photo: Irish Times)

The opening meet of the Kilkenny Hunt, November 1929. Hector Toler-Aylward on Anama, Sir Otway Cuffe on Punch and Zinna Toler-Aylward on Mary Anne at Barneyglissawney.

(Courtesy of Mr. & Mrs. Harry McCalmont)

St. Patrick's Day, 1930. The first meet at Kilkenny Castle since 1882.

he was mounted. Dermot relied on his kennel huntsman Davy, to liaise with farmers and landowners. Davy was immensely popular and solved many a problem with a bottle of whiskey. Second horsemen, immaculately turned out, in their liveried jackets, bowler hats and well boned boots followed the field, frequently giving assistance and always ready to provide the McCalmonts with their fresh horses, when required.

Lady Helen always had two Rolls Royce cars following her, one transported hampers with food while the other was equipped with liquid refreshment, and she would offer refreshments to one and all. She was generous almost to a fault, "Take my Rolls Royce and get help" she insisted on one occasion, to an astonished farmer who was in trouble with a cow. However, there were limits as far as Dermot was concerned. One very cold day at Knockroe nothing much was happening. Jack 'Priesty' Brennan of Ardaloo, a slim man and a noted pole vaulter in his day, who was employed as a chauffeur at Mount Juliet, noticed Lady Helen's fur coat lying idle in the car. He donned it in order to keep warm. Although the incident caused a ripple of laughter amongst the field, Dermot was not amused. The following week Jack was nowhere to be seen; his duties had been changed.

The Ormondes provided the picture gallery in the Castle, as a venue for a small number of hunt balls, until someone's prank, which involved the valuable collection of statues being dressed up, met with the Ormondes' severe disapproval. Premises in Patrick Street, Kilkenny, later Stathams Garage, then became the venue, as did the Mayfair Ballroom for a period. The Mount Juliet employees were engaged for the staffing of these events. However hunt balls were soon phased out. Dermot considered them unnecessary, and there was no longer any great need for subscribers to raise funds. Instead hunt members were regularly treated to lavish entertainment at Mount Juliet. As social occasions, these more than compensated for the loss of the annual hunt ball. The gentlemen generally wore white tie and tails or pink coats and at dinner each guest was attended by a footman.

(Courtesy of Mr. John Kirwan)

A group at Kilkenny Castle, including Victor McCalmont, Mrs. Binty Marshall, Lady Sybil Ossory and Charles Carlos Clarke.

(Courtesy of Mr. & Mrs. Harry McCalmont)

Dermot McCalmont, Victor McCalmont and Davy McMinn passing through Mile Post village in 1932.

By the 1930s despite the agricultural depression, the Kilkenny Hunt was at its twentieth century zenith, secure and in the complete control of a benevolent man of considerable expertise and ability. It coincided with a period when hunting was fashionable, and regarded as "the thing to do". In 1930, on the Saturday after Christmas, the hounds ran a point of nearly five miles in 50 minutes from Killeen to Booleyglass. Dermot was providing top quality sport.

The Kilkenny hounds became virtually impossible to beat at the Clonmel hound show. In 1936, they won nine out of a possible ten classes. They were beaten in the best single unentered bitch class by Carlow Dorothy, who was by the Kilkenny hound, Dolphin.

The combination of good sport and fashion attracted many visitors. In Kilkenny a hunting hotel opened to take the overflow of guests who could not be accommodated at Mount Juliet. It was owned by Major McCalmont, and managed by Col. Collie Eccles. Another hotel opened in Thomastown in 1930. Horses could be hired from a variety of sources. Jimmy McClintock, of Kells Grange, kept some hunters for visitors. He was the equivalent of "the master of the horse" at Mount Juliet, a beautiful rider, who rode the country with great ease. Paddy Power from Kilmoganny also kept a supply of hirelings.

In the season of 1933-34, Dermot, his wife and his mother were masters of three separate packs of hounds. Lady Rose (now in her seventies) was master of the Kildare Hunt from 1932-34 and Lady Helen, master of the County Limerick Hunt from 1933-36, surely an unique situation.

(Courtesy of Mr. & Mrs. Harry McCalmont)

Mrs. Binty Marshall and Lady Helen McCalmont.

The McCalmonts encouraged the breeding of hunters within the county by making stallion services available, free of charge, to Kilkenny farmers. Some were also given well-bred mares, retired from the hunting field, in order to increase the quality of the local stock. In an attempt to impress the McCalmonts and their friends, it was common practise for those with home-bred hunters for sale, to enlist the services of a young lad to ride up at the front of the hunt, in the hope of being noticed. Some of these horses changed hands for considerable sums of money, making the whole exercise worthwhile.

(Courtesy of Mr. Kevin O'Donnell)

Davy McMinn and Dermot McCalmont at Barneyglissawney lead the Kilkenny Hunt to the next draw.

Cap money was collected from all hunt members and subscribers. However, the field masters were not always consistent in their approach to its collection, some were more lenient than others. Gilbert Butler would never expect landowners or children to pay, but Sir Otway

(Courtesy of Mr. Kevin O'Donnell)

The Kilkenny Hounds in the hunt kennels at Mount Juliet.

Cuffe of Lyrath expected all those who could afford it to pay up. Much employment was given by the main hunting families. In the season of 1932-33, the McMorrough Kavanaghs of Borris had nine hunters in their yard, for the use of the family. Their horses hunted 113 days that winter and a total of £96 was paid in subscriptions to the neighbouring packs of hounds. It was divided between the following hunts: Kilkenny £45, Mount Loftus £33, Carlow £23 and Mr. Alexander's £12.

For the wealthy families who hunted regularly, the whole winter was devoted to the sport. Arrays of servants were kept busy with the associated duties. Valets, lady's maids, chauffeurs, grooms, stable lads all had their own jobs to do, to make certain that their employers, as well as the hunters, were properly turned out. The life of the grooms was not an easy one; following a long day's hunting, they would generally return after nightfall with tired, dirty horses which then had to be rubbed down and fed. Likewise, with the other servants, the day's work would not be finished until the tack, clothes, boots and the remainder of the hunting kit had been scrubbed clean, so that it would be ready for use the following day. Their employers would treat themselves to a welcome bath on their arrival home and then change into the fresh evening clothes that had been laid out for them. Hot water was always in great demand, after a long, cold, wet day, but even in the grandest houses turns had to be taken in sharing the bath water. High tea usually consisting of eggs and bacon was served at 6 p.m., on hunting days only. It was followed by dinner at 8 p.m.

(Courtesy of Miss Maura Toler-Aylward)

Miss Murdoch winner of the Ladies' Race at the Kilkenny Hunt races, riding Mrs. F. Wise's "Lady Sprey", clearing the last fence.

Amongst the good horsewomen hunting with the Kilkenny Hunt were Rosie Springfield and Binty Marshall, both of whom rode side-saddle. Rosie, towards the latter end of her life, lived at the Rocks, Maddoxtown. An indomitable lady, she refused to drive a car with the Kilkenny registration IP(ee), preferring a Tipperary registration. Her boyfriend had reputedly been killed by a train while out hunting, and in his memory, she wore only grey or purple for the rest of her life. She never married, disliked children, and was frequently heard to say "Go on you silly child, you are getting in my way!" Her groom was not

(Courtesy of Miss Maura Toler-Aylward)

Mr. J.E.N. O'Brien, Lady Helen McCalmont and the Hon. Lady McCalmont.

permitted to ride her hunter, in case he tired the horse out. Instead he had to lead the horse from his bicycle while she drove her decrepit old Ford car to the meet. She hunted until late in life. At her funeral, Dermot McCalmont blew "going home" over her grave. In recognition of her love for hunting she left a legacy to the hunt. It paid for the planting of a covert, near Lukeswell, a small square covert enclosed by a stone wall, named Springfield in her honour. Binty Marshall was a superb horsewoman who rode hunters and showjumpers for Lady Helen. The best of these was Whitegate, named after her home on the Freshford side of Kilkenny City. A plaque to Whitegate may still be seen in the hunters' yard at Mount Juliet. From a child's point of view,

Mrs. Marshall was less frightening than Rosie Springfield and had a reputation for being kind to children in the hunting field.

Lionel Edwards, the artist, was a prominent visitor. He came to Ireland to paint hunting pictures for wealthy patrons. He noted in his *Irish Sketch Book* that an equivalent sized hunt in England raised over £2000 in subscriptions annually, whereas the Kilkenny Hunt raised only £500, demonstrating how enormously indebted the hunt was to the McCalmont family *(Edwards, 1938).* The 1930-31 hunt accounts indicate that all kennel and hunt staff expenses, including the provision and keep of hunt horses, were met by the Mount Juliet estate.

The War Years

The outbreak of the Second World War was to have a significant impact on everyone's hunting arrangements. Due to the rationing of petrol and associated transport problems, the country hunted had to be curtailed. Lord Waterford travelled to the meets in south Kilkenny from Curraghmore in a pony and trap, leading the hunter behind the trap. The Kilkenny Hunt stopped hunting what had been the Gaultier country up to 1934. Unlike many hunts which, because of the war, were forced to economise the Kilkenny Hunt continued to receive the full support of the McCalmont family and came through the war years relatively unscathed. Dermot hunted the hounds throughout the war years and Davy carried the horn on the rare occasions when he was away.

Those living in the big houses made adjustments to their way of life, this generally meant leading a considerably less lavish lifestyle. The numbers of servants were greatly reduced and they were never to be replaced. The male members of many families were abroad fighting and the women had to take on more responsibilities. In houses like Borris, the silver was no longer put out on the table for dinner and they ate at the earlier hour of 6 p.m. The hunt subscribers raised funds during the war years by holding dances in the village halls of Thomastown, Windgap and elsewhere, supplying teas and cakes themselves. Mrs. Moylan of Rathclough and Joan Butler, sister of Gilbert, arranged a series of hunt chases in the Bennettsbridge and Danesfort locality, also in an effort to raise funds.

During the Emergency (1939-1946) the puppy show was a small affair. In 1943 Mrs. Moylan walked Workman, but he lost part of his stern in a door when he was with her and it had to be amputated. At the show Mrs. Hall, the legendary master of the Carlow Hunt, judged him

(Courtesy of Mr. Nick Marshall)

Contrast in ladies' riding dress, prior to the Second World War. Miss Biddy Noble Johnson and the Hon. Lady Rose McCalmont, in her traditional habit, at an opening meet of the Kildare Hounds.

and said that he was such a fine dog that she could not resist giving him first prize. The prize-giving did not take place in the usual manner, instead the awards were quietly distributed at the Mount Juliet gymkhana.

Dermot's first wife, Lady Helen, had died in 1938, and was buried in Ennisnag. In her memory, Dermot presented the church with a beautiful stained glass window, designed by Catherine O'Brien, commemorating

Lady's Helen's love of animals and hunting. The Kilkenny saints Ciaran and Moling are depicted with some of their pet animals. St. Moling's repentant fox had many faults, he ate the monastery's hen, and endeavoured to make up for it by stealing one from the convent, which he gave to the saint as a peace offering. The saint was unimpressed and told him that he had now committed two sins. The fox is thus shown returning the hen to the surprised nuns, alongside a pleasant hunting scene.

In 1941 Dermot married June Patterson Nickalls, only child of Major Patterson Womersley Nickalls, D.S.O. Under her influence much of the extravagant lifestyle at Mount Juliet was curtailed. The number of employees was slightly reduced, but the hunters' yard continued to be run in a military fashion.

She was responsible for setting up the Kilkenny Hunt Pony Club in 1946 and encouraged local children to join, which they did, sometimes on half-broken ponies and often without riding hats or safe tack. They were all made welcome and anything that was required for pony or child was supplied by Mount Juliet. Dermot was in charge of the teaching of cavalry drill to the children, on their little fat ponies, a difficult task. The O'Donnells, who became a byword in point-to-point circles, the Hughes family of current international show jumping fame, and the Lawlors later to be breeders of international showjumpers, were all enthusiastic members. Each Christmas a party was held in the house for the Pony Club children. The excitement was intense, as they were let loose playing hide and seek throughout the big house. But the viewing of the cine-film, showing the high-lights of the summer months activities, was the moment all waited for. It was before the days of television and few had even been to a cinema, so it was a great novelty to see themselves filmed on their ponies.

Chapter 9

Johnswell and Mount Loftus Harriers

The hunt was not merely incidental to rural society, it was a legitimate and integral part of it. (D. Itzkowitz, 1977)

For a brief period Dermot hunted the entire county, something virtually no one had done since Sir John Power, and something which has since become impracticable due to the rise of other registered and unregistered hunts within the county. From approximately 1920 to 1927 a pack, owned by John Grace, hunted the Freshford area. John Grace was a local publican and undertaker, a member of the famous sporting family that included Dr. Pierce Grace and Father Dan Grace. The hounds were kennelled in the yard behind his premises, which is now Kavanagh's, on the north-west side of the square. They always met at Freshford, and it is said that when the hounds were released John always left the village at full gallop blowing "Gone away". The reason being that it was then the custom for the local butchers to hang whole carcasses of mutton and quarters of beef on hooks outside their shops – a practise not unnoticed by the harriers.

The Johnswell Harriers

The Johnswell Harriers were founded in 1924 by agreement with the Kilkenny Hunt. Their founder was Dr. William H. O'Brien, a native of Foynes, County Limerick, who together with Peter Duggan and Dr. Patrick Heffernan had been informally hunting the Johnswell country for some time. Other founding members were: Edward Hogan, Kieran Comerford, Pierce Keeffe, John Kirwan, Father Hughes, Thomas Butler, George O'Sullivan, Edward Hogan, Edward Drennan, Thomas Manning, Patrick Comerford, John Bennett, Edward Mulrooney, James Downey, Pierce Comerford, Peter Duggan and John Brennan. Their subscription rates were £2 for regular and £1 for non-regular members. The area hunted extended from Johnswell to Castlecomer and over to the Carlow border to the east, and included the districts of Johnswell, Revanagh, Castlewarren, Coolcullen, Uskerty, Coon East, Coon West, Muckalee, Ballyfoyle and Dunmore. The agreement with the Kilkenny Hunt made it clear that Major McCalmont did not allow the Kilkenny coverts to be drawn, so only outlying foxes could be hunted. This caused problems as they would often run foxes into the coverts. Matters eventually came to a head, and to discuss the crisis the harriers held a general meeting on April 19th 1925 at Ballysalla Cross Roads "at 3 o'clock old time" *(Minutes of the Johnswell Harriers, 1921-31).* Subsequently a meeting was called at the Club House Hotel, at which the county pack was represented by Major McCalmont and Major Kavanagh and the harriers by Dr. O'Brien, Edmund Hogan and Kieran Comerford. The following settlement was made:

> That Major McCalmont handed over to the Johnswell Harriers all the country north of Johnswell covert and also including Gaulstown Park, Freneystown, Castlewarren but he also reserved the right of visiting this country himself whenever he wished and to be retained for himself and his own use, all these coverts lying between Kilkenny City and Johnswell covert *(Minutes of the Johnswell Harriers, 1921-31).*

Once the above resolution had been agreed the relationship between the two hunts improved, the number of hounds in the Johnswell Harrier pack was increased to eight couples, and the average field numbered around fourteen. The best of their hunting country was on the open land adjacent to the Carlow border, as any fox found there had to run some distance to find covert. The hounds (originally eighteen inch harriers) were kennelled by Dr. O'Brien at Kilkieran during the hunting season, and for the remainder of the year most of them were trencher fed, greatly reducing the hunt's running costs. Any hounds that remained in the kennels were fed on an oatmeal cake prepared by the Misses O'Brien, the Doctor's sisters, who were assisted by Peter Duffy, loyal groom and kennel huntsman.

Unsuccessful Stag Hunting

In October in 1924, the harriers decided that they would acquire a stag for the benefit of the hunt. It was arranged that Tom Butler would collect the animal and the sum of £2 would be handed over to the vendor. Col. Gilheany undertook to accommodate the stag in the barracks in Kilkenny. On the 12th November, amidst great excitement, the stag was brought by horse and covered-in cart to Brown Mountain, where it was enlarged. He headed for Cretteclough forestry, where he disappeared and was never seen again. The harriers had not hunted him well, it was an experiment which was considered best forgotten.

Dr. O'Brien's methods of establishing the whereabouts of foxes was somewhat unorthodox, he depended on his patients to supply him with the required information. The best of these foxes was the Tullabrin one, which provided them with three good hunts, the outstanding one being:

> On a Thursday towards the end of February 1928. The meet was at the Kennels at one o'clock and Dr. O'Brien drew the country in the direction of Tullabrin, in the hope of finding this fox. There was a good turnout with some visitors from the Gowran area and two army Colonels from the Military Barracks, Kilkenny. When the hounds drew Tullabrin, Reynard was away at once and hounds hunted very fast to Muckalee and Clorinka from there to Coolraheen and on to Uskerty and over to Glenmullen wood near Castlecomer, nearing the wood the fox was coursed by a sheepdog and this upset the scent. However after some delay, hounds got on terms with him again and ran to Coolcullen and Revanagh and through Mr. Pierce Comerford's farm at Coolgreany, from there to Castlewarren wood where he was marked to ground. There were some very tired horses towards the end, but it was an enjoyable hunt over a good country, stone walls and single banks *(Minutes of the Johnswell Harriers, 1921-31).*

The harriers ran a point-to-point, with the approval of the Masters of Foxhounds Association, in 1926 on Tullabrin Hill. Sixty-seven horses were entered for the meeting. It was considered a success and it became an annual event for a brief few years until 1931. In 1928, on a bad misty day there was an unfortunate incident when the favourite, named Harrier, a winner of twenty point-to-points ran in the Open Heavy Weight race, broke its leg and had to be shot *(Butler, 1928).* Race Cups were presented by a variety of hunting families including the Smithwicks, the McCalmonts and the O'Briens of Rockview, Stonyford. It was initially hoped that the harriers would continue after Dr. O'Brien left for his new post in Graignamanagh. No new master could be found, so the country reverted to the Kilkenny Foxhounds. Once it became clear that the harriers were to be disbanded, Dr. O'Brien brought the hounds with him and, the following year, founded the Mount Loftus Harriers.

The Mount Loftus Harriers

The first pack of hounds based at Mount Loftus were the property of Sir Nicholas Loftus during the early nineteenth century. He was said to have ridden hard, drank as well as any man, loved wisely but too well – and pleased himself. Sir Nicholas took pleasure in bringing his guests down to inspect the hounds before going "back to the house for a hunt breakfast". This was usually washed down with plenty of liqueurs after which the hounds were "had out" *(Grattan-Bellew 1971, 28)* and the day's sport commenced.

The pack was infamous for purportedly having eaten the kennel huntsman, who reputedly still continues to haunt the old kennels with his screams. The Loftus family were away at the time of the incident. The huntsman took advantage of their absence and went to Goresbridge, got drunk and ended up spending a couple of days there. When he eventually returned to Mount Loftus, he failed to negotiate the steps up to his little house, and fell down some adjacent steps which landed him in the kennel yard. The starving hounds devoured him. Nothing remained, but his boots. In the fields above the old kennels, there was a racecourse that ran through the estate, dating from this period.

In 1930 Dr. William O'Brien brought six or seven couples of hounds with him from the Johnswell Harriers to Graignamanagh. There had been a pack of trencher fed harriers in the vicinity earlier in the century, but it is unlikely that they were still in existence by 1930. He wasted no time in forming a committee, obtaining permission from Major Jack Loftus to kennel the hounds at Mount Loftus and he then opened negotiations with the Kilkenny Hunt, regarding the extent of the country they would allow him to hunt. Dr. O'Brien became the master of the new pack and was later joined by the former hon. secretary, Patricia Loftus, as joint master. She looked after the hounds initially with the aid of the Carroll boys from the back gate at Mount Loftus.

When she took in the harriers she was unaware of the fate of her ancestor's huntsman:

> Five couple of trencher fed hounds arrived, coupled, in a lorry

(Courtesy of Mrs. Patricia Bayliss)

The Mount Loftus Harriers at Mount Loftus. From left to right: Mr. Challoner (kennel huntsman), Dr. O'Brien, Mr. Duffy (Dr. O'Brien's groom) and Miss Patricia Loftus.

without much warning. My father said I could put them in the Old Bull Yard where there was a larger stable, once the home of a famous racehorse called Hollyhock, whose mounted hoof we have, inside is a ballad written in parchment by his ostler (groom). Well anyway, the five couple were put in this paddock and I asked my father, if I could have a couple of youths from the Back Lodge to help me exercise and feed them…

The hounds in the paddock were making rather a lot of noise, and the boys scrambled up the nearest trees. Nothing would persuade them to come down.

Almost in tears I went into my Papa telling him that the boys had declared that the last huntsman was eaten by his hounds. "Is this true?" "Yes" said my Papa. So we got a professional kennel man from the Thurles and Kilshane Hounds and by degrees built up a pack of 25 couple *(Bayliss, 1999)*.

The Mount Loftus Harriers were a successful and popular pack from the first. Their opening meet was at Mount Loftus on November 2nd 1930, when they had a good day. Much of their country was quite trappy, but as the hounds were much slower than the Kilkenny Hounds, it was possible to get through it. On January 17th they met at Goresbridge and Joane McMorrough Kavanagh wrote in her hunting journal:

> The country varied more than any other hunt I have seen. Butlers, Graigue road, past Miltown, Glencoum. The first part was small and stony, up around Glencoum there were high narrow banks that one could jump anywhere, round Miltown there were enormous double walls and the last part was our own rough stony country. A pack of foxhounds would not have been able to hunt that fox for he twisted in every field, but except for one long check the Harriers hunted beautifully and at one time quite fast, approximately 1½ hours *(McMorrough Kavanagh, 1926-35).*

Point-to-Points at Doninga

The annual point-to-point at Doninga was another popular venture. It was run across Willie Mullins's land. He did not object to the course going through his barley, he said that the horses galloping through the seed did no harm and he just gave it a roll afterwards. It was a very stiff course, the first year four horses were killed. In the Ladies' Race that year, Patricia Loftus had a crashing fall over a low bank. Her mare missed her take off and somersaulted. She held on to the reins and was trampled across her face and chest. A member of the Mullins family picked her up and put her back on the horse and sent her off. Having completed the race she continued to carry out her duties as hunt secretary and it was only at the end of the day's racing that Dr. O'Brien reckoned that maybe she should have a few stitches. Being too drunk to do the job himself, his friend, Dr. Murphy from Enniscorthy, provided the required medical attention.

A deliberate case of mistaken identity occurred when the Ladies' Race was won by a man whose disguise had been applied by a professional hairdresser. There was a certain amount of consternation when the individual's true sex was discovered some three weeks later. The ladies were no weaklings when it came to race riding, Mrs. Moylan came off in a Ladies' Race at Doninga when her horse fell at a bank. She simply caught the horse by the tail and remounted and managed to finish in third place. The last Mount Loftus point-to-point was also held at Doninga and the mixed riders' race was won by Maureen Mullins.

Within that locality, the Mount Loftus hunt balls were the social event of the year and were a considerable source of income for the hunt. They were somewhat less formal than those held by the Kilkenny Hunt. At first they were held at Mount Loftus, but after a particularly riotous one which was not appreciated by the hon. secretary's step-mother, they were moved to Graignamanagh. They were always held on St. Stephen's night, after the day's hunting, the meet usually attracted a large field of up to 80 followers. The kennels eventually were moved from Mount Loftus to Red Bog, where the hunt's first professional whip, Dick Challoner, an Englishman, was in charge.

Their country extended from Mount Loftus to Gowran Demesne and they never crossed the bridge in Graignamanagh into the Carlow country, with whom they were not on the best of terms, having fallen out with Mr. Grogan who referred to them as "Miss Loftus and her bloody dogs". To the north, they met at Shankill Castle, a meet shared by the Carlow and the Kilkenny Hunt. The furthest south they hunted was beyond Brandon Hill at the Rower. It was a long hack of about one and a half hours travelling slowly with the hounds. They would usually arrive home in the dark at about 6 p.m. People, horses and hounds were very fit then. In the summer Patricia Loftus would walk the hounds on foot for about two hours before breakfast. Prior to her marriage she was master for five years during which time she also took on responsibility for the welfare of the hounds. The Doctor only saw them on the days that he hunted them, but the hounds knew him instantly and he had no problem naming them. The hounds were fed on soup which Patricia cooked in a large pig boiler. The soup was made out of donated cockerels, mixed with maize meal bought at £10 a ton. Mount Loftus provided free oats, hay and straw and many farmers paid their small subscription in kind. When she retired, Major McMorrough Kavanagh took over as master.

One season, while Patricia Loftus was still master, she was made aware of an outlying stag in the woods in the Gowran demesne. She rang Dermot to request permission to hunt it. "Hunt it, kill it, do anything you like with it, just get rid of it", he replied. They hunted it from Gowran to the river Nore, the stag was one field ahead of them all the time and they never caught up with it. On reaching the river it swam across and got away after a long point – thus giving the harriers their most successful stag hunt. Dr. Bill O'Brien was on friendly terms with the McCalmonts and they were supportive of the harriers. However, a time did come when Dermot, concerned that they were killing too many foxes, reckoned that the solution was to present them with a couple of stags. The first one was carted to the meet in something that looked like a converted tea chest. It was a complete disaster, as the harriers killed virtually as soon as he was enlarged. Determined that such an incident would not happen again, Col. Gilheany was instructed to protect the second stag and ride alongside as it crossed the country, the story does not relate what became of the Colonel or the unfortunate stag. A decision to revert to the more mundane sport of foxhunting was taken, following an incident, when a stag went to bay in an upstairs bedroom in a house in Gowran.

Tragedy hit the harriers when hunting near Paulstown. Nearly half the pack were killed when, having scrambled over a stone wall, they fell into a deep quarry. Two neighbouring masters, Major Dermot McCalmont and Bobby Hall-Dare, deeply upset by the accident, joined forces and presented the hunt with replacement hounds.

Loyal Hunt Supporters

Among the many supporters of the Harriers from the 1930s to the 1950s were the following: the Loftus family, Major McMorrough Kavanagh and his family from Borris, Willie Mullins of Doninga (a close friend of Ikey Bell's, he acted as hon. secretary and whip for many years), the Prendergast family of Graignamanagh, Tom Walshe T.D. and Minister for Agriculture, Dick and Jim Kelly of Knockeen, the O'Donnells of Clashwilliam, Father Ger Bennett, John Joyce, Michael Murphy, Ted Hughes of Graignamanagh, Dan Kirwan of Lower Grange, Paddy Healy of Paulstown Castle, Tom Green of Cloghala, Johnny Hughes of Kilmanaghan, Charlie Hayden of Cloghala, Maureen Doran of Kilcruff, the Little family of Spahill, Tom Blackmore of Tullaherin, Father Gerry Maher of Graignamanagh, Mick Gahan, Joe Doyle of Coolyhune, Ned and Larry Mahon of Blackwell, the Connolly family of Goresbridge, Micheal O'Donoghue of Lower Grange, Teresa Hoyne of Thomastown, Teddy Pilsworth of Thomastown, Miss Power of Kilfane and Tom Murphy of Brittas. Paul Kelly helped with settling claims made occasionally for damage caused by the hunt. Alice Kavanagh was the

(Courtesy of Mrs. Patricia Bayliss)

The Mount Loftus Harriers at the gates of Shankill Castle. From left to right: Mr. Willie Mullins, Mr. Duffy (Dr. O'Brien's groom), Miss Patricia Loftus, Dr. O'Brien and Mr. Challoner, the kennel huntsman.

last hunt member to ride side-saddle. Rosie Springfield also hunted regularly with the Mount Loftus Harriers. She was very sporting, but had a sharp tongue; one day hunting near Paulstown Castle, her bowler hat got caught in the branches of a tree, Willie Mullins, who was behind her, was shocked to observe that not only had the hat come off, but so had her hair. "Pick it up man, did you never see a wig before?" she bellowed at him.

The harriers, unlike the county hounds, were not opposed to hunting on holy days, when as many as sixty would be out. Farmers in particular were attracted to the harriers. On one such holy day the harriers were hunting at Skeoghvosteen. They were joined by a farmer's daughter dressed in a cotton dress, bare legs and shoes who was riding bareback a cart horse in blinkers. "Glory be to God, praise to the Almighty, may the Virgin help me get over this", she chanted in a loud voice as she clung to her horse's neck as it negotiated the most formidable obstacles and, at great pace, sometimes ahead of the master, followed the hunt all day. Alas the story does not record her name.

A fast run of at least eight miles from Healys' at Paulstown Castle to Castlewarren wood was one of the best days enjoyed by the harriers. During the run the hounds were not handled for five of those miles. Another good day saw some exceptional hound work when the line was carried along the top of walls. Elsewhere that same day, which included a six and a half mile point in one hour, the hounds had to jump from stone to stone on some very steep country. Shortly after her marriage to Commander Bayliss, Patricia was hunting a green horse from Coppenagh towards Graignamanagh over some very hairy ditches. Her horse fell into one and as people jumped over her, she heard someone shout "Come on Commander, your wife is dead in a ditch".

War Years and After

Like most hunts they found it difficult during the war years. In about 1943 the kennels were moved to the Prendergast farm at Tinnepark, Graignamanagh where Joe Turner, who had succeeded Challoner, looked after them. He remained whip for the rest of their existence.

After the war, the pack met weekly and held meets at Mount Loftus, Graignamanagh, Coppenagh, Dungarvan, Neigham, Red Bog, Doninga, Garryduff and elsewhere. The period from 1945 until the mid 1950s was a very stable time in the Kilkenny countryside, one member of the Mount Loftus harriers described it as real countryside, in which there was little discontent. Many of the coverts that they drew have now gone, as have the wooden gates, that were so easily jumped. The death of Dr. O'Brien in 1952 almost heralded the end of the harriers. For a while they continued to hunt under the mastership of Terence Vigors of Burgage. Around 1955 he took over the mastership of the Carlow Hunt and what remained of the harriers was merged with the Carlows.

(Photo: Michael O'Byrne. Courtesy of Kilkenny Archaeological Society)

Portrait of Sir John Power (2nd Baronet) with his hounds, Safety, Samson and Ranties by Sir Francis Grant.

George Bryan raises his hat
to call on the hounds,
hunted by his son-in-law,
Sir Edward Bellew.
Bryan's sister, Augusta Mary,
watches the stag's
enlargement with interest.
The 'chef d'equipe' is depicted
riding Bryan's favourite
grey horse.
The setting is near the Seven
Sisters in County Kilkenny.

From the painting by the
Kilkenny artist,
Edmund Fitzpatrick,
c. 1853.

(Courtesy of Mr. & Mrs. Andrew Kavanagh)

The Land War, 1881-1882, put a stop to hunting in some areas. The foxes picnic in safety from the hounds. The host invites his guests to "be aisy and take a dhrop of the 'crathur', sure you're ahl safe here be raysen o' them blaguards".

(Private Collection)

(Private Collection)

The hounds are in full cry and Sir Edward Bellew blows his horn to encourage the stragglers. Mr. Swift of Swifte's Heath, is depicted falling over the wall, while George Bryan, on his bay horse, is jumping it in the approved manner of the day. In contrast the gentleman behind appears to be 'hailing a cab' as he jumps. Once again Bryan's favourite grey horse is prominent. From the painting by Edmund Fitzpatrick, c. 1853.

(Courtesy of Mr. Nicholas Lambert)

A watercolour sketch of Nicholas Lambert and his kennel huntsman.

Nicholas Lambert,
from a portrait by H. Harris.

Lord Southampton.

(from the Spy print published in Vanity Fair.)

(Photo: Sally Kerr Davis. Private Collection)

Portrait of Isaac Bell
by Sir Alfred Munnings, 1920.
(With acknowledgement to the Sir Alfred Munnings Art Museum, Castle House, Dedham, Essex.)

Isaac Bell,
Master of the
Kilkenny Hunt,
1908-1921.

(Private Collection)

Dolly Bell winning a point-to-point riding side saddle, from a painting by Lionel Edwards.

(Private Collection)

Lawton's Last, Ikey Bell's brilliant hunter, later a successful sire, from a painting by Lionel Edwards.

(Private Collection)

Ikey Bell's yacht, Bloodhound, built in 1936, which won the Fastnet race.

(Courtesy of Mr. & Mrs. Harry McCalmon[t]

Dermot McCalmont as a young man in 1908, by Crawford McFall.

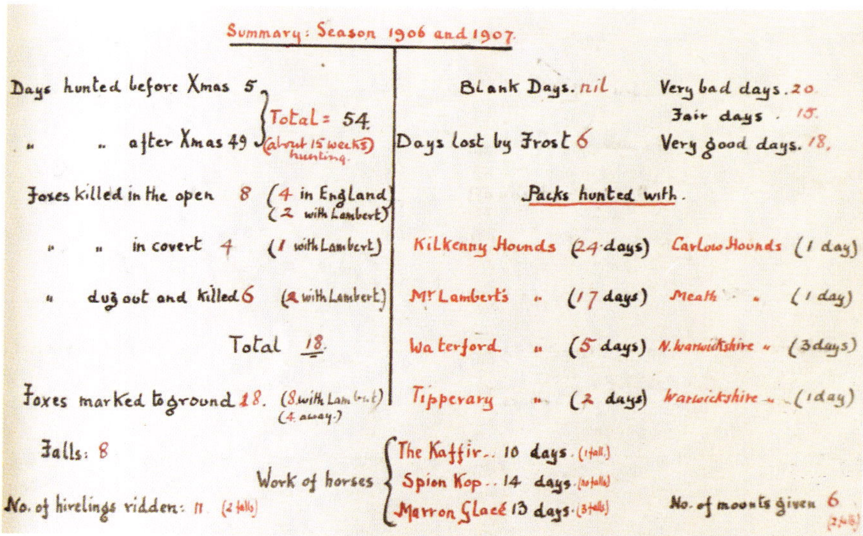

Summary: Season 1906 and 1907.

Days hunted before Xmas 5 } Total = 54 (about 15 weeks hunting)
" " after Xmas 49

Foxes killed in the open 8 (4 in England) (2 with Lambert)
" " in covert 4 (1 with Lambert)
" dug out and killed 6 (2 with Lambert)
Total 18.

Foxes marked to ground 18. (8 with Lambert) (4 away.)

Falls: 8

No. of hirelings ridden: 11 (2 falls)

Blank Days. nil
Days lost by Frost 6

Very bad days. 20
Fair days. 15.
Very good days. 18.

Packs hunted with.

Kilkenny Hounds (24 days) Carlow Hounds (1 day)
Mr Lambert's " (17 days) Meath " (1 day)
Waterford " (5 days) N. Warwickshire " (3 days)
Tipperary " (2 days) Warwickshire " (1 day)

Work of horses { The Kaffir.. 10 days. (1 fall.) / Spion Kop.. 14 days. (no falls) / Marron Glacé 13 days. (3 falls)

No. of mounts given 6 (2 falls)

(Courtesy of Mr. & Mrs. Harry McCalmont)

A page from Dermot McCalmont's hunting diary summing up the 1906-07 season.

(Private Collection)

A fox crossing the road near Booleyglass from a painting by Peter Biegel.

(Private Collection)

Hounds crossing the road near Ballyhale, from a painting by Peter Biegel.

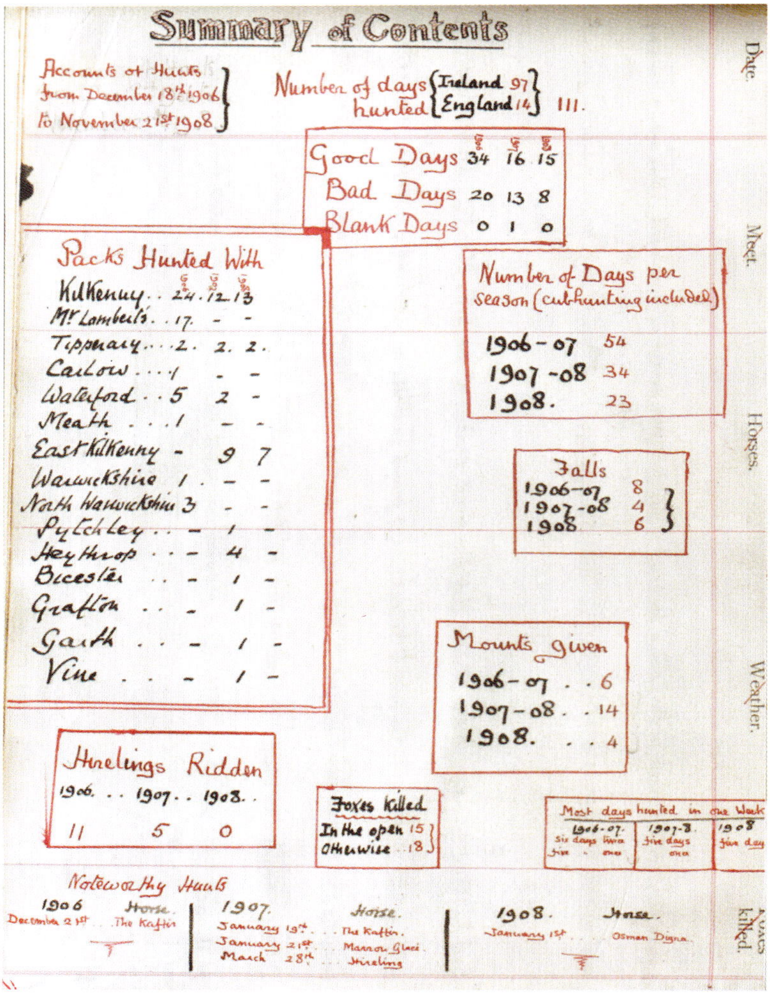

Summary of Contents

Accounts of Hunts from December 18th 1906 to November 21st 1908

Number of days hunted: Ireland 97, England 14 — 111.

	1906	1907	1908
Good Days	34	16	15
Bad Days	20	13	8
Blank Days	0	1	0

Packs Hunted With

	1906	1907	1908
Kilkenny	24	12	13
Mr Lambert's	17	-	-
Tipperary	2	2	2
Carlow	1	-	-
Waterford	5	2	-
Meath	1	-	-
East Kilkenny	-	9	7
Warwickshire	1	-	-
North Warwickshire	3	-	-
Pytchley	-	1	-
Heythrop	-	4	-
Bicester	-	1	-
Grafton	-	1	-
Garth	-	1	-
Vine	-	1	-

Number of Days per season (cub-hunting included)

1906-07	54
1907-08	34
1908	23

Falls

1906-07	8
1907-08	4
1908	6

Mounts given

1906-07	6
1907-08	14
1908	4

Hirelings Ridden

1906	1907	1908
11	5	0

Foxes Killed: In the open 15, Otherwise 18

Most days hunted in one week: 1906-07 six days twice, five once; 1907-8 five days once; 1908 five days

Noteworthy Hunts

1906	Horse	1907	Horse	1908	Horse
December 2nd	The Kaffir	January 19th	The Kaffir	January 1st	Osman Digna
		January 21st	Marron Glacé		
		March 28th	Hireling		

Summary from Dermot McCalmont's hunting diary, 1906 to 1908.

(Courtesy of Mr. & Mrs. Harry McCalmont)

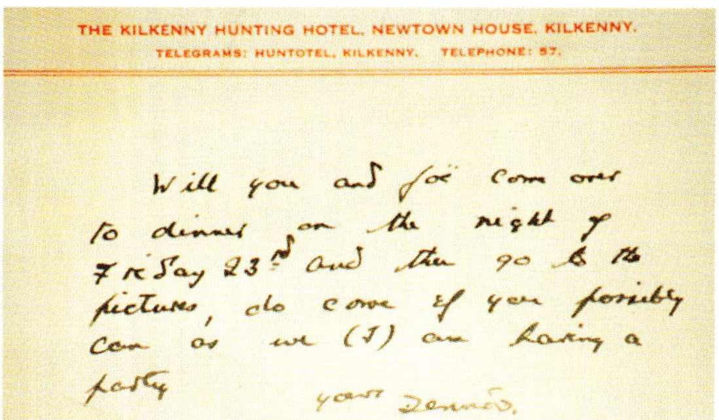

THE KILKENNY HUNTING HOTEL, NEWTOWN HOUSE, KILKENNY.
TELEGRAMS: HUNTOTEL, KILKENNY. TELEPHONE: 57.

Will you and Joe come over to dinner on the night of Friday 23rd and then go to the pictures, do come if you possibly can as we (I) are having a party

yours Dermod

An invitation to Miss D. Gabbett, Ballaghtobin, from a visitor at the Kilkenny Hunting Hotel.

Entrance ticket to the Kilkenny Hunt Point-to-Point races in 1909.

PRICE 6D.

KILKENNY HUNT

POINT-TO-POINT RACES.

AT

Lacken, near Bonnettstown,

On THURSDAY, APRIL 1st, 1909,
Commencing at 2 o'clock,
Under sanction of the Irish National Hunt Steeplechase Committee.

(Private Collection)

Victor McCalmont, age 4, on his pony.
Watercolour by his godmother, Rose Barton.

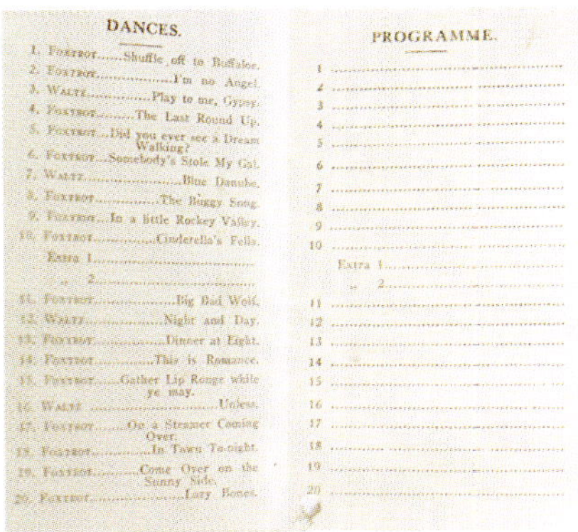

DANCES.

1. Foxtrot......Shuffle off to Buffaloe.
2. Foxtrot..................I'm no Angel.
3. Waltz..............Play to me, Gypsy.
4. Foxtrot.........The Last Round Up.
5. Foxtrot...Did you ever see a Dream Walking?
6. Foxtrot...Somebody's Stole My Gal.
7. Waltz..........................Blue Danube.
8. Foxtrot...............The Biggy Song.
9. Foxtrot...In a little Rockey Valley.
10. Foxtrot..............Cinderella's Fella.

Extra 1..
" 2..

11. Foxtrot.....................Big Bad Wolf.
12. Waltz.....................Night and Day.
13. Foxtrot..................Dinner at Eight.
14. Foxtrot................This is Romance.
15. Foxtrot......Gather Lip Rouge while ye may.
16. Waltz...................................Unless.
17. Foxtrot.......On a Steamer Coming Over.
18. Foxtrot..............In Town To-night.
19. Foxtrot.........Come Over on the Sunny Side.
20. Foxtrot...........................Lazy Bones.

PROGRAMME.

1 ....
2 ....
3 ....
4 ....
5 ....
6 ....
7 ....
8 ....
9 ....
10 ....
Extra 1..
" 2..
11 ....
12 ....
13 ....
14 ....
15 ....
16 ....
17 ....
18 ....
19 ....
20 ....

Dance Programme from the Kilkenny Hunt Ball, 1934.

(Photo: Seamus Corballis)

Above :
Major Victor McCalmont explains the rudiments of hunting.
Children's meet, Chapel Hill, 1992.

Opposite:
Major Victor McCalmont, Master of the Kilkenny Hunt, 1948-1993.
(Photo: Jim Meads, first published in 'The Great Hunts, Foxhunting Countries of the World' by Alastair Jackson, David & Charles, 1989)

(Photo: Patricia Vigors. Courtesy of Mr. and Mrs. Harry McCalmont

Bunny and Victor McCalmont
with their terriers and pekinese

(Courtesy of Mr. & Mrs. Roy Strudwick)

Roy Strudwick, Joint Master of the Kilkenny Hunt, 1987-1998

(Photo: Des McCheane)

Some of the field, Kilkenny Hunt opening meet, Gowran, 1998.

The beautiful window in Ennisnag Church by Catherine O'Brien, was presented by Major Dermot McCalmont in memory of his first wife, Lady Helen.

St. Patrick is said to have given St. Ciaran a bell. He was to found a monastery wherever the bell rang. It rang in Ossory. In the window St. Ciaran is shown with the bell at his feet along with four of his pets, a fox, a wolf, a stag and a badger. Above to the left are huntsmen and hounds. St. Moling is shown with his alsatian. His pet fox had many faults. In the lower right panel a monk makes the fox hand over a valuable book which he has buried. The same fox, penitent for having eaten the monastery hen, steals a hen from the convent as a peace offering. St. Moling tells the fox "Now you have committed two sins, you are to put the hen back in the Ladies' Cloisters". Top right, the sisters are depicted surprised at finding their hen restored. The panels between the tracery to the top of the window show a kneeling St. Ciaran, a partridge and a grouse.

(Photo: author, by permission of the Representative Church Body.)

Chapter 10

Kilmoganny and Gaultier Hunts

It is six to one that the fox will get away. Anyway you'd kill a rat, wouldn't you, why not a fox? (Mrs. Olive Hall, 1963)

The south and south-west of County Kilkenny was well hunted by the Curraghmore Hounds prior to their demise in 1884. Hercules Langrishe then reclaimed the country on behalf of the Kilkenny Hunt.

Herky had one of his best days hunting in that region, when hounds ran from Windgap Gorse, past the snowy cairn on top of Slievenamon at 2,346 feet to the rocks above Killurney Glen overlooking Lord Ormonde's shooting lodge at Ballyknockane, where hounds marked their fox to ground. It was a hunt of twelve miles as the hounds ran, an eight mile point from the covert to the mountain top *(Records of the Kilkenny Hunt, 1899-1908)*.

Since Ikey Bell spread his hunting area to include almost the entire county, hounds were not meeting in the south west as frequently as heretofore. Many of the 25 or 30 hunt followers in the area found that it took up to half a day to hack to Kilkenny Hunt meets in other parts of the county and transport was not readily available. Thus in the early 1920s when it became clear that Dermot McCalmont intended to increase the Kilkenny Hunt's country, by taking in the East Kilkenny Hunt country, it was felt locally that there was a need for a pack of harriers to provide the southern district with regular sport.

Father Larkin, the Windgap curate, and Pat Walsh of Coolaghmore House already had a mixed bag of beagles and hounds and, with the support of John Hawe, Patrick Shee of Newtown, Richard Curran of Cregg, and Patrick Moore of Kilmoganny, they formed the Kilmoganny Harriers. They augmented their pack with a draft from Col. Holroyd-Smith who had a private pack near Youghal *(Power. T)*. Initially it was hoped to amalgamate with the Carrick Harriers, run by the Bearys, who hunted carted deer on the Waterford side of the River Suir, however this was not to be.

(Photo: Des McCheane)

Typical Kilmoganny country in the Lingaun valley.

A peculiarity of twentieth century Kilkenny "harrier" packs is that they all hunted the fox exclusively. The Kilmoganny Harriers did likewise from the start, though in deference to the Kilkenny Hunt, they maintain green livery. The country was lent to the Kilmoganny, on condition that the Kilkenny Hunt retained the sole right to draw certain coverts. Phil Cuddihy recalled their first meet:

> It was at Grand Gates, Piltown and there were six horses at the meet. Bessborough was in its heyday then and in great shape with lovely rides in the woods. Four of us, Jack McEnery, Paul Beary, Charles Jameson and meself went in and from eleven o'clock until four in the evening never stopped hunting... We never left the demesne and although we had little jumping we had plenty of galloping *(Power, T)*.

In 1922 Jack McEnery became master and the hounds were kennelled at his home, Rossenara House. He was on good terms with Dermot and this eased the way forward for the harriers. Famous for having married Lady Lavery's daughter, from her first marriage, Jack was a fabulous horseman, with lovely hands and very good to cross country, and he always knew what hounds were likely to do next.

His hounds had a extraordinary midnight hunt, when they broke out one night. It was not the first time, Paddy Herne remembered hearing them when he was a young lad in bed at night. "It happened several times when I was young... they used to... come across from the hill above McEnerys' and across to the Long Wood above and they'd hunt Castle Morres half the night. 'Twas the grandest thing you ever heard of a night". On the occasion of the midnight hunt 'The Jock' Herne went and told Jack that they were out, they both got horses and 'The Jock' went to the road while Jack took to the hills with a flash-lamp, and with its help jumped all the banks and ditches he met, until the fox was killed *(Power, T)*.

In 1931 Captain G.A. Langley Ellis of Belline took over the mastership. He moved the hounds to Belline and Jim Power acted as whipper-in. The hounds had a magnificent hunt in 1934 on December 20th. They picked up a travelling fox on Kilkeasy Hill on a great scenting day and finished in Tullogher, an 8 mile point, twenty miles as hounds ran. Only three riders survived to the end. Amongst those out that day were Capt. Langley Ellis, Mrs. Ellis, Miss Pearl Beary, Miss Springfield, Jack McEnery, Matty Brennan, J. Power, Neil Shee, P. Power and M. Walsh.

A certain hunt follower was out ferreting rabbits one day when he heard the hunt up the hill and in his own words:

(Courtesy of the Shee family)

St. Patrick's Day meet of the Kilmoganny Harriers, at John Delaney's, in 1946. From left to right: Robert Dowley, Jack Dowley, D. Dowley, Martin Keating, Pat Shee, Gerard Quirke, Matty Brennan (father of Tommy Brennan), Neil Shee (master), Phil Cuddihy, D. Nix, Mick Costello, Jim Moore, Mary Walsh and Ted Townsend.

> Well you know when a fella is ferreting he of times wipes his hands on the arse of his pants and he'd be stinking from it. So anyhow I was going down the field when they started coming down and looking serious. So I knew they had me smelled and were after me. I legged it down the field, and only they stopped at the cross below, and I leapt over the bleddy ditch into me own place they had me ate. 'Twas wicked and they nearly killed me. I'll never forget it, but you can't blame them cos I smelt gamier than any fox *(Power, T)*.

Langley Ellis's mastership did not last long, three years later it reverted to Jack McEnery. New kennels were built on Brown Mountain near

Booleyglass, where the Tennyson brothers kept and whipped-in the ten couples (they were mainly foxhounds with Welsh cross). From the start the Kilkenny Hunt enforced their stipulation that no coverts were to be drawn. One long day after drawing ditches and headlands without luck, Jack drew Glasscourt covert, found immediately and had a smashing evening hunt. Dermot McCalmont heard of the incident and called Jack aside saying "if this happens again, I will give up the country and stop hunting the hounds". Jack replied that he did not mind for then he would hunt the Kilkenny country himself *(Power, T)*. Things soon settled down and it was accepted that the county pack held the traditional rights to hunt the country.

The second world war broke out with all its attendant difficulties for hunting. Rather than disband, the decision was taken to trencher feed the pack for the duration of the war. The committee appointed Michael Costello and Matthew Brennan of Dunamaggin as joint masters with Neil Shee of Newtown as huntsman. Neil had only one arm but this did not hinder his horsemanship. Despite the restrictions and shortages of the war years, the hunt kept going until once again the hounds were kennelled as a pack at Newtown, in 1945 *(Reilly, 1988)*.

After the War

Neil Shee married and went to live in Clonmel, where he became master of the Clonmel Harriers *(Reilly, 1988)*.

In 1946 Charles Blacque of Castletown Cox, near Carrick-on-Suir became the sole master. His mother, a Beresford, was related to the Waterfords of Curraghmore. He immediately began to build up the pack and was helped and encouraged by Ikey Bell, who arranged the procurement of some well-bred old Tipperary hounds and they started crossing them with some drafted from Mount Juliet. Charlie Blacque always considered the Kilkenny hounds were much too fast and, as Dermot was happy to give away some of his slower rejects, the foundations were laid for a well-bred Kilmoganny pack.

There was a certain amount of friction between the masters of the two packs and this filtered down to their followers. Most families staunchly supported either one hunt or the other, though in the Sullivan family even brothers were divided in their loyalties. Matters came to a head, Charlie had at this time been breeding hounds for about ten years and now had a very good pack. The harriers were maturing into a more professionally run outfit and the "old Major" saw this as a threat. Since

(Courtesy of Mr. & Mrs. Charles Blacque)

Kilmoganny Harriers in the village of Piltown 1947-48. Jim Creeny, whipper-in, Charles Blacque and Tom Shelly.

the northern country had been lent on a long-term basis to the North Kilkenny Hunt, the Kilmoganny region was visited more often by the county hounds. Many local farmers who were deeply involved in the running of the Kilmoganny Harriers also owned land that included the coverts reserved by the Kilkenny hunt. They felt entitled to invite Charlie Blacque to draw these coverts, particularly if they were having a poor day. This caused a certain amount of aggravation between the two packs. A meeting to try to resolve the issue was held at Mount Juliet. Fortunately by this time Victor McCalmont had joined his father as joint master, and as he and Charlie Blacque were good friends, confrontation was avoided and it was agreed that as the Kilmoganny country was under pressure the Kilkenny Hunt would visit that area less frequently.

Kilmoganny Point-to-Points

Since the harriers did not have anything like the financial resources of the Kilkenny Hunt for fencing and other repairs, the members returned the day after a meet to put right any damage. They were welcome almost everywhere. There was no electric fencing or winter corn and only a little plough and occasional wire. The rough country around Booleyglass, Lismatigue and Windgap provided good hunting, but most popular of all was Black Bog with its great banks.

Black Bog became the home of the Kilmoganny point-to-point for 35 years. Considered by many to be the equal of Punchestown, it was a serious galloping track with five double banks (three all the more testing on an uphill approach), up-banks and a long pull up on the straight to test even the best of horses.

At the first Black Bog point-to-point in 1923 the members' race was won by Paddy Beary. Though Turf Club rules dictated that all point-to-points be held before 30th April, special permission was granted, with Dermot McCalmont's help, to hold the Black Bog meeting in the first week of May, due to the nature of the going. John Hawe worked hard raising funds for the races and he organised the entire meeting. If any scrubeens (hawkers selling apples or the trick-of-the-loop men) arrived, John would get very upset and do his utmost to scatter them *(Power, T)*. Lady Helen McCalmont's Amber Wave and Tom O'Gorman's Clare County were two Irish Grand National winners to compete and win at Black Bog. Famed lady riders to race at Black Bog included Miss Murdoch, Mrs. Masters and Mrs. Pilsworth.

The last point-to-point run on the course was in 1958, when the owners began to consider the risk of racing their valuable horses, over natural banks, too great and demanded the safer bush fences. The last hunt race held there was won by the hunt honorary secretary, Tommy Brennan, later to become the international showjumper and course designer, son of Matthew Brennan.

The Kilmoganny Harriers met at noon and attracted some fearless

(Photo: Des McCheane)

Michael Buckley and Rory Dicker judging hounds at Clonshire in 1996.

horsemen, including Mick Costello. He had a large family, hunted regularly, and nothing daunted him across country. One day near the demesne wall of the Rectory at Kells, Mick, riding a little athletic, roan horse called Patsy Fagan, in familiar country was well up with the hounds. Unaware that his friend, George Sherwood and his sister were motoring past on the far side, he put his horse at the wall. Horse and rider cleared the obstacle, and landed briefly on the back of the truck, before changing legs and galloping on. He waved a gesture of thanks to the surprised motorists and carried on with the hounds. Amongst other hunting enthusiasts were Jimmy Murphy, who bred Boomerang, Jimmy Walsh from Lismatigue, Ted Townsend, Jim Finnegan, John and Ned Sullivan and the Shees. Frank Fitzgerald used to hunt occasionally with the Kilmoganny Harriers. Riding short like a flat race jockey, he liked to show the regulars how to cross the country and in Michael Curran's

(Photo: Des McCheane)

Michael Kennedy shows evidence of Kilmoganny success at the IMFHA Hound Show at Clonshire in 1996. Michael whipped-in to Peter Thomas, before becoming kennel huntsman with the Kilmoganny. He left to hunt the Laois hounds in 1998.

words he succeeded one day at Grangemockler:

> "Frank was riding a goodish horse and halfway through burst the two girths. He rode the last half hour of that hunt barebacked holding the saddle on the horse's withers in front of him. Charlie was hunting the hounds that particular day" *(Power, T)*.

In the early years hunt balls were in Castle Morres. It was uninhabited at the time and the only electrical plant ran on batteries. Biddy Weiner was in charge of the band and Mrs. Lawlor the catering. It was always a struggle to make a profit after the out-goings had been met *(Power, T)*. The Kilmoganny Hunt Ball was later held in the Ormonde Dance Hall in Carrick-on-Suir. More recently the ball moved to the Ardree Hotel in Waterford and then to the Newpark Hotel in Kilkenny and became hugely successful.

Twenty-Five Years as Master

Charlie Blacque hunted the Kilmoganny Harriers for twenty-five years and it was only in his last years that he had a field master. Prior to that it was unnecessary as they were a popular pack, their country was small and they were on good terms with all the farmers over whose land they hunted. As master he always welcomed visitors at the meet, but made a point of informing them that should they ride over the hounds they would be sent home.

Once mounted on his horse Charlie Blacque's mind was solely on the job in hand. Occasionally, in exasperation on a bad day, he could be heard 'encouraging' his horse or hounds in French. Regarded as a good master, he was always well mounted and enjoyed the support of the hunt committee.

Michael Curran of Cregg joined Charlie Blacque as master from 1963-1972. The highlight of this successful partnership was the Templeorum meet on Sunday, January 30th 1966 when a dog fox was found in Kilmogue, Harristown. He went to the east of Carricktriss, skirted Booleyglass village and crossed the main road at the school-house. Passing the Ballinteskin bogs he crossed the Ballinteskin to Newchurch road. Hounds then checked briefly before hitting the line to run over the old Blackbog racecourse, he then ran through Wall's covert, on to Foran's, over the main Carrick-on-Suir road, swinging

(Photo: Des McCheane)

Patricia Brennan, daughter of Charles Blacque, follows in her father's footsteps as Joint Master of the Kilmoganny Hunt.

right handed towards Rossenara hill and the hounds eventually ran out of scent on entering the walls of Brownstown. A fifty minute run over some of the very best bank country, a five mile point and over seven as hounds ran. Amongst those out were Charlie Blacque, Michael Curran, Tim Falvey (whip), Mick Fitzgerald (whip), Francoise Blacque, Rita Hayes-Jones, Tyrone Waterford, Dorothy Ronan, Niall Quirke, Pat Shee, John Shee, K. Barry, Michael Norris, Olly Meagher, P. Lenehan, Kevin Dowley, Tommy Brennan, T. Kiely, L. Byrne, Mary Dunphy, Gillian O'Brien, Jacqueline Quirke, Susan Curran and Miss Kennedy.

In the early 1970s Charles Blacque and Michael Curran resigned in favour of a triumvirate of young farmers, Thierry Blacque of Cregg,

Patrick Murphy and John Costello, of Dunamaggin, who hunted the harriers. From time to time consideration was given to the amalgamation of the two packs as, the Kilmoganny, hunting a small country, could often, during a good run, find itself trespassing into Kilkenny territory. The harriers finally rejected the proposal. The Kilkenny Hunt eventually ceded the country to the Kilmoganny. George Murray-Smith and John Costello negotiated the deal, in 1976, on behalf of their respective hunts. It included the surrender of the Kilkenny Hunt's rights to any coverts in the south-west of the county and in return the Kilmoganny Hunt gave them the rights to hunt Hugginstown. Each pack now had its own country clearly defined.

In 1983, Rory Dicker who had previously hunted the Laois hounds became joint master with Patrick Murphy and the following year they were joined by Michael Morris. Tim Falvey who had been whip and kennel huntsman relinquished his position to Pat Meehan *(Power, T).* Eventually, in 1987, the pack re-registered as foxhounds, and it was fitting that this was the year in which Patricia Brennan, daughter of Charles Blacque, joined Rory and Michael, as joint master. The quarry they had been hunting since 1918 was now officially recognised by the Irish Masters of Foxhounds Association.

A 1987 March meet from Booleyglass, produced a point of just over 5 miles in 1 hour and 50 minutes and 16 miles as hounds ran. A fox was found in the Kilmoganny hunter-trial course at Catstown, a quick circle was had taking in some of the obstacles until hounds marked in a bank. He was soon bolted and run east down the valley to Lismatigue and on to Harristown. Here hounds swung left handed and crossed the Mullinavat to Harristown road at Keatingstown, into the Kilkenny Hunt country, crossing the Dublin railway line and eventually Reynard took refuge in gorse halfway up the Greywood quarry. He headed off again towards Knockmoylan. After a brief check hounds crossed the Kilkenny to Waterford road marking to ground two fields on, just opposite Knockmoylan school. This hunt took in the best of the Kilkenny Hunt stone wall country. Rory Dicker and his wife, Mary, were the McCalmonts' guests at Mount Juliet that night and rumour has it that they faced a fearsome debriefing.

In 1990, Jimmy Keane of Mayfield, Portlaw, became huntsman and joint master with Seamus Molloy, and a year later they were joined by

(Photo: Des McCheane)

Michael Higgens, Master of the Kilmoganny Hunt from 1993-1999. Previously he was master and huntsman of the four-day-a-week Tipperary Hunt.

Ivan Dowley. Michael Higgens hunted the hounds from 1993.

Like elsewhere, the Kilmoganny countryside continues to change, the enclosures have become wired up in recent years and consequently it has become necessary to have a horse trained to jump wire. The intensive management of the countryside affects most wildlife, foxhunting ensures the maintenance of a number of habitats which benefit both the fauna and flora therein. From a hunting point of view, there is less useful covert, and the increasingly large forestry woods act as a hindrance. Over the past few seasons only seven or eight five mile points have been recorded, and on these occasions few have been able to keep in touch with hounds throughout .

Gaultier Harriers

Joe Widger and Dayrell Gallwey hunted parts of the country around Waterford city with their harrier packs prior to the First World War. These packs did not thrive and the War of Independence continued to hinder their sport. In 1923, Dayrell Gallwey gave up his remaining hounds to Sir Robert Paul of Ballyglan, Waterford. Paul restarted the pack under the new name as the Gaultier Harriers. He obtained permission from Major Dermot McCalmont to hunt the section of his country left vacant by the East Kilkenny Hunt. The Gaultier Harriers started with twenty couples of hounds kennelled at Gaultier, near Woodstown. Jack Boland, became the loyal kennel huntsman, who remained with the pack for many years. Ed Geraghty assisted him as second whip.

They drew the east of County Waterford and the south-east of County Kilkenny. Mooncoin and Kilmacow were particularly popular Kilkenny meets. In January 1926, they drew the famous Mount Neil covert from a meet at Mooncoin, found and ran in the direction of Carrigeen, turned right towards Granagh, leaving Portnahully and Curraghmartin on the right. They crossed the Carrick road and bearing left met the railway line at Rathcurby, giving a fast 30 minutes without a check. They hunted on almost to Dangan, where hounds were stopped at a slight check as most of the horses were beaten. The point was 5½ miles and hounds probably ran twice as far. Amongst those out on that day were: Sir Robert Paul, Lady Paul, Mrs. Chipley, Mrs. Anderson, the Misses de Bromhead, Miss Coughlin, Mrs. Bowe, Miss Bloomfield, Father Larkin, David Power, Mr. E.A. Gibbon, Mr. N.A. Gibbon, Messrs. J.H. and P.J. de Bromhead, Tom Murphy, Mr. R. Widger, M.B. Nolan, Mr. Conway, Mr. Connolly, Mr. Aylward, Mr. Barry and "many sporting farmers from the neighbourhood" *(UNC).*

Sir Robert Paul hunted them until 1930 when John H. de Bromhead took over. The latter was a superb horseman, with a good eye for a horse. The de Bromhead family was a large one and they were associated with the Gaultier Harriers from the start. There were so many de Bromhead children hunting that the kennel huntsman, Boland, normally a silent and taciturn man, was once heard to say "I dreams of little de Bromheads". They had a habit of riding hard on his tail. John took over the horn, at the age of 18, when Sir Robert Paul was ill. When John eventually became master, his opening meet was an undistinguished one, as the hounds, having found on their way to the meet, set off in full cry. John failed to stop them and ended up arriving at the meet without his hounds. He went on to produce much good sport over the next fifteen years, with his popular pack.

(Courtesy of Mr. & Mrs. Harry de Bromhead)

Sir Robert Paul and Jack Boland, kennel huntsman and whipper-in with the Gaultier Harriers.

(Courtesy of Mr. & Mrs. Harry de Bromhead)

Members of the Gaultier Hunt at Woodstown, January 1931. From left to right, front row: Tommy Gallwey, Larkie Murphy, M. Murphy, Major Jones, Dodo Goff (later Mrs. Beaumont), John de Bromhead, Robin & Desmond (smaller) Hall, Sir Robert Paul, Betty Murphy, Jack Widger. Middle row: T. Goff, Nancy McCoy, Ernest Goff, Betty Nolan, Mrs. Olivia Roche, Mrs. de Bromhead, Mrs. Bright, Mrs. Hall, Evelyn de Bromhead, Olivia Widger, Fidelma Bailey and Miriam Rohan. Back row: Mary Jennings, Rachenda Galloway, Ray Galloway, Major Carew, Dick Leonard and Bella Leonard (née de Bromhead).

County Waterford, being nearer the coast than Kilkenny, has a milder climate. When severe frost hit Kilkenny and the ground was too hard for hunting, the "old Major" and his entourage would descend upon the Gaultier Hunt. At a meet near Waterford, John, under pressure to show sport to his visitors, drew several of their best coverts to no avail. It approached 4 o'clock and the day had been uneventful. Suddenly, a report of a fox eating a dead cow, half a mile away, was brought to his attention. The hounds were brought on and, in full cry, flew after the fox for two fields, before killing him. The fox was too full of dead cow to run anywhere, but to John's consternation Dermot announced to him that it was the worst bagged fox that he had ever seen.

By 1934 the Kilkenny Hunt had lent a large portion of their northern country to Mr. Alexander's Hounds and it was apparent that its successors, the North Kilkenny Hunt, intended to carry on. To make up for the loss of country in the north, the Kilkenny reclaimed the Gaultier section of the country.

After the war Mrs. Alison Crosby, a gutsy and brave woman to cross country, hunted the Gaultier Harriers. She re-registered the pack to ensure their official recognition as a pack of foxhounds. Jack Boland remained on as kennel huntsman and first whip. Briefly, from 1947-48, she hunted the south Kilkenny country. The hounds were kennelled at the Manor of St. John, Waterford, and there are those who recall her riding through the city after dark with the hounds on their return from a long day's hunting. The diminished area of their country proved too restricting and by 1956 the Gaultier had to disband.

Chapter 11

The North Kilkenny Country

A master of hounds is one of the most difficult characters in life to fill; hence it is not surprising that there are but two sorts – the best fellows under the sun – and the nastiest brutes going.
("The Analysis of the Hunting Field", 1845-6. Anon)

Ikey Bell began to hunt the northern end of the county in 1909. The area was subsequently hunted by the county hounds up to the end of the 1930-31 season. By the late 1920s Dermot McCalmont was finding it increasingly difficult to cover such a large tract of country adequately. His wife, Lady Helen, is believed to have been instrumental in persuading him to permit John Alexander of Milford, County Carlow to form a pack of hounds to hunt the Freshford/Castlecomer country.

This arrangement was ratified at a public meeting in Freshford on March 30th 1931. According to the minutes the following were present: Lord Bellew (Chairman), Lady Bellew, Richard Brennan (Eden Hall), Rev. W. Briscoe, John Bergin, G. Brennan, R. Cahill, Sir Otway Wheeler-Cuffe, Senator Dillon, P. Joyce, S. Dobbs, Dr. Farrell, C. Fowler, T.F. Frisby, Captain and Mrs. McCheane, Dr. and Mrs. Moore, Dr. Mitchell, Dr. C.S. Purdon, George Reid, F. Renehan, J.E. and Mrs. St. George, W. Seale, T. Tynan and Dr. White. Apologies were received from Captain Prior-Wandesforde, Major A. Kavanagh, T.B. Ponsonby, Captain R.B. Gahan, Edward Staunton, James Gibbons, William White, Patrick Dowling, N.J. Harrison, Miss Shortall, Thomas Whiteford and Michael Maher (of The Square, Freshford). Many of these played a prominent part in the formative years and the descendants of some are involved in the affairs of the hunt to this day.

Initially John's kennels were at Rathvinden, Leighlinbridge, and the hunt horses were stabled at Uppercourt, Freshford. The hunt coverts included in the north country were Ballyring, Acragar, Ballymartin, Punchbowl, The Rock, Persses and Killeen. The kennels were later moved to Ballyragget House, the property of the Marquess of Kildare. Some of the hounds objected to the new set-up and walked back over the hills to their old home at Rathvinden.

About 40 mounted followers attended John Alexander's opening

(Courtesy of Mr. & Mrs. Andrew Kavanagh)

John Alexander and Major Kavanagh, with Mr. Alexander's Hounds

meet at Freshford on October 30th 1931. Charlie Hall-Dare was whip. At the end of their first season, the hounds met by invitation at Ballingarry, in the Tipperary country and enjoyed a particularly good day. Prouts produced a right-handed ring ending close to Wilford after 48 minutes. Later from Mardyke they ran straight and hard past Killenaule to ground at Mortlestown in 35 minutes.

Pack re-named the North Kilkenny Hounds

Regrettably John resigned after two seasons. He subsequently became joint master with Lady Helen McCalmont of the County Limerick hounds. Paddy Regan, his whip, also went to Limerick.

A committee was formed and Dermot McCalmont agreed to grant the country on similar terms to the new committee, which decided that the pack should henceforth be known as the "North Kilkenny Hounds".

John's hounds were valued at £195, a sum the committee could not afford. Capt. Henry Bramwell, the newly appointed master, agreed to purchase the hounds, subject to the committee having the right to repurchase at any time, at a valuation. Capt. Bramwell (remembered

(Courtesy of Mr. & Mrs. Andrew Kavanagh)
Joane Kavanagh on Molly, with Sir Hercules and Lady Langrishe at the opening meet of Mr. Alexander's Hounds in Freshford.

chiefly for his volatile temper!) resigned after only one season. With difficulty the committee succeeded in raising the money to redeem the hounds.

George Angel, who married a member of the Poe family of Kilkenny, was appointed master for the 1935-36 season and subsequently for the 1936-37. The hounds remained at Ballyragget demesne and the hunt committee, ably led by Bobby Cahill as secretary, was responsible for the building of new and modern kennels in the castle yard.

During the 1930s hunt dances were held at Ballyconra and at Kilrush House, also at Kilcreene by permission of Mrs. Bell. In 1939 Lord and Lady Kildare hosted the hunt ball at Ballyragget House in lavish style. They had a large house party, and the music was supplied by Major "Huby" Watt MFH and his United Hunt Band *(Tatler Issue No. 1962)*.

In 1937 Lord Kildare and Dick Prior-Wandesforde took over as joint masters and the hunt prospered. However at the outbreak of war, both

(Photo: Kilkenny People)

Betty and Des McCheane at the North Kilkenny opening meet, 1937.

men were called up to join the war effort. A committee of four, Rodney Purdon and Bobby Cahill together with Tommy and Betty McCheane as field masters, kept the hunt going for two seasons.

Father John Kearns' timely rescue

By the end of the 1940-41 season, funds were exhausted and it was decided that the hunt had no option but to close down. However, one of the greatest sporting priests Kilkenny has known, Father John Kearns, a curate in Ballyragget at the time, persuaded the farmers to rally round and save the hunt. The hounds were within a day of being put down.

An entirely new committee was formed with the goodwill of everyone. Jack Murphy and James Campion were appointed as joint masters with Michael O'Reilly and Paul Murphy as honorary secretaries. Mick Phelan who had joined the hunt staff in the 1930s continued as huntsman, a position he held until 1950. Prominent members at this time included Tom Fitzgerald, Jimmy Phelan of

(Photo: Alan Moran)

Michael O'Reilly and Father John Kearns

(Photo: Kilkenny People)

St. Patrick's Day meet 1953 at Ballyconra House. Included are Lt. Col. Eccles, Mrs. Seale, Billy Grogan, Jean Seale, Rufus Keogh, Mick Phelan and Jack Murphy.

Finnan, Jimmy Phelan of Rathbeagh, Sonny Fitzpatrick, Mick Stapleton, James Cantwell, James Carrigan and Michael Frisby. The latter, was a popular vet who hunted his own pack of otter hounds. The hunt's problems were compounded in 1945 when Father Kearns left to deploy his undoubted talents on the mission fields and Ballyragget House was sold to become a Mercy convent. The hounds had to leave their kennels and there was no money to build again. James Dillon's offer to accommodate them temporarily at Tullaroan was gratefully accepted and once again they were saved.

After Father Kearns' return to the diocese in the 1950s as curate in Dunamaggin and later as parish priest in Castlecomer, he continued to smooth the path of the hunt he had rescued from oblivion and he opened up much country in the Castlecomer area. When Father Kearns died in 1985, his horse with boots reversed in the irons preceded the hearse and the hunt's greatest enthusiast was laid to rest with full hunting honours.

North Kilkenny Hunt Masters from 1941

Jack Murphy has continued as joint master to this day. He celebrated his 50th season in 1990 and is listed in Baily's Directory as the current longest serving MFH world-wide. Michael Maher of Gleneven House, a popular local landowner, replaced James Campion as joint master in 1947. In the same year 50 acres of land at Ballyring were purchased by the hunt club and the existing outbuildings were converted to accommodate the hounds, a turning point in the fortunes of the hunt.

A memorable run at this period resulted from a meet at Balleen with Mick Phelan hunting the hounds on December 29th 1948. The Kilkenny Journal reported:

> ...Next draw was at Persse's Gorse where a fox left almost immediately running through Fitzgerald's farm, past the old Spa House, almost to Creenkill, wheeled left through Dwyer's and Brennan's Gorse and past Ballycuddihy Castle to Lower Ballyspellan, wheeling left again through Patrick and Robert Tobin's farms at the back of Johnstown village where Christmas shopping was in full swing and great excitement caused by the sound of hounds and horn in full cry almost in the village street. Past the old school, Johnstown chapel and St. Mary's church, where the fox crossed the main Kilkenny road running in the direction of the rectory and wheeled right crossing the main Dublin—Cork road at the new cemetery, through William Seale's farm at Violet Hill, and was marked to ground at Frank Renehan's farm on the banks of the Ghoul *(KJ).*

A good sized field, all finished this seven mile point over stiff country in 1¼ hours.

Rufus Keogh (1950-1957) of County Carlow extraction, was the first joint master to regularly hunt the hounds himself. Mick Phelan reverted to kennel huntsman and whip, Rufus was in charge when on New Year's Day 1954 they had an outstanding day's sport. They...

> ...found several foxes in Uppercourt, hunted one out through Butler's Hill, on through Adamstown, through Barrington's Hill, by Green Hill, Comerford's Hill, Kildrinagh and on to the

> edge of Kilcooley, where hounds were stopped. Time 2 hours *(McCheane, 1920-1970).*

The point was about 6¾ miles and probably 8½ miles as hounds ran. The cap collected on the day was £2-2-6, from a field of seventeen, more than usual, on account of the holiday. At the opening meet that season, only 10/- was collected, an indication of the meagre income on

(Photo: Kilkenny People)

Rufus Keogh leading the North Kilkenny hounds away from Ballyconra, 1954.

which the hunt was surviving. By 1957 the finances were in a precarious position. Rufus Keogh left to go as huntsman to the Rome Foxhounds and popular Johnstown bloodstock breeder, Tom Nicholson, who had rendered sterling service to the hunt over the previous decade became joint master and hunted the hounds for the winter of 1957-58. Amongst his many successful horses were Vulpine, winner of the Power's Gold Cup in 1966 and the Irish Grand National in 1967, and Bigaroon, three times winner of the Irish Caesarewitch

Barry Tate, a successful engineer, who had participated in the rebuilding programme in Germany after the war, injected hope and cash as a new and enthusiastic joint master in 1958. He made improvements to the kennels and introduced some fresh hound blood from England.

When Barry regretfully left after only one season to take up a mastership with the Llangibby, Tom Nicholson once again generously stepped into the breach until Major T.G. Wilkinson was appointed joint master in 1960. Major Wilkinson is remembered for his racehorses, principally Flying Bolt, often favourably compared to his contemporary, Arkle. Both were trained by Tom Dreaper and it is

(Photo: Des McCheane)

Loughlin Bowe, joint master (1970-1980) of the North Kilkenny, in the saddle again in 1996.

more than a coincidence that they never met on a racecourse.

Dapper Freshford businessman, Ollie Maher, was a popular and stylish joint master for two seasons (1963-65). James Bowe, of Gathabawn, worked very hard to revive flagging interest in the hunt during his five season tenure from 1965 and it is to the credit of the joint masters and a handful of die-hard followers that the hunt survived this critical period.

Landscape changes affected hunting in the north of the county to a greater extent than elsewhere. Avonmore, the dairy co-operative, made a huge impact in the late 1960s, when they began to encourage modern

(Photo: Des McCheane)

Successor to the traditional role of sporting priest in North Kilkenny, Father Willie Hennessy.

dairy farming. Land prices rose and more drainage grants were allocated to the northern third of the county than to the remainder. It was not all to the detriment of hunting, as too much covert had grown up in certain areas, and the more efficient farming practises helped to clear much of the scrub, forcing the foxes to make a clean break. The biggest problem for the field, following drainage, was the barbed wire that was erected afterwards, though this did not deter the hounds.

The decision, controversial at the time, to hunt on Sundays coincided with the appointment of Loughlin Bowe of Creenkill, Gathabawn, as joint master in 1970. In the early 1970s the lucrative market for fox pelts resulted in enormous numbers of foxes being shot. Initially the hunts feared that they might be shot to extinction, but it actually resulted in producing better and stronger foxes that were well able to travel the country, providing good sport. Fields steadily increased tenfold to over 90 out. Loughlin hunting hounds with Willie White and John Hickey turning them to him formed a team that produced hectic sport. Hunting men came from far and near. Michael Purcell, Timmy Hyde, P.P. Hogan, the Dwans, Denis, Kevin and Jack from Tipperary, Dessie and Harry Lalor from Laois, the Hanlons and Tommy Byrne

(Photo: Des McCheane)

Michael Dillon, Liam Murphy and Jack Murphy with the North Kilkenny at Seskin, St. Patrick's Day 1993.

from Carlow, Kevin O'Donnell from Gowran, Billy McKenzie the hunting vet, were all courageous men across country. Many were to be found, hours after hunting had ended, in the nearest pub, clothes still steaming and 'the craic was mighty'. Michael Dillon of Tullaroan, was appointed a third joint master with special responsibility for the field in

1975. Loughlin continued to hunt hounds until the end of the 1979-80 season.

Throughout the 1980s and early 1990s Jack Murphy and Michael Dillon were joint masters with Michael carrying the horn with distinction and showing good sport. They were joined by Jack's son, Liam, in 1997 and Billy Phelan, who had previously hunted the Laois, came in as huntsman. For the 1998-99 season John Hickey, for many years the popular kennel huntsman, shared the mastership with Jack and Liam Murphy and Billy Phelan continued to hunt the hounds. Whips to the hunt over recent years included Sean Doheny, Ted Murphy, Liam Murphy and James Brennan.

Financial Arrangements

While others have served periods as secretary and treasurer, it was always either Michael O'Reilly or Bobby Cahill who shouldered the considerable burden of administration and successfully steered the hunt through the crisis periods. The minutes recall how on different occasions each agreed personally to guarantee the overdraft or give a loan. They also bear witness to the frustrations that arose from a seemingly endless chain of problems. "It appears (one) is never out of one trouble until you are in another" *(North Kilkenny Hunt Minutes, 21/10/1950).*

During the first 40 years of the North Kilkenny Hunt's existence, subscriptions and field money provided only a fraction of the income required to run the country. Many and varied were the fund raising events – not only the point-to-points, gymkhanas, hunt balls and dances but also raffles, garden fetes, children's parties, bridge sessions and even a pantomime. For several years the hunt joined forces with the local Macra na Feirme in organising successful carnivals in Ballyragget. Apart from the masters and secretaries, others deeply involved in the running of these necessary events included Rodney Purdon, Edmund Tynan, Patrick Ryan, Margaret Stanley, Jean Seale, Agnes Gibbons, Larry O'Reilly and Billy Julian.

Balleen Races

The first North Kilkenny point-to-point was held at Adamstown near Tullaroan in 1934. The following year the course moved to Balleen. By the mid-1940s the annual Balleen point-to-point on Easter Monday was attracting enormous crowds and had a festival atmosphere. The course was very well built and some of the banks can be still discerned to this day. It is said that races were won or lost in the dip, where a part of the course was out of view to most spectators.

Many a match was made at the race night dance either in the hall, Ballyragget or in the Odeon Cinema, Freshford, where Jimmy Carroll's band provided the music, admission was 5/-.

Jack Murphy's brilliant little bay, Vanguard II, will always be associated with Balleen. Piloted by Jack himself, he was the local

(Photo: Des McCheane)

Jack Murphy blows the opening note to start his 50th season as joint master of the North Kilkenny, Freshford. November 1990.

banker and never let down his legion of fans. Jack and Vanguard II travelled to distant point-to-points on foot, transport was non-existent during the Emergency. Vanguard II is credited with winning at least 14 point-to-points and with third place in a feature race at Punchestown.

Not until 1954, by which time birch fences had become a necessity, did the point-to-point switch from Balleen to Knockdav for some years. Joint ventures were run with the Laois Hunt at Ballyconra from 1962 and at Gowran Park from 1969-1972. From 1973 the Laois Hunt ran theirs at Thurles and the North Kilkenny continued at Gowran Park.

The present excellent course on "Murphy" land at Parksgrove, with a natural raised viewing area, has recaptured at least some of the atmosphere of the old point-to-point. For many years Priscilla Flanagan has been a hard-working and efficient point-to-point secretary.

Courses for Horses

A hunter-trial course has been constructed on the hunt's own land at Ballyring where the North Kilkenny Hunt hold their hunter-trials once or twice a year. The hunt members co-operated with St. Kieran's College in 1990 and with Kilkenny College in 1991, in holding the inter-schools hunter-trials at Ballyring.

In the 1980s and early 1990s the North Kilkenny Hunt consistently had competitive hunt chase teams. Liam Murphy, Ted Murphy, Michael Bowe and Marie Brannigan represented the hunt to win the Furstenberg Trophy at the Dublin Horse Show in 1987. The following year the same team (with Anne Marie Dunphy deputising for Marie Brannigan) represented Ireland at Stoneleigh where they lost narrowly to the Zetland in the final. The hunt went one better in 1993 when the North Kilkenny Hunt team of David Ryan, John Hickey, Gillian Dillon and Tom Hogan won the hunt chase at Stoneleigh.

Hunt members have bred and schooled many top showjumpers and sport horses over the years. Martin Walsh of Firoda won the Young Irelander at Millstreet in 1987 with a King of Diamonds youngster bred by John Lacey of Ballymartin. Martin also supplied Carraig Dubh to the Army. He retains a share in Diamond Cliff which won the Grand Prix at Windsor in 1998 for John Whittaker.

Chapter 12

Victor McCalmont succeeds his father

Continuity is everything. It is the essence of successful hound breeding. It gives confidence to landowners, farmers and shooting tenants. It gives permanence to hunt staff. (M. Berry, 1933)

Dermot's son, Victor, left the Royal Dragoons in 1947 and soon immersed himself in the hunt, whipping-in to his father. Unlike many kennels in these islands, the pack had come through the war in good order. In 1949 he became joint master and took over the horn from Dermot, who had carried it for 29 seasons. The "old Major", thus called to differentiate him from his son, Victor, remained deeply involved in the running of the hunt and still did a tremendous amount on its behalf. He would also stand in for Victor, on occasions when he was absent from the hunting field.

Victor had married Beryl (Bunny) Sutton in 1945 and they resided at Rathvinden, near Leighlinbridge in County Carlow. Bunny designed the garden there which included a topiary running fox, a replica of the one on the hedge at Mount Juliet, near the occulus. She too was a great hunting enthusiast.

Victor, who had previously hunted his own pack of beagles, quickly became a top class huntsman, he had an affinity with his hounds which allowed him to exercise great control over them. Within a couple of seasons they were no longer silent. He differed from the "old Major", who had hunted for the thrill of having a good horse under him while he crossed the country at speed. Victor jumped only because he had to jump to stay with his hounds, he was a hound man first and foremost.

He understood the nature of foxes and intuitively knew what a fox was going to do, and thereby aided his hounds. Fox numbers continued to increase and the likelihood of having a blank day diminished. He had whips who went well, Tommy Monahan, in particular, was a good man to go and Victor was not averse to taking a lead from his whips over a difficult fence. Crossing the country carefully, he preferred the stone wall areas of Ballyconway and Ballyhale. He gained his reputation for producing excellent sport early in his career as huntsman. On January

(Photo: Irish Times)

Major Victor McCalmont raises his cap in a salute to the President's Box, as he parades the Kilkenny Hounds at the Dublin Horse Show.

18th 1950 he had an outstanding hunt from Poulnassy to the wood at Graigue, a twelve mile point. Only one strand of wire was encountered and there was virtually no plough. Frank Fennelly was amongst those who were out that day. He had hacked his horse from Callan to Ballintee, about ten miles away, where it was left with a farmer over night. Frank's father being a vet, had a supply of petrol, at a time when it was scarce, so he brought Frank back home for the night. The following morning he joined his horse again and hacked on for another ten miles to the meet at Mullinavat. Between 2 p.m. and 2.30 p.m. he rode back into the yard at home, the family on seeing him assumed the hunt had been cancelled. They could hardly believe him when he described the hunt from Poulnassy. The hounds had not run too fast, so nearly everyone had finished the hunt, they had only checked once, at Booleyglass. The following year on January 20th they ran in the

(Photo: Frank Meads)

Victor McCalmont on Philip, watching his hounds work, near Mullinavat.

opposite direction from Booleyglass to Clonassy.

The hounds were still capable of hunting at break-neck speed. From a meet at Delaney's pub near Tullahought, McGrath's was drawn, it was then owned by the hunt. They quickly found and ran in what seemed like ten minutes to Davis's Gorse in Windgap, absolutely flat out for five miles, and on this occasion there were horses everywhere, as many failed to finish the run.

The good sport attracted a large number of visitors, it was not an infrequent sight to see at least twenty red coats in the hunting field. The McCalmonts entertained and mounted their friends, others stayed locally and rented hirelings from Paddy Power and elsewhere. Paddy Power, a publican, was based in Kilmoganny and had about 10 or 12 hirelings. Victor would often ask him to go on point duty around the back of a covert, he was always ready to help, but famous for beginning every sentence with "Oh Hell!" Never in a hurry out hunting, he crossed the country brilliantly always there at the end apparently arriving out of nowhere. He stood the well-known sires, Sandyman and Battleburn. County Kilkenny was renowned for breeding good horses. Paddy's brother, Jimmy Power, was whipper-in with the Kilmoganny hounds for Capt. Langley Ellis *(Power, T)*. Paddy Comerford in Kells broke several that later went on to compete in the Olympic Games. He hunted the young horses prior to selling them and the good quality hunting was conducive to the production of showjumpers, point-to-pointers and national hunt horses, as it was an ideal training ground.

The continuing generosity of the McCalmonts

Cub-hunting under Victor's regime commenced at 6 a.m. early in the season, when they would draw places like Flood Hall and Castle Morres. It was a comparatively private affair for the masters, their few guests, local landowners and the hunt staff.

The Kilkenny Hunt has always been very lucky in having a plentiful supply of loyal puppy walkers. Mrs. Moylan of Rathclough, was amongst the most successful. She walked puppies from 1932 up to her death in 1996, each year she always chose her pup carefully, and won in excess of 25 prizes. The valuable prizes were much sought after, silver cups, hip flasks, silver tea and coffee pots were presented each year by the McCalmonts.

Hundreds were invited to the annual puppy show in the 1950s. A large marquee was erected near the kennels and the caterers came down from the Dolphin Hotel in Dublin. Some of the guests had never seen anything like it before, but all enjoyed themselves, and many a pioneer pledge was broken. Afterwards Dermot would invite those who remained to the pub, where the tables were laden with bottles of whiskey and gin. Many people were only used to drinking pints, so it was necessary, afterwards, to have cars laid on for the purpose of returning everyone home safely.

The McCalmonts inspected their horses every Sunday at 10 a.m. They were all trotted out and the list, noting who was to hunt which horse, in the forth coming week was handed over to the head groom. It was not unusual to see up to thirty hunters regularly exercising around the roads near Mount Juliet. Both Dermot and Davy McMinn were small men and Dermot had traditionally bought small quality horses between 15.2 and 15.3 hands high, often buying them from Larry

(Courtesy of Mr. Kevin O'Donnell)

Kevin O'Donnell winning the Open Race on Brunnador II, at the Kilkenny Hunt point-to-point, Woollengrange, 1957.

O'Byrne of Kilmacthomas. However, Victor and Bunny preferred a more substantial animal for hunting.

The majority of subscribers still paid a £10 subscription in the 1951-52 season, unchanged since Herky Langrishe's time, but the standard of turnout still rivalled anything found in the shires. You could see your reflection in the shine on the hunting boots worn by the members of the McCalmont family. The sight of twenty red hunting coats hanging up on a clothes line, that greeted one hunt member on a visit to the kennels, well illustrates the scale on which the hunt was still being run. The hunt staff and the grooms were all kept supplied with new breeches and some staff members were given a new suit every year, they all received free milk and electricity.

The spectacle of the Mount Juliet grooms unloading the horseboxes was one never to be forgotten. From two or three boxes, up to fifteen horses would be unloaded, a mile or two from the meet. The grooms wore livery, topped by a long overcoat and a flat cap and the second horsemen wore charcoal coloured riding suits, stocks, leggings and bowler hats. They would hack the horses to the meet at a smart trot, so that they would not be too fresh for the visitors, some of whom were inexperienced or elderly riders. The horses were always impeccably turned out, manes plaited, tails pulled, trimmed with a hunting clip and they all appeared to be about the same height, around 16.1 hands high. A constant supply of horses was required, and they were bought from all over Ireland. Danny Kinane from near Mullinahone made many of them, he was a lovely horseman with good hands. He rode the young horses at the back of the hunt while he got them going.

Amongst those regularly hunting were: the Dowlings, Willie O'Grady and Jimmy McClintock, all great men to go. Paddy McCann, the stockbroker, who generally stayed at Mount Juliet. Peter Duggan, would cross himself before jumping and Jack Freeman, a vet and a top-class horseman from Clonmel, sitting as straight as a die with a great length of leg, would take on any fence. Eileen de Bromhead and Mrs. Alexander finished a particularly good hunt from Harristown, up over Booleyglass to the plantation at the top of the hill at Windgap. The hounds never checked that day, the bitch pack had flown. There was a lot of jumping in that locality, one had to be sharp to stay in touch. They were really too fast for the country, with its small enclosures. Binty Marshall still hunted, she had become somewhat crippled and her groom would follow her with the pony and trap and take her from

(Courtesy of Mr. & Mrs. Harry McCalmont)

"To ground, Mount Juliet" by Peter Biegel, November 1st 1962.

covert to covert, so she might avoid the long hacks. Tragically she found her disability too depressing and after hunting one day, she gave her horse to her groom, drove south and threw herself off the bridge at Fiddown. A sad end for a remarkable horse-woman.

Lord Waterford, was always extremely well mounted and was a serious man to cross the country. He detested anyone following him, and if he thought he was being used as a pilot, he would choose places that were virtually impossible to jump and make them look easy. This lulled the unfortunate riders behind him into a false sense of security, and almost invariably they would end up being buried in a ditch. He impressed Bunny McCalmont one day by jumping the demesne wall into Castle Morres. His wife, another a superb horsewoman, would take her own line, usually in the opposite direction.

The halcyon days of hunting in County Kilkenny continued through the 1950s. Land was of little monetary value, rural electrification was just in its infancy, the banks were kept clear of growth as they were constantly being cut to provide fuel. When riding a line across the country, it was safe to pick your spot from the middle of the field, as wire was still quite rare. The cattle wintered out, herds were small and there were virtually no large continental breeds. Many were weak and in poor condition during the hunting season and thus did not require much in the way of fencing to keep them in. Some even walked the roads grazing the "long acre", but as there was little traffic it did not matter. In areas like Black Bog where the Kilmogannys held their point-to-points, the field used to be able to charge at the large double banks, all spread out, and cause relatively little damage. The Mullinavat country was considered the cream of the Kilkenny Hunt country with narrow stone faced banks, sometimes with a small ditch on either side, they could be jumped anywhere, but frequently caught out those horses that were used to the wider banks of Black Bog and elsewhere.

The area managers looked after the notice cards that were sent out to inform farmers when the hounds would be next in their locality. They also handled complaints of damage after hunting, there was a back up team from Mount Juliet who dealt with the necessary fencing and repairs. The McCalmonts always ensured that any farmer who had suffered damage by the hunt, was adequately compensated for the inconvenience, with new gates made available to replace broken ones and anything else that might be required. There was constant demand for compensation from the poultry fund, claims amounting to £759-17-6 were paid out in the season of 1950-51, a vast sum considering that subscriptions in the same year only raised £551-5-0.

In the 1950s petrol again became freely available and horseboxes were used by those who could afford them. Some had grooms to drive their cars around following the hunt and take their horses home at the end of the day. For those less fortunate, long hacks were still the order of the day. To hack twelve miles to a meet would take about two hours and hounds might well run in the opposite direction to home, so the parting words were "expect me when you see me". However to facilitate those who had to hack home, hunting did tend to finish earlier, rarely later than 4 p.m.

(Photo: Frank Meads)

Paddy Macdonald leads the hounds, followed by Alf Wright and Victor McCalmont, in the Mullinavat West country.

It was common for horses to be out of their stables for up to twelve hours on hunting days. Many relied on their one horse for the whole winter, hunting perhaps twice a week and it was not unusual for the same horse to be ridden to collect shopping or other messages, or even do light agricultural work in between hunting days. Many claim that hunters in the 1950s stayed sounder than their modern counterparts.

Kept very fit, they had to be extremely well-schooled and sure-footed. Young horses were always lunged and ridden over a variety of obstacles, long before they were ever introduced to hunting. People too were fitter, the sedentary lifestyle of modern riders was not for them. In the country there was always work to be done. Before the introduction of marts, farmers drove their cattle on foot to fairs, often leaving home as early as 3 a.m. If they did not sell or buy replacements, the round trip on foot could be twenty-five miles or more.

Victor rejuvenated the hunt club, members were entitled to wear a top hat and the hunt buttons on their hunting coats. Social divisions remained very marked, many farmers who hunted with the Kilkenny Hunt tended to keep to themselves. Others preferred the more relaxed atmosphere of the harrier packs. The hunt was still run in a regimental fashion, which was generally beneficial, although it could be tough on those who did not conform to the "old Major's" high standards, as Lady Nesta Fitzgerald discovered aged about 16, when she went cub-hunting with her half brother, Andrew Kavanagh, in the mid-1950s. Their grandfather had been a friend of Dermot's and a fellow officer. Dermot, seeing Andrew looking miserable at the prospect of starting prep school later that day, generously gave him 2/-. But, when he noticed that Nesta was wearing an 11th Hussars tie, the only one that she could lay her hands on, he sent her home saying, "Young lady, when you are entitled to wear that tie you may, until then kindly go home". Frank Fitzgerald, a well-known horseman who went well, suffered a similar fate, he had borrowed a hunting coat, which happened to be a red one. Soon after his arrival at the meet, he was promptly shown the way home by the "old Major".

Changing Times

Alf Wright, from the South Dorset Hunt, took over from Davy McMinn in 1957 as kennel huntsman. He did not have the same flair as Davy for crossing the country, but he was a good hound man and whip, and he had greater respect for his horses. He was much quieter than his predecessor. A tall man who looked thin, seldom rode horses that were quite up to his weight. One day Ollie Partridge, from Tipperary, was poised to jump off the top of a bank, when Alf suddenly emerged from below looking distraught pleading "Don't jump madam!" He had fallen into a ditch full of water, had lost his false teeth and was trying to find them in the water. George Murray Smith took over the management of the country after Davy's retirement, while Alf concentrated on the kennels.

In 1959 Paddy Macdonald came to work at Mount Juliet. Born and reared in the Wexford Hunt kennels, he had been second horseman to Colonel Cairns and had also whipped-in to Ned Fitzsimons, the kennel huntsman there. When he moved to Kilkenny, his wages were £4 a week, and the "old Major" said, "if you suit me and I suit you, on November 1st, I shall give you a 10/- rise". Hacking down the main road at Kilmacow, just prior to the start of the season, Dermot tapped him on the shoulder and said "do you remember the words we had on 1st May? It will be in your pay packet tonight when you go home."

Alf Wright remained kennel huntsman and first whipper-in, Paddy was the second whipper-in, and they worked together for more than twenty seasons. They hunted four days a week, and there were nine people employed in the kennels, looking after 60 couples of hounds.

(Courtesy of Mr. Nicholas Lambert)

Paddy Macdonald, Ollie Lambert and Alf Wright at Knocktopher, 1963.

(Photo: Frank Meads)

Anne Tupper clears a Kilkenny wall on Nutmeg in 1971.

Dick Butler was head kennel man and Willie Kavanagh was second kennel man. They were aided by Harry Wylie, the terrier man, and Johnny Wall who did the skinning. Also there were two or three other lads to do the sweeping and odd jobs. The hunters' yard contained about twenty-two horses overseen by the head groom, Nicky White from Portlaw. Prior to Paddy's arrival, he had been second whip. He

(Courtesy of Mr. & Mrs. Andrew Kavanagh)

Andrew Kavanagh on Irish Grand National winner, Vulpine, wins at Gowran point-to-point races in 1968. Ann Brogan in second place .

began working at Mount Juliet in 1930, at a time when there had been over sixty horses on the property, between hunters, racehorses and jumpers.

The whole McCalmont family hunted during the 1960s, including Victor's children, some of whom were not quite as enthusiastic as their parents might have wished. His wife, Bunny, like Lady Helen, adored her hunting and was a great sportswomen, she had many crashing falls, but was very brave. Her generosity was immense and she always had huge picnic baskets in her car, following the hunt. She would administer apricot and blackberry brandy to cold and wet children, which never failed to perk them up. Several second horsemen, including Jimmy Minoge and Tom Grace (who kept an eye on the McCalmont children) were always, ready to exchange their fresh horses for tired ones.

In 1963 Sir Terence Langrishe, chairman of the Kilkenny Hunt Club, presented to Dermot, on behalf of the hunt members, two oil paintings by Peter Biegel. The "old Major", master for 42 years, on receiving the paintings at Knocktopher Abbey recalled the first day he ever hunted with the Kilkenny Hunt as a schoolboy, the meet was at Knocktopher Abbey, and Sir Terence's father was hunting the hounds. He also paid tribute to the staff who worked at Mount Juliet in the hunters' yard and in the kennels. Mick Collins and Dick Butler were mentioned in particular, as they both came to work for Dermot in 1921 and were still in his employment 42 years later.

An example of the good sport that Victor was showing was a run from Mrs. Sutton's covert at Kilmacow, over Tory Hill to the valley of Mullennahone. At that time there was no forestry on Tory Hill and only one strand of wire was cut. Out of a field of seventy, only a small number finished, including: Victor, Bunny, Lord Waterford, Major Sutton (Bunny's brother), Larry Byrne and Paddy Macdonald. In 1963 hounds found in Booleyglass covert and ran a very straight line towards Piltown. Travelling flat out, the field were able to go where they wanted, no wire and only one piece of forestry which they skirted. Major Murray Smith was acting as field master that day and he was surprised to see hounds catch their fox on his own front lawn at Belline.

The extent of the country further diminished when Victor gave up

(Photo: Mary Tarry)

Victor McCalmont with his daughter, Diana.

(Photo: Mary Tarry)

The Puppy Show at the kennels at Mount Juliet, May 1979. Sitting on the bench are Rosie Wallace, Kay de Vere Hunt and Bunny McCalmont. Alf Wright showing the hounds.

hunting the Shankill to Ballysallagh region, this despite the fact that, in March 1957, they had a very good hunt from Ballysallagh, across the hills to Old Leighlin. While hunting was good in the 1960s, it was not particularly popular. Many people, due to rising wages and increased costs, could no longer afford to hunt in the style that they had once known and preferred to cease hunting rather than cut back. Others, on the other hand, though no longer able to afford grooms or to keep second horses, were unable to resist the lure of the hounds. Field numbers were small. The increased traffic on the roads meant it was no longer safe to hack home long distances in the dark and the use of a trailer, with a safe ball hitch, became a virtual necessity for anyone hunting regularly.

Kilkenny Point-to-Points

The Kilkenny Hunt held their point-to-point at Stonecarthy in 1948, a total of 47 horses were entered in five races. Prior to this they were held at Knockadrina over a natural bank course, which varied from year to year. By 1949 the location had changed to the popular Woollengrange course, near Bennettsbridge, where they remained until it was decided that the natural course was no longer suitable. The course consisted of two bush fences before horses went out into the country, where they were faced with a couple of double banks, a stone wall, a drop bank and two "up" banks. The undulating ground tested the horses' stamina, particularly by the time they had completed the second circuit and were approaching the finish *(O'Connell, 1998)*.

The winner of the open farmers' race was eligible to win outright a challenge cup presented by Major Dermot McCalmont if he won it three times, not necessarily in succession. By 1964 the previous winners of the race were: Mr. John Cass's Ballyroberts (1957, 1959 & 1961), Mr. T. Blackmore's Kilfane (1958), Mr. T. Hutchinson's Paddy's Pick (1960) and Mr. P. O'Hanrahan's Lady Rabirio (1962). 1964 was the last year that the races were held at Woollengrange. Owners who had runners in 1964 included: Mr. P. Berry, Mr. Tom Brennan, Mr. P. Butler, Mr. E. Cash, Mr. John Codd, Miss Ita Connors, Mr. M. Costello, Mr. George Doran, Mr. P. Fennelly, Lady N. Fitzgerald, Mrs. M. Fitzgibbons, Mrs. S. Flood, Brig. B.J. & Mrs. Fowler, Mr. Gannon,

(Photo: Mary Tarry)

Michael Glynn, chauffeur and butler to the McCalmont family, 1981.

(Photo: Mary Tarry)

The Mount Juliet dining room table set for lunch, prior to the 1980 Puppy Show.

Mr. R.M. Harvey, Mr. T.P. Hutchinson, Mrs. Johnson, Mrs. McCalmont, Mr. W. A. McLernon, Dr. P. D. Murphy, Mr. A. S. O'Donnell, Mr. J.J. O'Neill, Mr. W. Seabrooke, Mr. F.J. Stafford, Lady Ursula Vernon, Capt. S.H. Walford, Mrs. F. Warren, Lt.-Col. T.G.

(Photo: Mary Tarry)

Major Victor McCalmont thanking the puppy walkers for their good work at the Puppy Show, May 1980. Sitting beside him are Pam O'Mahony, Brian Fanshawe and Bunny McCalmont.

Wilkinson and Mrs. Wilson. The new venue in 1965 was Gowran Racecourse, where the point-to-point races are still held.

Master of the Wexford Hunt

In 1964 Victor was invited to become master of the Wexford Hunt. Colonel Cairns carried the horn on Wednesdays and Victor brought his hounds from Mount Juliet each Monday and Friday and hunted them in Wexford. This arrangement lasted until 1974, when Victor resigned his Wexford mastership, as the running of two hunts had become an impracticable and onerous task.

Capt. Ronnie Wallace, an old friend of Victor's, advised him on his hound breeding program. They crossed the old Kilkenny lines

(Photo: Mary Tarry)

Sir William Blunden and the Marchioness of Waterford.

(containing old Heythrop blood) with the new Heythrop blood. This combination was successful in producing both winning hounds on the flags and good hounds in the field. All through the seventies there was great rivalry between Kilkenny and Tipperary as to which pack would win the most prizes. The new breeding program produced a lighter, whiter in colour and more wiry hound, of which Dermot did not entirely approve. Although their tendency to go fast through the country should have satisfied him.

Big changes were made in farming practises during the 1960s. Land began to become more valuable, and traditional farming was coming to an end, as mechanisation was slowly introduced. Much drainage and reclamation of land came about, largely due to generous government grants. Hunts began to lose coverts, especially those that were planted on good land, many ditches were excavated or ripped out and the knocks of gorse (which so often held a fox) were bulldozed. This all increased the value of land, some of which had been almost worthless in previous decades. The Kilkenny Hunt's ownership of Bishopslough (a classic example of a hunt covert) and other hunt coverts, ensured the

(Photo: Mary Tarry)

Kilkenny Famous (centre) back home, after winning the bitch championship at Peterborough hound show in 1978.

(Photo: Mary Tarry)

Enjoying Bunny's blackberry brandy. Betty Guinness, Nora de Montmorency, Bunny McCalmont, Vincent Poklewski-Koziell and Tony Tarry.

survival of these small, but important, areas of woodland and gorse. In the late 1960s some very good sport emanated from Bishopslough, a perfect square in the middle of rich limestone farmland, planted for hunting and for the preservation of foxes. On one memorable hunt hounds ran from Bishopslough to Shamrock Lodge, up in the hills near Coppenagh, but it was gradually becoming more difficult to get through that part of the country, with the increase in tillage. The general decline in cover was lamented at the time, but appears to have improved the sport, by forcing the foxes to travel.

Major Dermot hunted until he was about 80 years old, attended by a groom. He found it most satisfying to see the hounds hunting well and it always put him in a good humour. But like many a good huntsman, he resented growing older and found it difficult seeing his sons pass him out on the hunting field. He died suddenly in Rhodesia in 1968, while on a visit to his son, Pat. There were those who were surprised to find the hounds meeting at Ballyhale before the "old Major" was even buried, but they were not aware of his request that the hounds were not to miss a day's hunting on his death.

The following year Victor and his family moved into Mount Juliet and he became the sole master of "a magnificent going concern" as he put it.

By 1974 Ireland had joined the Common Market, this led to significant changes in rural Ireland. Greater emphasis was placed on productivity, which brought about more intensive farming practises, and this in turn caused a rapid increase in the price of land, making it too valuable to sustain hunting in certain cases. Fox fur gradually became a valuable commodity, peaking in the years 1978-80 *(Sleeman, 1997)* when vast numbers of fox pelts were exported to supply the fashion industry. The corresponding reduction in fox numbers did not prove the disaster that many hunting people had predicted. Fewer foxes,

(Photo: Mary Tarry)

The Marquess of Waterford jumping a Kilkenny wall.

(Photo: Mary Tarry)

The second horsemen: Bun Doolin and Tom Grace.

but in view of the on-going opening up of the country, they often travelled further and provided some good hunts. In 1975 Victor reported to J.N.P. Watson that the Kilkenny Hunt had one of their best days in years, on a bye day when they hunted a fox slowly for two hours and then a fresh fox gave them a five mile point in 55 minutes, there were only fifteen people out *(Country Life, 13/1/76).*

Sometimes coverts seemed to disappear overnight. Victor was hunting the hounds near Windgap and hacked to a covert he planned to draw, from which they had had an exceptional run in 1971. When they arrived all that they found were stumps of trees and bushes, it had been bulldozed. Victor called Charlie Blacque up to explain, "did you know this had been done?" to which Charlie replied "Yes, but I did not know where you were going!" as he winked at a hunt member. The infamous walls of "murder mile", between Ballyhale and Kilcasey, remained relatively intact. This was the country most favoured by Bunny and Victor.

In 1974 a large hunt party was given by Mr. & Mrs. Gilbert Butler to celebrate Victor's twenty-fifth anniversary hunting the hounds. A presentation of some Waterford Glass was made on behalf of the hunt subscribers to the master.

On the few occasions, that Victor was unable to hunt the hounds, Alf carried the horn. After years in Kilkenny, he knew every inch of the

(Photo: Mary Tarry)

Alf Wright on the Donegalls' horse, Digby

(Photo: Mary Tarry)

Bunny McCalmont on Carrigeen, October 1982.

county, including all the short-cuts, every lane and gap. On a good scenting day, at Knockroe, he was in charge when the hounds sped away from the covert, with the field close behind. There was no sign of Alf during the hunt, but when the hounds marked to ground, Alf appeared on the bank and nobody knew how he got there. Alf's proudest moment came at Peterborough hound show in 1978, when after winning an earlier class, he showed Kilkenny Famous to take the bitch championship, the climax of any hound breeder's dream.

Last of the Hunt Club Dinners

An undemocratic committee, comprised of hunt club members, aided Victor in the running of the hunt. Meetings were held at Mount Juliet with George Salmon acting as secretary. If Victor, or in earlier times, his father, were absent from a meeting any decisions made would be referred to them for approval the next day. If approval was not forthcoming the decisions were rescinded. The system worked well and no one objected to the hunt being managed in this manner, as the McCalmonts were honourable and knowledgeable masters who took care of everything. Although members paid a subscription, it was essentially a nominal amount when compared to the subvention provided by the McCalmonts.

In accordance with tradition, occasional dinners were held, as custom dictated, in the Club House Hotel in Kilkenny. They were men-only affairs, much to the chagrin of Bunny and of certain other hunt ladies. The dinners although expensive, were non profit-making events. The food was traditional, plain and simple fare, but of the best quality. Desmond Lambert of Dysertmore provided the salmon for the first course, this was followed by old-fashioned roast beef. One year, Jack Dwan succeeded in procuring some unpasteurised beer in the cask from the brewery in Kilkenny. It was so palatable that copious quantities were drunk and Jack was afterwards accused of having laced it with poteen. Generally, nothing but the best claret and vintage port were served, the club maintained its own wine cellar. The dining table was decorated with three Ascot Gold Cups, from the safe in the Mount Juliet basement. These were taken off the table when dinner was over and driven back to Mount Juliet to ensure their safety. Members of the Hunt Club included: Lord Waterford, Sir Terence Langrishe, Sir William Blunden, Major Desmond Lambert, Col. Palmer, Major David Thomas, Charlie Blacque, Jack Dwan, Gilbert Butler, James Butler, Paddy Fennelly and Edric Dowley.

The club was disbanded during Sir William Blunden's chairmanship and its cellar of fine claret and vintage port was sold off. The drink driving laws hastened the club's demise.

Chapter 13

The Harrier Packs

Up a hill hurry not,
Down a hill flurry not,
On level ground spare him not. (An old country milestone)

Foxhunting in south Kilkenny has been a way of life and a tradition that has affected a great number of people in varying ways. Some have derived enormous enjoyment from it and contributed greatly to its survival, some have simply enjoyed it, more have accepted it as inevitable and maybe some more have hoped it would go away – but it never has. The farming community has supported it enthusiastically and are mainly responsible for its survival as a rural sport.

The Mullinavat Harriers

The fifty year old Mullinavat Harriers or to give them their full title the "Mullinavat and District Harriers" are an example of a successful local farmers' pack. They were officially formed as a club in 1947, with Bill Burke as the first chairman. They appear to have taken over from the Kilmacow Harriers who hunted as a mounted pack, an area slightly south of Mullinavat, prior to 1940. Their master and huntsman was Mr. Conway from Kilmacow.

The founder of the Mullinavat Harriers was Jimmy McDonald of Ballintlea, who it seems, was always interested in dogs and hunting. It is not exactly clear how he acquired his first hounds, but it is likely that the following tale has something to do with it:

> Jimmy was a regular puppy walker for the Kilkenny Hunt and the "Major" as he would be described locally or more accurately the "old Major" (Dermot McCalmont) in those days. Some would say that the "major" was not great at collecting his pups, others would say that occasionally Jimmy or the pups might be missing when he'd arrive, but either way, there were a few stragglers left that Jimmy and Jack Gaule (his farm labourer) hunted with a few greyhounds on a Sunday and

> of course the "Major" could hunt on McDonald's land on a week day – so everyone was happy *(Conway, 1999)*.

Towards the end of the Second World War, Jimmy McDonald, Jack Bolger, John Walsh and Paul Sullivan went to the south west of Ireland to Cahirciveen and Waterville for hounds. Their journey was facilitated by petrol coupons supplied by Jackie Whelan of the sack and bag factory in Newrath. This was the first introduction of Black and Tans, at least of the four legged type, to Mullinavat. Larry Byrne, master and huntsman for 25 years, believes that the blood of these original hounds is still in the kennels.

(Courtesy of Mr. Patrick Holden)

Paddy Holden leading out the hounds in the 1950s.

A second trip was made, in an Austin 55, to County Kerry. Jimmy McDonald, Larry Byrne and Wattie Power brought back ten more Black and Tan hounds. They had been trencher fed, and had a tendency to work in pairs initially. Whether it was their background or breeding is not certain, but on occasions a hound or two might be "unavailable" at going home time after a day's hunting with the Mullinavat Harriers. On Monday mornings children walking to school in Mullinavat, from

(Courtesy of Mr. Larry Byrne)

From left to right: Jimmy McDonald, Pat Kinsella and Larry Byrne.

the Killandra or Ballyquin direction would not be surprised by the sight of a hound making its way home up the Chapel Road, particularly if the hunt had been on the far side of the parish, the pervious day.

Those who lived on the east side of Mullinavat near the kennels, would occasionally have a musical treat late at night:

> For a number of years the practice was for the kennel man, Philip Maddock to bring the hounds to the meet behind the bicycle – he always seemed to pass down by the church gate with the pack in tow as the people came out from 11 o'clock mass, i.e. 11.50 a.m. at best! Philip of course would bring home the hounds by the same means in the evening and if they had to occasionally make "a call" in the village – well, Black and Tans aren't given to hanging around, so by 8 or 9 at night they could be in full cry up the valley under Kilbeacon, Glendonnel and onto Ballyquin or up by Killandrew and Ballynooney towards the three Friars. For some reason they always sounded louder and much clearer in the stillness of the night. Of course they were invariably interrupted sometime before midnight by Philip calling from around the Big Tree *(Conway, 1999)*.

In the early days, when the hounds were kept in an old cow house at Jimmy McDonald's, the fields were small, Jimmy, Jack Gaule, Philip Maddock, Pat Conway, Luke Doyle on his pony and Larry Byrne in short trousers were the only regulars.

In February 1947 the hounds were moved to the kennels in Ballyquin, their present location. Philip Maddock moved into the adjacent cottage, both the cottage and kennels are on McDonald's land, and he lived there as kennel man for 29 years. Pat Conway describes how he visited him:

(Courtesy of Mr. Larry Byrne)

Betty Byrne, Andy Doherty, Willie Mullally and Larry Byrne.

> on his first night in the kennels and most nights for the next twenty or so years. The kennel house became the place to visit for many years, Jimmy and Mick McCarthy, Pat Delahunty and Willie Aylward were regulars, the venue for many a good hunting story, even of ones that nearly took place *(Conway, 1999).*

The kennel grounds later became the schooling ground for young horses on their way to local gymkhanas. These events produced some notable horses, like Lock an Easpaig (ridden by Davy McMinn to jump 7 feet 2 inches, in Callan) and Earlsrath Rambler who both won at Wembley.

The land is now owned by Tom McDonald who hunted with the harriers in his youth.

With Jimmy McDonald as huntsman and master, regular members of the field included George and Mick Connors (with the one eyed pony), John, Tom and Richie Walsh, Jim Freyne, John and Richard Aylward, Anna McDonald (Jimmy's wife), Mickey McCarthy, Pat Delahunty (breeder of Lock an Easpaig), Jamie Foskin, Martin, Paddy and Jimmy Raftice, Pat Kinsella of Roselier fame, Mick and John Knox, Tom Maddock, Maurice Murphy, Jimmy Holden and John Campion who often rode Earlsrath with the harriers.

Paddy Holden succeeded Jimmy McDonald as huntsman in the mid fifties and was noted for his good voice in the covert, which he still enjoys in his eighties. Paddy occupied the position of club chairman for over 25 years. This was not a demanding task as meetings were not popular in those days. A seasoned member described meetings as places where "minutes were taken" and "hours were wasted" and consequently "we weren't much into meetings or committees" *(Conway, 1999).*

Another man to hunt the harriers was Tom Walsh assisted by a young Richie Hendrick, both entered the world of racing with some success. Tom's brother, John, acted as club treasurer for a considerable period. Jack Cranley, the only man with a horsebox at the Mullinavats up to the early 1970s, took over as huntsman for two or three seasons until he handed the horn over to Larry Byrne in 1964.

Larry hunted the Mullinavat Harriers for 25 years with only a break of a year or two when Tommy Mullally took charge, although Larry officially remained huntsman and master. He ran the whole operation for most of those 25 years. Larry was assisted by Tommy Mullally and

(Courtesy of Mr. Tommy Mullally)

Tommy Mullally and Larry Byrne with the hounds.

(Courtesy of Mr. Larry Byrne)

At the Rochestown Cross meet, near Glenmore. From left to right: Tommy Mullally, Johnnie Grennan, Jimmy McDonald (on foot), Maura Kelly (mounted on dark horse), Robert Kent (on the grey pony) and Fidelis Doherty (on foot).

Seamus Freyne who was club treasurer and later by Johnny Grennan. They bred and fed hounds, walked pups, kept and maintained the kennels, drew flesh, did the fencing, managed the cemetery and generally kept the hunt running smoothly. Amongst Larry's other helpers were, Andy Doherty, Victor Mullally, Sean Kinsella, Brendan Holden and Micheal Kennedy, who now hunts the Laois hounds.

Larry's strategy for dealing with hounds, reluctant to return to kennels at the end of a day's hunting was simple, provided the location of the meet allowed it, he would organise his draws back towards the general direction of the kennels. "It took some of us years to understand what "working our way back to the kennels" meant *(Conway, 1999).*

Prominent hunting members in Larry's day were Peggy, Sheila and Maureen Mullally, Mary Doherty, Tom Duggan, Dinny Hogan and Ned Fitzgerald and Jimmy Murphy who was so tragically drowned in the Grey Wood quarry where he went to wash his horse on his way home from hunting in Harristown. The Suttons, Foskins and Holdens were all hunting families and most households in Mullinavat and the surrounding parishes had a member who had hunted at some period.

Jack Waters was a regular helper with Larry around the kennels as was Jimmy Fitzgerald and John Wallace in more recent times. John Corcoran succeeded Larry Byrne and hunted hounds for six seasons up to 1998, assisted by Sean Aylward and Robert Kent who takes over as huntsman in the 1999-2000 season.

The Mullinavat Harriers were run almost exclusively on a voluntary basis, with cap (in the early days) of half a crown and membership of one pound. Funds were raised by the annual "Harriers Dance" in Harney's Hall in Mullinavat, gymkhanas in Mackies Field on the main road between Lukeswell and Mullinavat and in more recent years by the "Harriers Dinner Dance". Fund raising was extended to include cabarets and discos and in 1999 by a share in the joint hunter-trials held at Coolmeen.

The Mullinavats were always blessed with great farmer support, not alone from Mullinavat but from the surrounding areas as well, possibly brought about by the service provided by the kennels which were kept open all year round. As a farmers' pack they always welcomed locals hunting, particularly children and had a huge foot following. People like Jim Doyle, Paddy Shalloe and Jimmy Grennan on their Raleigh bicycles, Paddy Grennan on his Honda and Johnny Gaule in the Prefect car were regular followers on the road with the hunt. Car followers are still a big feature of the harriers and on a fine Sunday it is a family outing for many. A local recently described it thus "those harriers are more of a 'movement' than anything else".

The Nore Vale Harriers

The Nore Vale Harriers came into existence in the early 1940s, probably in 1944. The principal founding members included Michael Bookle, John Doody, Jim Bolger, Jack and Danny McDonald, Harry Murphy, Peadar Laffan and Eddie Hanrahan.

They hunted the parishes of Thomastown and Inistioge, as well as parts of Graignamanagh and Tullogher. In the early days the annual highlight was a joint meet held with the neighbouring Mullinavat Harriers on St. Patrick's Day. These meets are remembered more for the mutual hospitality than they are for the length of the points or for the number of foxes found. During its first decade, the Nore Vale was a footpack with the occasional mounted follower.

(Courtesy of Mr. Andy Galavan)

Pat Barron, Master and Huntsman of the Nore Vale Harriers for almost 30 years.

By the opening meet of October 1954, at Dangan Cross, almost all the followers were in the saddle. Michael Bookle was their first huntsman and he kennelled the hounds at his farm in Brownsbarn, near Inistioge. By the early 1960s the hounds had moved to Jim Bolger's farm in Dangan, where they remained for two or three years.

In 1966 or 1967 Kilcross, Inistioge became the new home of the harriers under the mastership of Pat Barron, with Paddy Clifford and Richard Doody as whips. Pat continued to hunt the hounds for almost thirty years until his death in 1995. He was a man who loved hunting above all else, a natural huntsman. As a teenager he was frequently seen on cold winter Sundays, setting out for a day's hunting alone, on his pony with his one couple of hounds. The summer months could never pass quickly enough for him. In the hunting field, Pat did not suffer fools gladly, but "if severe in aught, the love he bore to hunting was at fault". In later years he introduced a large number of local children to the joys of hunting, often training horse and rider together in the field behind his house.

On the death of Pat Barron, the Nore Vale Harriers were reorganised under an elected committee with Richard Doody and, more recently, Paddy Clifford as huntsman, with Shane Croke and John Clifford as whips *(Kavanagh, Martin)*.

Chapter 14

Looking to the Future

No organisation is so dependent on goodwill as hunting... Goodwill must prevail. (Owen Conway, 1995)

Realising that one of the strengths of the Kilkenny Hunt had been its ability to accept change during the past 200 years, Victor was determined that hunting should continue to adapt to and meet the challenges of the late twentieth century. Harry, his youngest son, and Peter Thomas joined Victor McCalmont as joint masters in 1983. Victor gave up carrying the horn in favour of Peter. It was the first season for 62 years that there was not a McCalmont hunting the hounds.

Peter Thomas's commitment to the hunt was total and he brought renewed vigour to it. Peter's equestrian skills were not the most polished, he had taken no interest in horses as a child and when asked why, he would reply that he had been too busy playing with bits of string in the manure heap. Notwithstanding, he was a fearless horseman who rode for one reason only, and that was to stay with his hounds, this led to some terrifying falls early in his career as huntsman, though he seemed seldom aware of them. When hounds were running he would expect his horse to jump virtually impossible places. Seemingly impenetrable to all behind, blind hedges would open up to let him through and close again afterwards. However the new huntsman and his horse usually succeeded in reaching the other side intact and, as time passed, occasionally in great style.

Peter never forgot that he was a farmer and always showed due respect to those over whose lands he hunted. He made a point of knowing personally as many landowners as he could. He was a man of his word and if asked not to enter a field on horseback he was just as happy to run through on foot with his hounds.

Some of the best days sport seen in recent years were achieved by Peter. He soon overcame his inexperience and it quickly became clear that he had all the required attributes for his new position. During his first season the meet at Knockmoylan stands out, described as follows in his own words:

(Photo: Mary Tarry)

Peter Thomas hunting hounds in his first season.

12 ½ couple. Clear and dry. East wind. Aylwards' and Railway line blank. Found in Daltons' bog by Corcorans' house. Ran for bogs by main road and along river towards Mullinavat. Turned up hill through Gearys' and then parallel with Mullinavat – Hugginstown road, above Anthony Knoxs' and Corcorans'. Crossed road in Ballinarahy and through small covert by Noel Butler's. Checked here for a while until we hit

> it off beyond cattle foil. Ran for Flynns' bogs in Ballyhemin. He lay down here until we refound him. Crossed road into Killeen, through Andy Frisby's yard and silage pits, then recrossed road at Red Acres and back to Flynns' bogs. Left bogs running south as far as a cul de sac road. Made it good over the road, to no effect. Fox must have turned short on road and back to bog. 2 hrs *(Thomas, 1983-90).*

At Victor's request Charles Blacque became chairman of the Kilkenny Hunt in the 1980s. It was at a difficult time. No longer was it feasible for the hunt to continue in the extravagant style of the past sixty years. Changes were slowly introduced. Until 1986 the hounds were fed oatmeal, cooked flesh and soup with minced-up mangles and cabbages.

(Photo: Mary Tarry)

From left to right: Johnny Alexander, Lady Waterford, Nicholas Lambert, Sean Aylward, Michael Morris, Mary Couchman, Diana McCalmont, Stephen Lanigan O'Keeffe and Caroline Murphy, 1981.

(Photo: Mary Tarry)

Peter Thomas, Victor McCalmont and Alf Wright.

This system was labour intensive, it took the kennel huntsman from 9 a.m. to 12 noon to feed. The change to raw flesh was eventually made when oil and oatmeal became too expensive.

Victor and Bunny would have up to ten horses out regularly, including those for their visitors (whom they always mounted) and their second horses. When Victor retired and gave up riding in 1983, there were big cut backs in the hunters' yard at Mount Juliet. Only Tom Grace and Bun Doolin were left to work in the yard looking after Bunny's horses.

It was a formidable task to introduce changes. The members had been indulged by a succession of four extremely wealthy and understanding masters, who had provided a top class hunt for close on one hundred years. They were content with the manner in which the hunt was managed, they paid little for their sport and were seldom required to concern themselves with the running of the club.

The chairman made it clear to the subscribers, that the McCalmonts were no longer in a position to sustain the extent of their funding. Members would have to raise money themselves and become more active in the running of the hunt in the future. Nevertheless, it was characteristic of Victor that when Jack Dwan took over from Richard St. George as honorary treasurer in 1989, Victor was still paying claims for damages and paid off a substantial hunt overdraft unbeknownst to the majority of the hunt subscribers in the same year.

The new regime proposed that landowners be given the materials they required to repair any damage caused by the hunt. Peter, together with Ned Fitzpatrick, appreciated that this was an insufficient gesture and that it was in the best interests of the hunt to rectify damages without delay, so they introduced the practice of having a fencer following the field. Any additional work was done the following day by Peter and his team of helpers. It was not an uncommon sight on dark winter mornings to see him waiting in his brown jeep for the sun to rise in order to have enough light to fix a gap. After the hunt ball he would

(Photo: Des McCheane)

Juliet Brown, Honorary Secretary of the Kilkenny Hunt, 1982-1993.

(Courtesy of Mr. E. Fitzpatrick)

Ned Fitzpatrick and Peter Thomas MFH.

never go to bed but would head straight out to the country where the hounds had run the previous day to put right any damage that might have occurred.

Peter Thomas played a key role in maintaining an equilibrium while the changes took place. He provided good sport and was completely dedicated to the Kilkenny Hunt. He was convinced that there was only one way to do things and that was the right way. Although it was not an easy time for foxhunting or for the Kilkenny Hunt, Peter's commitment to hunting was total. Savings were continually having to be made. There was a big increase in sheep numbers which resulted in the appearance of more wire and electric fencing.

In 1986 Victor and Bunny decided to sell Mount Juliet, the magnificent home of the McCalmont family for 81 years was put up for sale. The hunt kennels, which were excluded from the sale remained intact. Mount Juliet house was opened as a hotel and an internationally acclaimed 18 hole golf course, to the design of Jack Nicklaus, was created. The hunters' yard was converted and extended to house the golf club, accommodation and a leisure centre.

The appointment of Roy Strudwick of Ballygallon, Inistioge, as an additional joint master in 1987 eased the pressure on Victor, who never missed a day's hunting following his beloved hounds in his jeep. Sadly, Bunny McCalmont died that year, after a fall in the hunting field. She and Victor were just about to move into their new home, adjacent to Mount Juliet.

Peter's hunting diary shows constant concern for the farmers and their land, as well as the condition of the land. He often mentions his efforts to minimise damage and pays great attention to detail, particularly in recording landowners' names.

(Photo: Des McCheane)

Kilkenny Hounds jumping a gate.

(Photo: Des McCheane)

Owen Conway.

Peter appreciated that a good day for the hounds was not always a good day for the mounted field. Typically, he never expresses any concern for himself, not even when faced with the barrel end of a shotgun, an incident, mention of which he omits. A day at Ballyfrunk on February 16th 1987, must rate amongst his most memorable:

> 14½ couples. It took a long time before we could persuade a dog fox to leave Ballyfrunk covert. He ran an indirect route to Ballycuddihy plantation. The hounds pushed him out of this and for the gorse under Comerfords' farm. From here they ran towards Ballycallan chapel then left-handed over the road and towards the covert. However they crossed the stream in Pat Murphy's and lost him on the Tullaroan road. We then found in the small gorse opposite Jack Murphy's gate in Kilmanagh. They ran very fast over a stiff country to Ballyfrunk covert.

> The fox ran the fence of this before heading for Golden Fields and the top of Knockdreelan hill. He bore slightly left-handed here and after crossing two roads the hounds checked in Walton's cattle, Remeen. Hit off the line again over the earths opposite Waltons' gate and ran down through Oldtown for a mile before returning to the earths. Could not be certain if he got in a break or not as it seemed there was a fox stopped inside the earth. A good hunt. 1 hr 40mins *(Thomas, 1983-90).*

In the 1988-89 season Peter had eleven particularly good days hunting

(Photo: Des McCheane)

From left to right: Paddy Macdonald, Barry O'Reilly, Kevin O'Donnell (Jnr.), John Hughes, Pat Loughlin, Jack Dwan and Arthur St. George move off with the hounds from the opening meet in Gowran.

(Photo: Des McCheane)

Pat Loughlin, Gowran publican and supplier of hirelings to visitors hunting with the local packs.

and showed consistent sport throughout the winter, accounting for 16½ brace of foxes. It appeared as though the Kilkenny Hunt was blessed, with their enthusiastic huntsman coming into his prime. Unfortunately fate decided otherwise. Tragically, in February of 1990, Peter Thomas died from cancer, at the age of 41. It was an enormous shock for his family and the entire hunting community, the future of the hunt had been vested in him and his dedication and commitment to it had been exceptional.

Paddy Macdonald, who had been Peter's first whip, took on the job of hunting the hounds. Michael Kennedy whipped-in to him for one season, then Barry O'Reilly took over. Amongst Paddy's best days hunting hounds was a meet at Knockroe, when the hounds ran from Cloran to Wellbrook, in the North Kilkenny country near Freshford, a good five mile point. Another good run was from Poulnassy, Mullinavat, past the Grey Wood Quarry to Jimmy Brennan's covert, the Haystack, Kilcasey. Paddy Macdonald continued to hunt the hounds with the aid of Barry O'Reilly as first whip and John Hughes as amateur second whip until 1996. He worked in the kennels for one more year before completing a record 38 years of service with the Kilkenny Hunt.

As has been the norm for the Kilkenny Hunt for most of the twentieth century, the hounds were still very fast and sometimes Victor was often inclined to forget who was hunting them. He would be seen travelling across fields at dangerous speeds in his latest four wheel drive jeep, the fear always was that he might take on the ditch ahead. Victor had a great memory for a hunt, he would often accurately recall runs from many years past. This, together with his superb and unsurpassed knowledge of both the country and of the lines that foxes were likely to take, enabled him to follow the hounds successfully from his jeep. On occasions he would reach the end of a hunt before the hunt staff or field

(Photo: Des McCheane)

The Kilkenny Hunt field at Bramblestown.

(Photo: Fiona Jackson)

Mount Juliet, seat of the McCalmont family and home to the Kilkenny Hunt since 1921.

arrived, and would be wondering where everyone had got to. Not appreciating that wire and modern farming practises, were continuing to close up parts of the country, slowing down the field.

For many riders hunting was all about taking one's own line across the country after hounds. This has become increasingly difficult, as the century draws to a close. From the hounds' point of view the worst innovation is the introduction of electric fencing powered from the mains supply. On receiving the shock the hounds imagine it is their huntsman rating them and they loose concentration. Wire is found throughout the county, frequently on both sides of a bank. Coverts are not static, some famous ones have gone, but in other places covert has grown along ditches which were previously bare.

Victor was very good with children and encouraged them to enjoy their hunting. In latter years he made a point of attending the children's meet and talking to them before the first draw, ensuring the next generation's enthusiasm and respect for hounds. Victor had followed in his father's footsteps. He achieved considerable success with the show hounds, and won many championships. The Kilkenny hounds were always the ones that the other packs wanted to beat. The final tribute to his skill in hound breeding came, sadly, the year after his death, when Paddy Macdonald swept the boards at the hound show in Limerick. It was the culmination of a lifetime's work.

The point-to-point took place each March at Gowran Park and was an important money earner for the hunt. In addition to it, in the spring of 1993, preparations were in hand for hunter trials at Kilmanahan. Victor, as always, was the driving force, and over the previous three years had done all in his power to ensure that the subscribers fund raising venture should succeed. The day before the hunter-trials, the shattering news broke: the Major had died suddenly and unexpectedly. Despite the committee's insistence that the hunter-trials be cancelled as a mark of respect, characteristically, the McCalmont family requested that the hunter-trials should proceed. They were held according to plan, and Victor was laid to rest in the family grave at Ennisnag.

One of Victor's last moves had been to send out a circular to all members of the hunt on "Foxhunting etiquette – or – How to make your sport work". A sign of the times and indicative of the changes taking place. Interestingly, it was not the first time that such a document was deemed necessary, the Kilkenny Journal had published a remarkably similar list of instructions entitled "Hints to Huntsmen" in December 1835, describing the correct manner in which to behave while on the hunting field to ensure good sport.

The McCalmont era was only rivalled by that of one other famous father and son duo, the two Sir John Powers. It is largely thanks to these two families that the hunt founded in 1797, reached its bi-centenary, one of only a handful to have done so.

(Photo: Des McCheane)

Jim Quinlan (huntsman) leads the Kilkenny Hounds towards Knockroe. Chris Smith (whip) follows on the grey.

Postscript

After Victor's death, it became clear that a new master would be required to assist Roy Strudwick. In 1994 Rodney Day was appointed. Jim Quinlan became huntsman in 1997, and in 1998 Chris Smith took on the job of first whip. Tom Burns and Sarah Hatton joined Rodney Day as joint masters in 1998.

With the new team at the helm, the Kilkenny Hunt enters its third century revitalised and confident that it will rise to meet any challenges that the future may present.

Kilkenny, Kilkenny, the land of the chase,
Where horses and hounds always go the best pace;
The season is o'er, but we must not forget
The good sport we have had, the good fellows we've met.
(R. Frankland, 1845)

GLOSSARY

Bag fox	-	a captured fox, released for hunting.
Country	-	territory over which a pack may draw.
Couple	-	pair.
Covert		undergrowth or a wood which foxes inhabit. Pronounced *cover.*
Cub-hunting	-	a period before the hunting season, in which the young foxes are scattered and young hounds are trained.
Draw		the sending of hounds through a covert to push out a fox.
Earth	-	a fox's burrow.
Field	-	mounted hunt followers.
Harriers		technically hounds that hunt hares.
M.F.H	-	Master of Foxhounds.
Music	-	cry of hounds.
Stern		tail of a hound.
Trencher fed	-	a pack in which individual hounds are kept by hunt members and not together in a kennel.
Vulpicide	-	killing of a fox, excluding hunting.

APPENDIX I

KILKENNY HUNT FINANCES IN THE 1800s

Foxhunting became a popular pastime in Kilkenny during a period of slow economic expansion in the latter half of the eighteenth century, when gentlemen had the time and leisure to partake in the sport. Landlords benefited from a buoyant economy until 1815 when the Napoleonic Wars ended. Rents paid well and agriculture was booming. The lack of timber outside their estates favoured those with well-wooded demesnes. In 1801 John Power advertised "40 ton of well-saved oak bark" *(Gulliver and Silverman, 1995, 70)*. The healthy state of the economy was conducive to the establishment of a county hunt, although sporadic agrarian unrest caused moments of concern. The Irish Yeomanry, a part-time, voluntary, local defence force was formed in 1796. According to the official records of the District Corps, the Thomastown Cavalry was set up that year with the Earl of Carrick as Captain. Later John Power commanded the Kilfane Infantry and became known as Captain Power.

From its commencement the Kilkenny Hunt was a subscription pack, dependent not solely on its master for funds, but also to a lesser degree on its members. The first evidence for this is the following advertisement:

> Kilkenny Hunt, 20th. February. Last date for subscriptions; 5 guinea pa. Thomas Geery, Secretary. NB: The Club Meets 1st. Feb. Kilkenny Club House *(LJ. 2:2:1805)*.

Other early subscription packs are known to have existed in counties Cork and Meath *(Lewis, 1975)*, although most were supported solely by their masters. In 1815 John Power received almost £600 in subscriptions from 10 individuals, others paid in kind *(Anon., 1897)*. This was a small sum considering that in 1825 in England a professional huntsman would expect wages in the region of £300 per annum and a two day a week pack cost in the region of £1170 to run *(Itzkowitz, 1977)*. There is little to show how the other packs hunting within Kilkenny supported themselves, but it is reasonable to assume that most were privately owned and funded.

Hunt finances fluctuated with the fortunes of their masters, as they traditionally funded the bulk of the expenses. No complete set of accounts have been found for any period until 1895, and during the course of research carried out for this book, it has not been possible to determine the sources of the wealth of many of the masters who succeeded the Powers. A number, like Lord St. Lawrence, Sinclair Butson and Capt. Hartopp were not local men as, presumably, it was impossible to find someone from within the county with sufficient funds to finance the hunt. Furthermore, it is not always clear why they resigned their positions. The Kilkenny Hunt was in a weakened position after the Famine, but in spite of showing reasonable sport, George Bryan was unable to remain as master and handed over the running of the hunt to a committee, who found the raising of finance a major problem. The amount raised by the subscriptions continued to be minimal in comparison to the overall expenditure. Lord James Butler attempted to address the situation, but it was not until 1856 under Lord St. Lawrence that the finances improved.

During Meredyth's heyday in 1863, Sir John Power (2nd Baronet) wrote to Sir Charles Cuffe outlining the precarious financial situation of the hunt *(Power 1863).* Fifteen non-hunting men were contributing in excess of £200 and six hunting men subscribed £250, the bulk of which was donated by George Bryan. The preservation of several coverts and woods was also underwritten by both groups. In the same letter, he outlined his extreme concern for the future of the hunt:

> The question now is not one of merely concerning the Hunting men – it is a county affair. Is fox-hunting to be given up in our county? Once we let it fall to the ground and it will not like the Phoenix rise from its own ashes and depend upon it, the tone of society in Kilkenny will be very different to what it is at present. Our social and hospitable reunions will be few and the opportunity of creating a good and friendly feeling amongst all classes will, in a great measure cease *(Power, 1863).*

A letter purporting to be from "a trader of the city" throws light on the effect of hunting within the local economy. The letter was published in the pro-establishment Kilkenny Moderator. One must bear in mind that there may be some exaggeration in the figures quoted:

> There are at least 50 hunting men, keeping on an average 2 horses each, costing for their "keep" £3,600, all spent in the locality. All the oats, hay and straw for them is bought in the county. It may be calculated that 100 hunters employ 50 groom – generally the offspring of the agricultural population and consume annually about 20,000 barrels of oats, 100 tons of hay and beans in proportion. Every tradesman, professional man and trader is benefited by hunting men – tailors, bootmakers, blacksmiths, saddlers, brewers, druggists, surgeons and veterinary surgeons etc. *(KK Mod. 15:1:1870).*

He also notes that 15 tons of oatmeal and the carcasses of almost 100 old horses, consumed by the 42 couple of hounds, were bought each year. However, there is evidence in England *(Itzkowitz, 1977)* that the farmers did not always benefit directly from hunting by the sale of their crops, there were many dealers who bought the produce and kept the profit for themselves. In the Irish context, however, anything that kept landlords resident was generally beneficial to the county, thus hunting provided employment and created a local market for a variety of goods, which in turn kept money in circulation.

Hunting requires money and country, the raising of sufficient funds was a constant worry. Henry Briscoe had the goodwill of the country behind him. He had hunted his own Tinvane Hounds in south Kilkenny as well as the Curraghmore Hunt, he had an excellent track record. Unfortunately, he was not a man with enormous private funds, so when he undertook to become master of the Kilkenny Hunt and to hunt them three days a week, he required a guarantee of £1,285 per annum. Additional funds were to be raised by subscription from the hunt members. At the time the subscriptions were £500 in deficit, but half of that was made up promptly. The majority of members and subscribers were non-hunting men who felt it in their interest to contribute. Lord Ormonde, who could not ride and was reputed to have hated hunting, was the largest subscriber *(KK Mod. 22:8:1879).* He continued his generous support in the following years and in 1875 paid off a debt of £500 to save the hunt *(British Hunts and Huntsmen, 1911).* It was estimated that in 1881 the average master's expenditure was in the region of £1500 per annum.

In 1884, after the Land War, Lord Desart bought hounds from Tipperary and sold them at half price to the hunt. Prior to 1886 Lord Clifden paid off a hunt debt of £550 and made a donation of £100. Things became desperate, a number of hounds were sold and the remainder threatened with sale, but in 1886 Edmond Smithwick came to the rescue and bought twenty couple of Kilkenny Hounds to save them for the hunt. James Connellan became master in 1887 and bought the hounds from Edmond Smithwick *(British Hunts and Huntsmen, 1911).* Financial problems persisted until Sir Hercules Langrishe bought the pack in 1890. The hunt committee had considered buying them from Connellan *(Kilkenny Hunt Minutes, 1887),* but deemed it unnecessary once Langrishe became master.

National economic trends affected hunting in Kilkenny to a certain degree, but overall its economic well being was dependent upon the wealth of the masters.

APPENDIX II

Packs of Hounds in County Kilkenny:

Harvey Morres's Hounds	c.1732
Lord Carrick's, Mt. Juliet.	18th Century
Mr. Butler Cooper's, Ballyduff	18th Century
Mr. Agar's, Gowran	1768
Kilkenny Hunt	1773-75,1788-89
Merry Harriers	1774-1785,1788,1796
Lord Clifden's	1777
Sportsman's Club	1785-1790
Kilkenny Hunt	1797 to date
George Pack's Hare Hounds	1805
Webbsborough Hunt	1805
Mr. Hunt's Jerpoint Harriers	pre 1809
Mr. Elliott of Clonmore's Iverk Harriers	1827
Edward Cooke's Harriers (the Redcaps)	1827,1831,1842,1858
Capt. Poe's Harriers, Rossmore	c. 1830s
Henry Briscoe's father's Harriers	pre 1832
Tinvane Hounds	1832-c.1859
Ballydine Hounds	1833
Mount Loftus Harriers	pre 1835
John Walsh of Fanningstown, Harriers	c.1840s
Major Izod's Harriers	c.1840s
Ossory Hounds	c.1843
The Marquess of Worcester's Otter Hounds (visiting)	1849
Curraghmore Hunt	1852-1884
Mr. Alexander Hamilton's Woodstock Harriers	c.1859
Mr. Bryan's Harriers	c.1860-1861
Mr. Smithwick's Kilcreene Harriers	1862,1863,1869
The 20th Regiment's Beagles	1870
Mr. Ponsonby's Otter Hounds	1870
The Earl of Desart's Harriers	pre 1880
Carlow (occasionally hunted north east Kilkenny)	1880-1930
Sir Hercules Langrishe's Harriers	1880-1890
Major James Connellan's Otter Hounds	c.1890
Sir Charles Nugent Humble's (Portlaw)	1891-1893
New Ross Hounds	1894-1904
Lord Duncannon's Harriers	1898-1906
Castlecomer and Queen's County Hunt	1898-1909
Mr. Lambert's Hounds	1904-1907

Gowran/Graiguenamanagh Trencher Harriers	c.1904-1920
East Kilkenny Hunt	1907-1921
John Grace's Harriers	c. 1920-1927
Johnswell Harriers	1924-1931
Mr. Hodgkin's Harriers, Luke House	c.1920s - 1930s
Father Larkin and Pat Walsh's Hounds	pre 1920s
Gaultier Harriers (hunting in Kilkenny)	1924-34,1947-48
Kilmoganny Hounds	c.1922 to date
Mount Loftus Harriers	1931-1955
Mr. Alexander's Hounds	1931-1934
Mr. Frisby's Otter Hounds	1930s-1940s
North Kilkenny Hunt	1934 to date
Kilmacow Harriers	pre 1940
Nore Vale Harriers, Inistioge	1944 to date
Mullinavat Harriers	1947 to date

The above list includes mainly mounted packs, it is not a definitive list.

(Photo: Des McCheane)

Rodney Day, Joint Master of the Kilkenny Hunt.

APPENDIX III

KILKENNY HUNT MASTERS

1797 - 1844	Sir John Power (1st Baronet)
1840 - 1850	Sir John Power (2nd Baronet)
1850 - 1852	George Bryan
1852 - 1855	Committee
1855 - 1856	Lord James Butler
1856 - 1861	Lord St. Lawrence
1861 - 1870	Henry William Meredyth
1870 - 1876	Henry Briscoe
1876 - 1880	Col. Frank Chaplin
1880 - 1882	Capt. Hartopp
1882	Committee
1882 - 1884	The Earl of Desart
1884 - 1886	Capt. Sinclair Butson
1886 - 1887	Capt. Chaloner Knox
1887 - 1890	Major James Connellan
1890 - 1908	Sir Hercules Langrishe
1908 - 1921	Isaac Bell
1921 - 1968	Major Dermot McCalmont
1948 - 1993	Major Victor McCalmont
1983 - 1990	Peter Thomas
1983 - 1998	Harry McCalmont
1987 - 1998	Roy Strudwick
1994 - To date	Rodney Day
1996 - 1997	Kevin O'Donnell (Senior)
1997 - 1998	Billy Jones
1998 - To date	Sarah Hatton
1998 - To date	Tom Burns

(Photo: Des McCheane)
Sarah Hatton, Joint Master of the Kilkenny Hunt, riding side-saddle at a fund raising meet.

(Photo: Des McCheane)
Tom Burns, Joint Master of the Kilkenny Hunt.

APPENDIX IV

KILMOGANNY HUNT MASTERS

1918 - 1922	Pat Walshe
1922 - 1931	Jack McEnery
1931 - 1936	Capt. Langley Ellis
1935 - 1939	Jack McEnery
1938 - 1945	Neil Shee
1946 - 1972	Charles V. Blacque
1963 - 1972	Michael Curran
1972 - 1987	Patrick Murphy
1972 - 1982	John Costello
1972 - 1977	Thierry Blacque
1983 - 1990	Rory Dicker
1984 - 1989	Michael Morris
1987 - 1990	Patricia Brennan
1990 - 1993	Jimmy Keane
1990 - 1992	Seamus Molloy
1992 - To date	Ivan Dowley
1993 - 1999	Michael Higgens
1993 - To date	Patricia Brennan

NORTH KILKENNY HUNT MASTERS

1934 - 1935	Capt. H. Bramwell
1935 - 1937	George Angel
1937 - 1939	The Marquess of Kildare
1937 - 1939	R.C. Prior-Wandesforde
1939 - 1941	Committee
1941 - To date	Jack Murphy
1941 - 1947	Jimmy Campion
1947 - 1950	Michael Maher
1950 - 1957	Rufus Keogh
1957 - 1958	Tom Nicholson
1958 - 1959	B.D.N. Tate
1959 - 1960	Tom Nicholson
1960 - 1963	T. G. Wilkinson
1963 - 1965	Oliver Maher
1965 - 1970	James Bowe
1970 - 1980	Loughlin Bowe
1979 - 1998	Michael Dillon
1997 - To date	Liam Murphy
1998 - To date	John Hickey

APPENDIX V

COST OF ERECTING KILKENNY HUNT KENNELS AT DESART COURT

DATE 1886

Jul-30	Aylward, Carpenter; 2 days at 3/- per day	£0-6-0
Jul-30	Aylward, 5 ditto	£0-15-0
Jul-31	Rail Carriage of timber from Waterford	£0-3-6
Aug-02	Men drawing flags	£0-2-6
Aug-03	Lime	£0-4-0
Aug-06	Flags £3-17-0, Men drawing same 15/9	£4-12-9
Aug-07	Langford, Slator	£0-15-0
Aug-08	Dunphy, Carpenter	£0-10-0
Aug-14	Lime	£0-5-0
Aug-14	Dunphy, Carpenter	£1-7-6
Aug-14	Langford, Slator	£1-6-0
Aug-21	ditto	£0-6-8
Aug-21	Rail Carriage of Cement from Dublin	£0-5-1
Aug-21	Flanagan, Mason, 4 weeks at 9/-	£1-16-0
Aug-21	Dockerell ½ ton Cement	£1-8-9
Aug-21	Bill of Corrugated Iron & Bolts	£2-1-9
Aug-21	Graves' Bill of Timber	£1-2-7
Aug-21	Langford Slator	£0-8-8
Aug-23	New Window for Kennel	£0-5-6
Aug-10	Lime, 5 Brls at 1/- per	£0-5-0
Aug-10	ditto, 6 Brls	£0-6-0
		£18-13-3

APPENDIX VI

KILKENNY HUNT
Subscription List for Season, 1897-98

Subscribers	*Annual Sub.*	*Club Sub.*
Annaly, Lady	15-0-0	
Aylward, H.J.C. Toler	5-0-0	5-0-0
Allen, H.A.	1-0-0	
Alexander, Major, John	5-0-0	
Butler, John	5-0-0	
Bainbridge, Major	5-0-0	
Butler, George	5-0-0	5-0-0
Bryan, Hon. G.B.	5-0-0	5-0-0
Butler, Lord A.		
Butler, Colonel Somerset	5-0-0	5-0-0
Bradley, Mark	3-0-0	
Bellew, Hon. Richard	5-0-0	
Barry, John (V.S.)	3-0-0	
Buggy, M.J.	2-2-0	
Brennan, J.	2-0-0	
Browne-Clayton, Miss	2-0-0	
Connellan, Major J.H.	10-0-0	5-0-0
Considine, T.J.	3-3-0	
Considine, P.B.	3-3-0	
Dennis, Miss	2-0-0	
Dyer, Miss	2-0-0	
Dwane, Miss	2-2-0	
Desart, the late Earl of	20-0-0	5-0-0
Forbes, W.B.	5-0-0	
Fitzpatrick, Jerome	2-0-0	
Gregory, H. Charles	5-0-0	
"Gone Away"	2-0-0	
Hanford, C.B., Col. J.C.	30-0-0	5-0-0
Hutchinson, John	5-0-0	
Hourigan, W.P.	3-0-0	
Hore, Walter	5-0-0	
Hunt, Mrs. Helsham	3-0-0	
Hastings, Hon. Osmond	10-0-0	
Hastings, Hon. Aubrey	5-0-0	
Hodgens, R. Devereux	10-0-0	
Hely, Miss Florence	3-0-0	
Izod, Col. William	5-0-0	5-0-0

Subscribers	*Annual Sub.*	*Club Sub*
Jones, J.H.	2-0-0	
Kavanagh, Walter, McM.	20-0-0	5-0-0
Knox, Captain R.J.	5-0-0	
Knox, Col. R. Chaloner	10-0-0	5-0-0
Knox, Lindesay		
Kough, Miss Constance	3-0-0	
Keatinge, Col. Den	5-0-0	5-0-0
Kinlough, Col.	5-0-0	
Loftus, Capt.	4-0-0	
Lalor, N.J.	3-0-0	
May, Walter	5-0-0	
Maude, E.H.	3-0-0	
Marsh, R.M.	5-0-0	5-0-0
Murphy, T.F.	3-3-0	
McCreery, James	2-2-0	
McEnery, W.	6-0-0	
Marescaux, G.C.A.	2-2-0	
Maher, James	2-2-0	
McCreery, Col.	5-0-0	
Newport, G.B.	10-0-0	
Officers "The Buffs"	50-0-0	
Ormonde, the Marquess of, K.P.	20-0-0	5-0-0
O'Carroll, D.	5-0-0	
O'Keeffe, P.D.	3-0-0	
Power, Sir John	20-0-0	5-0-0
Power, L.J		
Power, Thomas		
Power, Henry		
Power, Rev. G.B.		
Pilsworth, W.T.	15-0-0	5-0-0
Poe, James, Senr.	5-0-0	
Poe, James, Junr.	15-0-0	5-0-0
Prior-Wandesforde, H.W.		5-0-0
Prior-Wandesforde, R.H.	20-0-0	5-0-0
Ponsonby, Hon. Mrs.	5-0-0	
Rainsford, R.C.	4-0-0	
Renehan, G. (M.R.C.V.S.)	2-0-0	
Smithwick, E.	15-0-0	5-0-0
Smithwick, George	3-0-0	
Smithwick, D.J.		
Smithwick, J.F.	6-0-0	
Smithwick, James	15-0-0	5-0-0
Smyth, M.	2-0-0	

Subscribers	*Annual Sub.*	*Club Sub*
Swifte, G.B.M.	25-0-0	5-0-0
Stopforde, Hon. E.B.	10-0-0	5-0-0
Seigne, John T.	5-0-0	
Sullivan, R.J.		
Stubber, R. Hamilton	10-0-0	
Smithwick, Miss May	3-0-0	
Thorpe, R.W.	3-0-0	
Tighe, E.K.B.	20-0-0	5-0-0
"Tally Ho"	5-0-0	
Waterford, The Marquess of	10-0-0	
Watters, L.J	10-0-0	5-0-0
Watters, Arthur	1-0-0	
Whitcroft, J.H	5-0-0	
Webb, Capt. D.	20-0-0	
Wilson, Major	5-0-0	
Webb, Capt. G.A.	4-0-0	
	Total £646-19-0	**£120-0-0**

KILKENNY HUNT 1951-52 Subscriptions

Subscribers	*Annual Sub*
Alexander, Major J.	20-0-0
Alexander, J.	15-0-0
Annesley, the Hon. Mrs. G.	20-0-0
Archer-Houblon, Mrs. D.	5-0-0
Barry, Capt. J.J.	5-0-0
*Butler, G.G,	15-0-0
Colfer, Mrs.	12-0-0
Cronyn, Mrs. W.	3-0-0
DeBromhead, Miss I.	5-0-0
DeMontmorency, Capt. J.	5-0-0
Dowley, I.	15-0-0
Douglas, E.P.	20-0-0
Duggan, P.	10-10-0
*Fairley, Col. W.M.	20-0-0
Fairley, Mrs.	15-0-0
Fanshawe, Lt.-Col.	10-0-0
Fanshawe, Mrs.	10-0-0
Fennelly, P.M.	10-0-0
Fennelly, F.	5-0-0
Fitzgerald, F.	10-0-0
Grey, C.	5-5-0
*Lambert, Capt. D.A.	5-0-0

Subscribers	*Annual Sub.*
Lambert, Mrs.	10-10-0
*Langrishe, Sir Terence	25-0-0
Lindsay, Mrs. B.K.	5-0-0
Madden-Simpson, Miss	5-0-0
Murray-Smith, the Hon. Mrs.	10-10-0
Murphy, P.	10-0-0
Murphy, D.	5-0-0
MacLeod, Mrs. E.	10-0-0
McCreery, P.	3-0-0
*McEnery, J.A.	20-0-0
McGrath, P.	2-0-0
*McMorrough-Kavanagh, Major A.	10-0-0
McMorrough-Kavanagh, Mrs	10-0-0
O'Donnell, K.	3-0-0
O'Donnell, J.	3-0-0
Parsons, N.	10-0-0
Palmer, Miss E.D.	5-0-0
*Pilsworth, W.J.	20-0-0
Pilsworth, Miss A.	10-0-0
Price, Mrs.	5-0-0
Power, Patrick	3-0-0
Ryan, G.	7-7-0
Sharrocks, Mrs.	10-0-0
Smithwick, J.D.	10-0-0
Solly Flood, Mrs.	5-0-0
Springfield, Miss Rose	3-3-0
Statham, Terry	10-0-0
Toler-Aylward, H.	5-0-0
*Wandesforde, Major Prior-	10-0-0
Walsh, Col. C.H.	20-0-0
Wilson, Capt. J.	10-0-0
Wilson, Mrs.	10-0-0
Harristown Gymkhana	20-0-0
Kilmoganny Harriers	5-0-0
Total	**£551-5-0**

(indicates the members of the Hunt Club)*

APPENDIX VII

RULES OF THE KILKENNY HUNT CLUB 1904

I. That the Members of the Kilkenny Hunt Club shall be duly elected from the Subscribers to the Hunt – but that from and after 1st January, 1894, no person shall be eligible for election to the Club, who does not subscribe at least £10 annually to the Hunt Funds.

II. That a Candidate for Membership to the Kilkenny Hunt Club, must be proposed and seconded by two Members who will submit the Candidate's name to the Honorary Secretary.

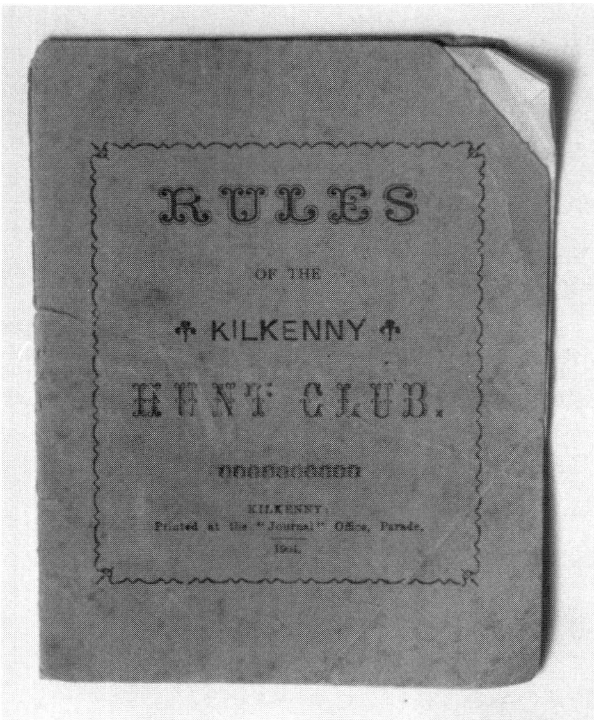

(Courtesy of Mr. Gilbert Butler)

The title page of the Kilkenny Hunt Club rule book, 1904.

III. That elections shall be by Ballot, and shall take place at Meetings of the Hunt Club, to be called for the purpose by the Honorary Secretary in November and January. The Honorary Secretary to be empowered to call a Special Meeting on a requisition signed by at least Three Members of the Hunt Club.

IV. That at all Meetings for the Election of Members of the Hunt club, five Members must be present to form a quorum, one black ball in five to exclude.

V. That an owner of a fox covert preserving and maintaining the same for the use of the Hunt at his own expense shall be considered a subscriber of £5.

VI. That the Members of and Subscribers to the Hunt may wear the Hunt Uniform with plain buttons, but that none but the Members of the Hunt Club, may wear the Hunt Button.

VII. That the Master of the Kilkenny Hounds shall always be considered an Ex-Officio Member of the Kilkenny Hunt Club, during his tenure of the Mastership.

VII. That all meetings of the Hunt Club be held in Kilkenny.

IX. That all Hunt Subscriptions must be paid annually, and that any member on arrears for more than one year, shall, *ipso facto,* cease to be a Member of the Club.

The following resolution also appears in the Minute Book: --
"That any Member of the Kilkenny Hunt Club may retain his Membership of the Club on leaving the Country, provided he continues to pay the annual Club Subscription of £5."

APPENDIX VIII

KILKENNY HUNT PUPPY WALKERS 1901

Mr. Phelan, Rossenara,	Windgap
G.B. Newport Esq.	Inistioge (2)
Mr. Barnes	Windgap (2)
Mr. M. Bradley	Kells Grange, Stonyford (2)
Rev. McCheane	Wellbrook, Freshford
– St. George Esq.	Kilrush House, Freshford
Mr. J. Millea	Mylerstown, Hugginstown
J. Smithwick Esq.	Kilcreene Lodge, Kilkenny (2)
Mrs. Darmody	Crowbally, Lukeswell
Mr. P. Darmody	Ditto
Mr. P.M. Darmody	Ditto
Mr. P. Aylward	Knockmoylan, Lukeswell
Mr. Fitzpatrick	Crowbally, Lukeswell
Mr. John Dunne	Ennisnag, Stonyford
Mr. John Cassin	Carrickshock
Mr. R. Cassin	Ditto
Mr. P. Keeffe	Ballyboden
Mr. J. Cody	Ditto
Mr. Rice	Ditto
Mr. M. Shea	Mullinbeg, Templeorum
Col. Hanford	Flood Hall (2)
Mr. P. Shelly	Kilmoganny (2)
Mr. Hawe	Foundry, Kilmoganny
Mr. J. Butler	Callan (2)
E.K.B. Tighe Esq.	Woodstock
Mr. Shea	Ballyquin, Mullinavat
Mr. Sheehan	Ditto
Miss C. Kough	Kilkenny
Mr. W. Leahy	Cloghala, Dungarvan
Mr. G.T. Williams	Tullow Lodge, Dungarvan
Hon. G. Bryan	Jenkinstown Park
John Whitcroft Esq.	Kilree House, Kilkenny (2)
Capt. Stopford	Norelands (2)
Major McFall	The Inch House, Kilkenny (2)
Mr. M. Cody	Thomastown
Mr. David Welsh	Westmoreland, Newmarket
Mr. M. O'Neill	High Street, Kilkenny
Mr. O'Connell	Norelands, Thomastown

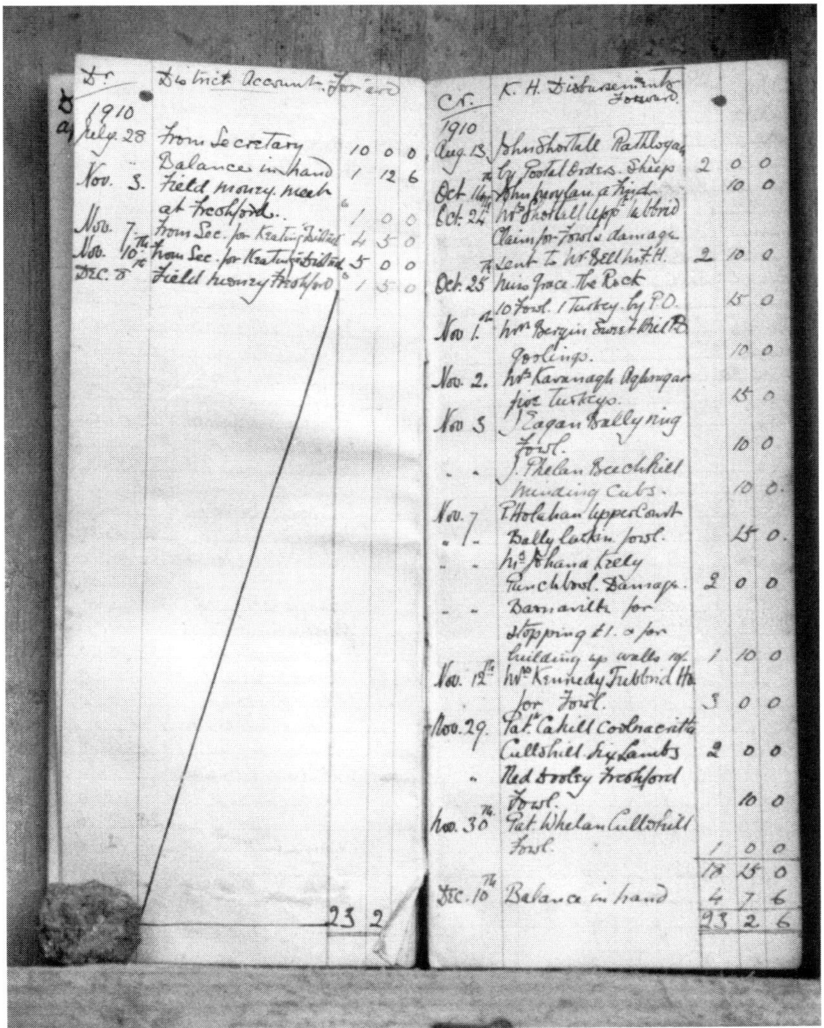

(Photo: Des McCheane)

Tommy McCheane's district accounts for 1910.

BIBLIOGRAPHY

PRIMARY SOURCES

ACCOUNTS:

Challoner Knox, R., Hunt accounts 1886-87.
Connellan, J., Kennel accounts, receipts and notes, 1887-1894.
Hunt account with the Kilkenny Moderator May - Oct. 1888.
Hunt ball accounts, 1886.
Hunt Expenditure in Thomastown district, for season 1889-90.
Statements of Accounts for Seasons, 1894-95, 1895-96, 1896-97.
Statement of Accounts and List of Subscribers, 1930-31.
Statement of Accounts and List of Subscribers, 1951-52.
Statement of Accounts and List of Subscribers, 1978-79.
Kilkenny Hunt Accounts, 1986-87, 1987-88.
McMorrough Kavanagh, A., 1930s accounts.

UNPUBLISHED ALBUMS & DIARIES:

Bell, I & D., Albums.
Blunden, W., 1790. Journal.
Butler, E., 1880. Diary.
Butler, G., 1928. Diary.
Butson, Capt. S., The Hunting Diary of Captain Sinclair Butson, 1884/85 – 1885/86.
Challoner Knox, R., 1876. Diary.
Martin, V., 1888. Diaries. Queen's University, Belfast Ms. NO. 17. Catalogue No. 874.
Marshall, P., 1929. Album.
McCalmont, D., Hunting Journal, 1903-1908.
McCalmont, D., Hunting Journal, Vol. III, 1913-1920.
McCalmont, D., Hunting Journal, Vol. IV, 1921-1926.
McCalmont, D., Hunting Journal, Vol. V, 1926-1931.
McCalmont, D., Hunting Journal, Vol. VI, 1931-1936.
McCalmont, The Hon. Lady Rose, Hunting Diary & Scrapbook, 1908-1933.
McCalmont, V., Hunting Journal, Vol. II, 1951-1958.
McCheane, B., Hunting Diary, 1920-1970.
McMorrough Kavanagh, J., Hunting Diary, 1926-1935.
McMorrough Kavanagh, Major A. T., Hunting Diary, 1904-1940.

Poe Album, Kilkenny Archaeological Society collection.
Richards, E., Diary, 1907.
Solly Flood, M., Album.
Toler-Aylward, M., Album.
Thomas, P., Hunting Diary, 1983-1990.
Scrap Album, ex-Mount Juliet, 1897-1898.

LETTERS:
Legal Correspondence between Lady Langrishe and Nicholas Lambert, 1907-08.
Sir John Power (2nd Baronet) to Sir Charles Cuffe, 1863.
Sir James Langrishe to Sir Charles Cuffe, 1863.

NEWSPAPERS & MAGAZINES:
Country Life, 15/1/1976.
Countryweek Hunting, May/June 1993, Obituary: Major Victor McCalmont by Capt. R.E. Wallace.
Finn's Leinster Journal.
Kilkenny Journal.
Kilkenny Moderator.
Kilkenny People.
Kilkenny People, *A Review of the Century 1892-1992,* (Kilkenny People, 1992).
The Hexham Courant, Nov. 1932.
The Tatler, No. 1962, February 1st 1939.
Sunday Tribune, 8/6/1986.
The Field, Obituary of Ikey Bell.
Unidentified newspaper cuttings.

PAMPHLETS:
Anon, 1870, *A Statement relating to the outrages committed against the Kilkenny Hunt, Dec. 27th 1869*, Kilkenny.

Bryan, G., 1870, *An account of the proceedings connected with the foxhunting in the county of Kilkenny for the last eighteen months*, Kilkenny.

Records of the Kilkenny Hunt during the Mastership of Sir Hercules Langrishe, Bart. 1899-1908, Kilkenny.

Records of the Kilkenny Hunt during the Mastership of Sir Hercules Langrishe, Bart. 1902-1908, Kilkenny.

OTHER PRIMARY SOURCES:

Bell, I., unpublished notes.
Bayliss, P., Letter, April 6th 1999.
Conway, O., *50 Years of the Mullinavats,* unpublished, 1999.
Dobbs, Harry B. (Canon), *Life at the Cottage*, unpublished.
Gaisford St. Lawrence, Mr., Family History Notes, Howth Castle, unpublished.
Entrance ticket, Bonnetstown Point-to-Point races, 1909.
Folklore Commission, Gowran Primary School, Lilly Kelsey, Bodal, Gowran, 23/7/1934. Told by Mr. Edward Brennan of Clashwilliam, Gowran, aged 85 years.
Kavanagh, Martin., *The Nore Vale Harriers,* unpublished notes, 1999.
Kilkenny Hunt Minutes, 1887.
Kilkenny Hunt Rules, 1904.
List of Covert Keepers, Ms. 25043, N.L.I.
List of the Kilkenny Foxhounds, Season 1987-88.
List of Puppy Walkers, 1901.
Minutes of Mr. John Alexander's Hounds, 1931-1934.
Minutes of the North Kilkenny Hunt, 1934-1977.
Minutes of the Johnswell / Tullabrin Harriers, 1924-1931.
North Kilkenny Hunt Ball menus.
North Kilkenny Hunt Dance invitation.
Point-to-Point programs, North Kilkenny: 1949.
Point-to-Point programs, Kilkenny: 1948, 1950 and 1964.
Power, Tony, *Kilmoganny Hunt*, unpublished notes.
Reilly, Elaine, *History of the Kilmoganny Hunt*, unpublished, 1988.
Solly Flood, M., *Memoirs of Six Reigns*, unpublished, 1978.
Thomas, P., *Stopping Notebook*, 1986-87.

SECONDARY SOURCES

AMERICAN FOXHOUND LEAFLET, *The Huntsman in the Field,* (1979).
ANDREWS, J., *David Aher and Hill Clements map of County Kilkenny* in *Kilkenny History and Society*, editors W. Nolan and K. Whelan, (Geography Publications, 1990).

ANON, *The Analysis of the Hunting Field 1845-6*, (London, 1847).
ANON, *The Young Lady's Equestrian Manual*, (London, 1838).
ANON, (Connellan, J.), *Memoir of the Kilkenny Hunt*, (Dublin, 1897 & 1911).
BAILY'S HUNTING DIRECTORY 1910-1911, (London, 1910).
BAILY'S HUNTING DIRECTORY 1937-1938, (Vinton & Co. Ltd. 1937).
BAILY'S HUNTING DIRECTORY 1976-1977, (J.A. Allen & Co. London, 1976).
BAILY'S HUNTING DIRECTORY 1998-1999, (Pearson Publishing Ltd. 1998).
BELL, I., 1947, *A Huntsman's Log Book*, (Dublin, 1947).
BENCE-JONES, M., *Twilight of the Ascendancy*, (Constable, London, 1987).
BOOTH, S., *A.J. Munnings*, (Sotheby's Publications).
BOWEN, M., *Irish Hunting*, (Tralee, 1953).
"BRITISH HUNTS AND HUNTSMEN", (The Biographical Press, London, 4 Vols. 1908-1911).
BURKE'S LANDED GENTRY OF IRELAND, (London, 1958).
BUTLER, H., *Escape from the Anthill*, (Lilliput Press, 1986).
BUXTON, M., 1987, *Ladies of the Chase*, (London, 1987).
CARR, R., *English Foxhunting: A History*, (London, 1976).
CORBALLIS, C., *Castlefield House*, in *In the Shadow of the Steeple*, No. 5, (Duchas, 1996).
CULLEN, L.M., *The Social and Economic Evolution of Kilkenny in the Seventeenth and Eighteenth Centuries*, in *Kilkenny History and Society*, editors W. Nolan and K. Whelan, (Geography Publications, 1990).
CUMMINS, J., 1988, *The Hound and the Hawk, the Art of Medieval Hunting*, (1988).
CURTIS, L.P. (Jr.), *Stopping the Hunt* in *Nationalism and Popular Protest in Ireland*, editor C.H.E Philpin, (1987).
DE BREFFNY, B., editor, *Ireland: A Cultural Encyclopaedia*, (Thames and Hudson, 1983).
DEBRETT'S PEERAGE, BARONETAGE, KNIGHTAGE, AND COMPANIONAGE, (London, 1948).
DESART, EARL OF & LUBBOCK, LADY, *A Page from the Past: Memories of the Earl of Desart by himself and his daughter*, (London, 1936).

DORGAN, D., *The Chapel District of Ballyouskill, Attanagh*, (Ballyouskill History Committee, 1996).
DOYLE, J., *An Historical Survey of St.John's, Kilkenny*. (Kilkenny, 1990).
DOYLE, J., *St. John's Parish*, (Kilkenny, 1989).
EDWARDS, L., *My Irish Sketch Book*, (Collins, London, 1938).
EDWARDS, L., *Famous Foxhunters*, (London, 1932).
EGAN, P.M., *Guide to Kilkenny*, (Kilkenny, 1884).
FAIRLEY, J., *An Irish Beast Book*, (Blackstaff Press, 1984).
FITZPATRICK, B.M., *Irish Sports and Sportsmen*, (Dublin, 1878).
FITZROY SOMERSET, H.H.A., *Foxhunting: the Duke of Beaufort*, (David & Charles Ltd., 1980).
GRATTAN-BELLEW, B., *The Loftuses of Mt. Loftus* in *Old Kilkenny Review*, (Kilkenny Archaeological Society, 1971) .
GULLIVER AND SILVERMAN, M., *Merchants and Shopkeepers*, (University of Toronto Press, 1995).
HARDAWAY, B.H., *Never Outfoxed*, (B.H. Hardaway, Georgia, 1997).
HARRINGTON, J.P., editor, *The English Traveller in Ireland*, (Wolfhound, 1991).
HORSE AND HOUND YEAR BOOK 1952-53.
HUNTING DIARY AND GUIDE, 1936.
HOWTH, LORD, *Leicestershire en France: or the Pau Hunting Field*, (London, 1894).
ITZKOWITZ, D.C., *Peculiar Privilege: A Social History of English Foxhunting*, (Hassocks 1977).
JACKSON, A., *The Great Hunts*, (David & Charles, London, 1989).
KELLY, F., *Early Irish Farming*, (Dublin Institute for Advanced Studies, 1998).
LAW, E., *A hunting we will go: the Merry Harrier Club*, in *The Old Kilkenny Review*, (Kilkenny Archaeological Society, 1995).
LEWIS, C.A., *Hunting in Ireland*, (J.A. Allen, 1975).
LEWIS, P., editor, *A Foxhunter's Anthology*, (London, 1934).
LOEBER, R., *Settler's Utilisation of the Natural Resources*, in *Wicklow, History and Society*, editors K. Hannigan and W. Nolan, (Geography Publications, 1994).
LYNG, T.P., *Castlecomer Connections*, (Castlecomer History Society, 1984).

LYNG, T.P., *Father Johnny* in *Deenside*, Winter 1996, (Deenside Committee, Boherkyle, Castlecomer, 1996).
MacEWAN, M., *Ten Great Irish Hunts*, (Punchestown Books, 1996).
MacLYSAGHT, E., *Irish Life in the Seventeenth Century*, (Irish Academic Press, 1979).
MAXWELL, C., *Country and Town in Ireland under the Georges*, (Harrup & Co., 1941).
MAYO, EARL OF, AND BOULTON, *History of the Kildare Hunt.*
McCALMONT, H., *Memoirs of Major-General Sir Hugh McCalmont*, (Hutchinson, London, 1924).
McCHEANE, D., compiler, *We grew up around Freshford*, (Wellbrook Press Ltd. Co. Kilkenny, 1982).
McCRACKEN, E., *The Irish Woods since Tudor Times*, (Newton Abbot 1971).
MEADS, J., *They will always meet at Eleven*, (Quiller Press, London, 1991).
MITCHELL, F., *The Shell Guide to the Irish Landscape*, (Country House, 1986).
MOORE, D., *Famous Foxhunters*, (Spur Publications, 1978).
MUNNINGS, SIR A., *Pictures of Horses and English Life.*
NEELY,W.G., *Kilkenny, An Urban History, 1391-1843*, (Belfast, 1989).
NEILSON, H.B., *The Adventures of Sam Pippins, Esq. with the Kilkenny Hunt*, (Simpkin, Marshall & Co., London, 1889).
NOLAN, W. & WHELAN, K., editors, *Kilkenny History and Society*, (Geography Publications, 1990).
O'CONNELL, J., *Woollengrange Races 1949-1964*, in *In the Shadow of the Steeple*, No. 6, (Duchas, 1998).
OSBORN, C., editor, *The Native Dogs of Ireland*, (Dublin, 1994).
O'SULLIVAN, H., *The Diary of an Irish Countryman, 1827-1835*, (Mercier Press, 1979).
PILSWORTH, W.J., *History of Thomastown and District*, (Kilkenny, 1972).
PRENDERGAST, P., *Of Hawks and Hounds in Ireland*, Journal Royal Society of Antiquaries of Ireland, (1852).
RHODERICK-JONES, R., *Ronnie Wallace*, (Quiller Press, London, 1992).
SCARTH DIXON, W., *Hunting in the Olden Days*, (London, 1912).
SCRUTATOR, *Horses and Hounds*, (London, 1855).

SLEEMAN, P., *Mammals and Mammalogy* in *Nature in Ireland*, editor J.W. Foster, (Lilliput Press, 1997).
SOMERVILLE-LARGE, P., *The Irish Country House – A Social History*, (London, 1995).
STRINGER, A., *The Experienced Huntsman*, (Blackstaff Press, 1977).
THE FOXHUNTER'S YEARBOOK, 1930-31, (Mayfair Press).
THE HUNTING DIARY AND GUIDE 1937-38.
TIGHE, W., *Statistical Survey of Co. Kilkenny*, (Dublin, 1802).
TRAFFORD, SIR H.F. de., editor, *The Foxhounds of Great Britain and Ireland*, (London, 1906).
VALE, M., *Gentlemen's Recreations: Accomplishments and Pastimes of the English Gentleman 1580-1630*, (Cambridge, 1977).
VINEY, M., *Wild Sports and Stone Guns*, in *Nature in Ireland*, editor J.W. Foster, (Lilliput Press, 1997).
VYNTER, R.T., *Notitia Venatica: A treatise on Foxhunting*, (London, 1847).
WATERFORD, LORD, *A Hunting Journal*, (Dublin, 1901).
WELCOME, J., *Irish Horse-Racing*, (Gill & Macmillan, 1982).
WHELAN, BISHOP J.B., *Homily* in *Deenside*, Winter 1996, (Deenside Committee, Boherkyle, Castlecomer, 1996).
WORCESTER SMITH, H., *A Sporting Tour through Ireland, England, Wales and France*, (Vol.1, South Carolina, 1925).
YOUNG, A., *A Tour in Ireland*, (Blackstaff Press, 1983).

RUNNING ON

The dusk is down on the river meadows,
The moon is climbing above the fir,
The land is crowded with creeping shadows,
The gorse is only a distant blur;
The last of the light is almost gone,
But hark! They're running!
They're running on!

The count of the years is steadily growing;
The Old give way to the eager Young;
Far on the hill is the horn still blowing,
Far on the steep are the hounds still strung.
Good men follow the good men gone;
And hark! They're running!
They're running on!

Will H. Ogilvie